THE
AUTO ROADSIDE

MAR   1996

THE AUTO ROADSIDE SURVIVAL GUIDE

by
David R. Solomon

IDG Books Worldwide, Inc.
An International Data Group Company

Foster City, CA ✦ Chicago, IL ✦ Indianapolis, IN ✦ Braintree, MA ✦ Dallas, TX

The Auto Roadside Survival Guide

Published by
IDG Books Worldwide, Inc.
An International Data Group Company
919 E. Hillsdale Blvd.
Suite 400
Foster City, CA 94404

Library of Congress Catalog Card No.: 95-77050

ISBN: 1-56884-377-1

Printed in the United States of America

10 9 8 7 6 5 4 3 2 1

1D/SU/QV/ZV

Distributed in the United States by IDG Books Worldwide, Inc.

Distributed by Macmillan Canada for Canada; by Computer and Technical Books for the Caribbean Basin; by Contemporantea de Ediciones for Venezuela; by Distribuidora Cuspide for Argentina; by CITFC for Brazil; by Ediciones ZETA S.C.R. Ltda. for Peru; by Editorial Limusa SA for Mexico; by Transworld Publishers Limited in the United Kingdom and Europe; by Al-Maiman Publishers & Distributors for Saudi Arabia; by Simron Pty. Ltd. for South Africa; by IDG Communications (IIK) Ltd. for Hong Kong; by Toppan Company Ltd. for Japan; by Addison Wesley Publishing Company for Korea; by Longman Singapore Publisher Ltd. for Singapore, Malaysia, Thailand, and Indonesia; by Unalis Corporation for Taiwan; by WS Computer Publishing Company, Inc. for the Philippines; by WoodsLane Enterprises Ltd. for New Zealand.

For general information on IDG Books Worldwide's books in the U.S., including information on discounts and premiums, contact IDG Books Worldwide at 800-434-3422 or 415-655-3000.

For information on where to purchase IDG Books Worldwide's books outside the U.S., contact IDG Books Worldwide at 415-655-3021 or fax 415-655-3295.

For information on translations, contact Marc Jeffrey Mikulich, Director, Foreign and Subsidiary Rights, at IDG Books Worldwide, 415-655-3018 or fax 415-655-3295.

For sales inquiries and special prices for bulk quantities, write to the address above or call IDG Books Worldwide at 415-655-3000.

For information on using IDG Books Worldwide's books in the classroom, or for ordering examination copies, contact Jim Kelly at 800-434-2086.

 is a trademark under exclusive license to IDG Books Worldwide, Inc., from International Data Group, Inc.

About the Author

David R. Solomon

David Solomon has been inducted into the Automotive Hall of Fame and Society of Automotive Engineers and is ranked as a World Class Technician for his accomplishments as a Certified Master Mechanic. Putting himself through school working as a mechanic, he also has a master's degree in psychology. People call him the "psyCARatrist" for his benevolence in helping motorists with his automotive newsletter and with his national live radio show, both called *Nutz & Boltz*.

He also works as an automotive forensic expert, does automotive instruction nationally in fuel injection and automotive computers, and writes for technical periodicals. David is on the *Bottom Line Personal* panel of experts and is a contributing editor for *Emission Monthly*.

Welcome to the world of IDG Books Worldwide.

IDG Books Worldwide, Inc., is a subsidiary of International Data Group, the world's largest publisher of computer-related information and the leading global provider of information services on information technology. IDG was founded more than 25 years ago and now employs more than 7,500 people worldwide. IDG publishes more than 235 computer publications in 67 countries (see listing below). More than 60 million people read one or more IDG publications each month.

Launched in 1990, IDG Books Worldwide is today the #1 publisher of best-selling computer books in the United States. We are proud to have received 3 awards from the Computer Press Association in recognition of editorial excellence, and our best-selling ...*For Dummies*™ series has more than 17 million copies in print with translations in 25 languages. IDG Books Worldwide, through a recent joint venture with IDG's Hi-Tech Beijing, became the first U.S. publisher to publish a computer book in the People's Republic of China. In record time, IDG Books Worldwide has become the first choice for millions of readers around the world who want to learn how to better manage their businesses.

Our mission is simple: Every one of our books is designed to bring extra value and skill-building instructions to the reader. Our books are written by experts who understand and care about our readers. The knowledge base of our editorial staff comes from years of experience in publishing, education, and journalism — experience which we use to produce books for the '90s. In short, we care about books, so we attract the best people. We devote special attention to details such as audience, interior design, use of icons, and illustrations. And because we use an efficient process of authoring, editing, and desktop publishing our books electronically, we can spend more time ensuring superior content and spend less time on the technicalities of making books.

You can count on our commitment to deliver high-quality books at competitive prices on topics consumers want to read about. At IDG Books Worldwide, we value quality, and we have been delivering quality for more than 25 years. You'll find no better book on a subject than an IDG book.

John J. Kilcullen

John Kilcullen
President and CEO
IDG Books Worldwide, Inc.

Dedication

For my son Skyler, my daughter Adriana, and all the wonderful subscribers, listeners, and friends without whom there would be no *Auto Roadside Survival Guide*.

Credits

VP & Publisher
Kathleen A. Welton

Executive Editor
Sarah Kennedy

Managing Editor
Stephanie Britt

Brand Manager
Stacy S. Collins

Editorial Assistants
Stacey Holden Prince
Kevin Spencer

Production Director
Beth Jenkins

**Supervisor of
Project Coordination**
Cindy L. Phipps

Pre-Press Coordinator
Steve Peake

**Associate
Pre-Press Coordinator**
Tony Augsburger

**Media/Archive
Coordinator**
Paul Belcastro

Project Editor
Pamela Mourouzis

Editors
Suzanne Packer
Tammy S. Castleman
Colleen Rainsberger
Michael Simsic

Technical Reviewer
Louis Pukelis

Production Staff
Gina Scott
Carla C. Radzikinas
Tricia Reynolds
Dwight Ramsey
Theresa Sánchez-Baker
Linda M. Boyer
Drew R. Moore
Anna Rohrer
Kathie Schnorr

Proofreader
Sandra Profant

Indexer
Sharon Hilgenberg

Cover Design
Kavish + Kavish

Acknowledgments

I would like to give special thanks to Alan "Ace" Elman, who was instrumental in bringing this book together.

(The Publisher would like to give special thanks to Patrick J. McGovern and Bill Murphy, without whom this book would not have been possible.)

Contents at a Glance

Table of Contents

Part V: Automotive Self-Defense 153

Chapter 13: Meeting Mr. Ripp U. Off: Mechanics and Other Rip-Off Artists 155

Introduction

. . . .

Welcome to *The Auto Roadside Survival Guide.*

Whether you love to tinker with your car or only want it to get you from point A to point B, you have to deal with cars at some level or another. Even if you aren't interested in learning how to torque your lugnuts or burnish your brake pads, you need to know some basics: how to fuel up, where not to take your car if it has mechanical problems, and what to do in an emergency situation, for example.

The Auto Roadside Survival Guide is a valuable tool that can help you get through any automotive-related situation, be it a crisis or a simple question. Designed to be fun to read, illustrated with plenty of cartoons, and written in language that even a novice can understand, this book has all the information you'll need to keep from panicking on the road.

How to Use This Book

You have two options: You can read this book cover to cover, or you can use it as a handy reference whenever you need information about a specific subject. I suggest that you do both, first reading it in its entirety and then keeping it in your glove box in case of an emergency. If your car acts up, you'll have a Certified Master Mechanic (me) by your side to guide you through any problem that you may face.

How This Book Is Organized

This book is divided into six parts, with an appendix at the end. Each part is organized into chapters that cover specific subjects. Because this book isn't written in a cumulative fashion, you can read the chapters in any order you want, picking out the topics that interest you and skipping the ones that don't. If there is more information about a particular subject that you're reading about in another chapter or section, I'll let you know that it's there.

The following sections summarize the contents of each part:

Part I: In Your Driveway

What better place to begin but at the beginning: in your driveway, before you even attempt to drive anywhere. The chapters in this part go through the main areas of your car that you should be familiar with, including the battery, brakes, and tires. You'll find basic car care tips and information about preventative maintenance that will help keep you out of trouble in the first place.

Part II: On the Open Road

This part tackles the tribulations of the open road: driving around big trucks, avoiding deer, and surviving those long road trips that never seem to end, to name a few. It also tells you how to handle driving in bad weather and get your car unstuck from snow, mud, or sand.

Part III: In the Breakdown Lane

It's bound to happen sooner or later: You _will_ have car trouble or — heaven forbid — an accident. The chapters in this part explain how you should react to these situations to make them as painless as possible and hopefully to keep yourself out of harm's way.

Part IV: On Your Way to the Shop

Many people think that some mechanics are from some other planet, speak another language, and use these things to their advantage to rip you off. This part tells you how to talk the talk and walk the walk (or at least fool people into thinking that you do) so that you can get what's wrong fixed correctly for a fair price.

Part V: Automotive Self-Defense

The information in this part may be the most important stuff in the whole book. It focuses on how to keep yourself safe from mechanics and other salespeople who try to rip you off and also from more violent criminals who aim to steal your car or physically harm you. Here, you can find self-defense strategies that will help keep your wallet fuller and yourself safer — being informed and aware are two of your best defenses. You'll also get information about what to do if you _do_ become a target of the infamous Mr. Ripp U. Off.

Part VI: The Part of Tens

This part of the book gives you zippy little lists of ten things for quick reference. Find out what to take along in your emergency road kit, what to do when your car breaks down, and more.

Appendix: Flowcharts

If your vehicle won't start, overheats, or pulls to one side or the other, check out these flowcharts to find out what to look for. These charts follow an "if/then" format, as in, "If the engine turns over but will not fire up, then you should check the fuel, ignition, and compression."

What the Icons Mean

This icon points out helpful hints that make dealing with your car even easier.

If you see this icon, watch out! It flags the procedures and situations that can hurt you or your car if you aren't careful.

This icon marks information that is worth making a mental note of: general rules of the road that you should commit to memory.

Feel free to ignore the stuff that's next to this icon, especially if you're an automotive novice and don't want to learn about the nuts and bolts of car repair. Some things are just too complicated and technical to explain without throwing around lots of mechanical lingo.

This icon points out the products and services that I particularly recommend. They may cost you a bit, but the expense is probably well worth it.

 This icon highlights the information that you can use to defend yourself in a threatening situation — threatening in either a financial sense or a physical sense. With these hints in mind, you can keep Mr. Ripp U. Off at bay and keep yourself from becoming a victim.

A Safety Reminder

Always keep safety in mind when you're working on your car. Remove all rings, bracelets, watches, necklaces, and so on and tie back long hair before you begin. Wear safety goggles or glasses to protect your eyes, and avoid wearing loose-fitting clothing that could get caught in something or catch fire. Make sure that the area you're working in is well lighted and ventilated, and always work with an assistant or buddy. Carelessness is the cause of far too many unnecessary injuries.

For More Information

Have a question that's not answered in this book? You can drop me a line at the following address:

Nutz & Boltz
Post Office Box 123
Butler, MD 21023

All letters with car questions will be answered, but you must write your questions clearly (typewritten preferred). Include year, make, and model of your car along with a legal-sized, self-addressed, stamped envelope.

For information about the Nutz & Boltz products mentioned in this book or the Nutz & Boltz Newzletter, you can call one of the following numbers:

National: 800-888-0091

In Maryland: 410-584-7574

Part I
In Your Driveway

In this part...

*T*his part tells you things that you can do yourself to save money on repairs — and maybe save your own life.

Chapter 1

Fluids and Filters

. . . .

In This Chapter

▶ Filling up your tank

▶ Checking your fuel filter

▶ Changing filters

▶ Changing your oil

▶ Dealing with low oil pressure

▶ Recognizing trouble signs at the end of your dipstick

. . . .

*I*n these days of self-serve gas stations, you need to know how to properly check and service the area under the hood of your car. Also, you can do many maintenance items yourself and save big bucks. This chapter will help you do the maintenance properly, without cutting corners and without using shoddy procedures. You'll also learn some of my best tricks and tips for working under the hood of your car.

Fill-Up Procedures

Filling the gas tank is a part of everyday life. Most people learn from watching Dad or Mom, but many don't get proper lessons on fueling a vehicle. The fact is, there's more to fueling your car than just pumping 'n' paying. This section gives you some tips for tanking up right.

Gas cap capers

First, memorize the gas cap's location. If you park on the wrong side of the pump and have to drag the hose over the car, you may damage your paint.

After you remove the gas cap, don't put it on top of the gas pump. Most gas stations have a big box full of gas caps that people have left behind. Instead, check to see whether the cover flap is equipped with a handy notch or holder for the gas cap. If not, put the cap on the fender directly above the filler hole or somewhere in plain sight so that you won't forget it when you finish!

Filling the whole tank properly

When pumping fuel, remember to stand upwind of the nozzle. Gasoline fumes are extremely hazardous to your health; avoid breathing them in at all costs. Here are the steps for getting a perfect fill-up without damaging your car:

1. *Carefully* **lower the gas nozzle into the filler neck.**

   Care is necessary because the last person may have left fuel in the nozzle, and this fuel may spill onto your paint.

2. **Insert the nozzle as far as possible into the filler neck.**

   This reduces the chance of the fuel "burping" out of the filler neck and onto your car and your shoes.

If the car doesn't take fuel well without making the nozzle click off, try inserting the nozzle upside down or even sideways.

3. **Shut off the pump at the second click.**

   Do not overfill the tank. If you are in the habit of filling the tank right to the top, you are wasting fuel, damaging the emission system, and hurting the environment. Overfueling causes excess gas to either run out on the ground or be drawn into the car's evaporative emission canister, ruining it. The canister is designed to store gas *fumes,* not liquid gas. If it becomes saturated with gasoline, its activated charcoal (used to store gas fumes) will be worthless, and the car will start to smell like gas after sitting in the sun on a hot day.

4. **Before removing the nozzle from the filler neck, make sure that all the fuel has drained out of it.**

   If you pull the nozzle out too soon, you will spill gas on the car, the ground, and you.

Static electricity can create a spark when you remove the gas cap and might ignite the fumes! In dry, cool weather, when a great deal of static is in the air, always lean against the vehicle with one hand and unscrew the cap with the other to prevent this from happening.

If you do spill gas on the paint, wash it off immediately with water. Wipe the area with some of your favorite auto polish as soon as possible to avoid gas stains. Do not use the windshield wash squeegee to wash off the gas — you'll contaminate the water bucket for the next user.

Lastly, I recommend against draining the fuel hose. If the next person prepays a precise amount, the pump will shut off at the nozzle and keep that person from draining the hose like you did. The customer pays for the gas it took to refill the hose but doesn't get to use it.

Debunking the High-Test Myth

Here are some commonly asked questions about gasoline:

> "Does my car need high-test? What about all the advertising that says that my car needs high-test to run properly? How do you know if using high-test really makes a difference? What if I want to treat my car to the very best? Is using high-test bad for any reason?"

Unless your engine is turbocharged, supercharged, or a multivalve, high-performance engine, you are probably wasting money on high-test fuel. One of the best ways to find out your engine's minimum fuel octane requirement is to check your owner's manual. If you can't find that information, check the area near the gas cap for a decal advising you of the vehicle's fuel requirements.

> "What happens if I use higher octane fuel than required?"

Some car-makers say that using high-test can cause drivability problems. High-octane fuels burn slower than regular fuels. If your engine is not designed to ignite the fuel early enough, the fuel won't have time to burn completely and will be wasted. The unburned portion of the fuel goes into the exhaust system, where it continues burning. This wasted energy goes right out the tailpipe, along with the money you spent on something your car didn't need. In some cases, using high-test can cause hard starting, stalling, hesitation, or engine surging.

> "Does it hurt to use regular when premium is recommended?"

Yes. If you constantly hear engine ping or knock, stop using regular. Constant engine pinging destroys the tops of the pistons and leads to the early demise of your engine. It can also lower gas mileage.

"What if my engine is supposed to use regular but knocks and pings unless I use premium?"

Have your mechanic repair the problem causing the knock. Likely candidates are lean air-fuel mixture, carbon build-up in the combustion chamber, and a faulty EGR (Exhaust Gas Recirculation) system.

 Use the lowest octane fuel that produces the highest mileage.

Some modern engines are equipped with knock sensors that prevent the engine from pinging. These engines can fool you into thinking that it's okay to use regular because engine timing is automatically retarded by the engine computer when the knock sensor detects ping. The engine will perform with less power and achieve less gas mileage. In the long run, you pay more for gas and get poorer performance than if you had used higher octane fuel.

Octane explained

Back in 1927, Graham Edgar proposed the idea of measuring fuel octane based on an arbitrary number scale. It became known as the *Research Method*. For this purpose, Edgar used two hydrocarbons — isooctane and heptane — as reference points based on their resistance to engine knock. Isooctane has a very high resistance to knock and was assigned a primary value of 100. Heptane has a low resistance to knock and was assigned a value of zero. The octane value became the volume percentage of the two ingredients.

In 1932, the American Society for Testing Materials (ASTM) got into the act and established its method for rating gasoline octane because reports indicated that Edgar's octane testing methods were showing poor correlation with what was happening in motor cars. ASTM wanted a test condition that more adequately reflected the results in actual real-world motors — not just lab motors.

The ASTM test was done at a higher fuel-air mixture temperature and engine speed than Edgar's research method. ASTM's corresponding numbers were called the *Motor Octane Number* (MON) and *Research Octane Number* (RON). This new procedure became known as the *Motor Method for octane labeling*.

Today's octane formula is expressed as the *gas Anti-Knock Index* (AKI) rating. The AKI is the measure of a fuel's capability to burn slowly or resist knock (ping) — a measure of its octane quality. The AKI number is the average of the Research Octane Number (RON) and the Motor Octane Number (MON), expressed as the equation $(R+M)/2$. This equation is displayed on a black and yellow decal on all gas pumps.

While you never know the actual numbers used to get at the final octane number posted on the pump, you do pick and choose octane levels. It's important to know that there exist big differences in fuel quality, based on how the fuel is blended. Just because one fuel is 93 octane may not mean that it is the same as another brand that lists 93 octane on the pump. The posted octane could have been created by using different levels of ingredients — producing the same octane result.

But the two different brands may perform differently in your engine. That's why it's important to try different brands of fuel until you find one that you and your engine like. Which one produces the best fuel mileage and pep and the least knock or ping?

Electric Fuel Pumpers

There is a science to the care and feeding of your car's electric fuel pump. Follow this advice and you will save both the pump and hundreds of dollars in repair costs.

First and foremost, keep the tank full. If you typically wait until the empty light comes on before refueling, you are inviting double trouble in two ways:

- Condensation (H_2O) will form in the tank. Water is the enemy of your fuel system. It is heavier than gasoline, so it settles at the bottom of the tank where it starts to attack the tank lining, causing flaky rust. Your fuel pump picks up the rust particles and is ruined. The best defense in this case is to keep the tank full, especially if you don't drive very often.

- The fuel pump will "starve." Modern electric fuel pumps depend on fuel for internal cooling and lubrication. Without fuel, the pump can be ruined in seconds. To avoid this problem, try to keep the tank at least one-quarter full at all times.

Be careful with gas additives. Don't use additives that contain xylene, toluene, acetone, or methanol (methyl alcohol). These can damage the rubber fuel hoses and fuel tank lining. The contamination caused by the attack damages the rollers in the fuel pump as well as causes a plugged fuel filter.

Forget the moisture. Modern gasoline already contains enough alcohol to absorb the moisture from the tank. Additional gas drying additives make a potent cocktail out of the water in the tank, actually pulling alcohol from the fuel where it is held in suspension. Then the fuel pump gets a big hit of water and additive all at once.

In general, don't use gas-drying additives unless you know that there is water in the tank. When in doubt, it's better to drain the tank to be sure.

Buy gas carefully. Don't buy gas from pumps that are seldom used and off the beaten path. You are more likely to get fuel that is contaminated or laced with water. Try to frequent a filling station that pumps a great deal of fuel — like one located at a busy intersection. They usually have better prices, too!

Change the fuel filter. Changing the filter is your best protection against fuel problems. Fuel filters not only remove solid particulates, but they also absorb a certain amount of moisture from the system. Larger filters can hold about three to four ounces of water; small ones hold less.

TIP

Some cars have *two* fuel filters; both should be changed.

Fuel Filter Testing

Fuel filters do the silent job of protecting the intimate parts of your car's fuel system. Many car-makers don't list change intervals in the owner's manuals, even though fuel filters should be changed every two years or 24,000 miles. A partly plugged fuel filter restricts the flow through the pump and causes it to wear prematurely. Replacing electric fuel pumps is costly, so changing the fuel filter is cheap insurance.

A partially plugged fuel filter also causes fuel starvation when the engine needs fuel the most — on heavy acceleration and at high engine speeds. For fuel-injected cars, a partially plugged filter is bad for the electric fuel pump because the pump needs fresh fuel to cool and lubricate its internal moving parts. Once the filter plugs completely, the engine will not run at all.

Save the old fuel filter, if possible. It is a great diagnostic tool. If you don't service your own car, ask your mechanic to save the fuel filter for you in a clean, clear, glass jar that you provide. Once you get the old filter, here's the drill:

1. **Find the arrow on the filter indicating the direction of fuel flow.**

2. **Blow into the filter in the *opposite* direction so that the contents of the filter go into the jar.**

   If you can't blow through the filter, this indicates a plugged filter and serious fuel contamination problems. Instead, use an air nozzle to blow through the filter.

3. **Examine the contents of the filter for potential fuel system problems, described in the following sections.**

4. **Let the contents of the jar sit for about 20 minutes to see what settles to the bottom of the jar.**

Read on to discover possible signs of trouble.

Black-colored fuel

This comes from deteriorating fuel hoses, indicating prolonged exposure of the hoses to alcohol, xylene, toluene, or acetone. These chemicals are found in cheap fuel and some brands of gas additives. Mechanics following improper fuel-injection cleaning techniques can also allow power-injector cleaning solvents to return to the fuel tank and damage the hoses.

 Make sure that you have a full tank of gasoline when having your injectors cleaned. If some of the injector cleaner chemicals are allowed to return to the tank, a full tank of gas will dilute them.

Water

If you see small, clear "bubbles" that stay on the bottom of the jar, you have water in your fuel tank. Infrequent use of the vehicle can cause moisture to condense in the fuel tank, or rainwater can enter the fuel tank through a cracked gas cap seal. No matter the reason, water leads to a rusted fuel tank, corrosion in the fuel rail, or damaged metal parts in the fuel system.

Gray-colored deposits

Fuel or fuel additives containing methanol or methyl alcohol cause the fuel tank lining to dissolve. Soon, the tank rusts.

Note that modern fuel tanks are now being made of plastic to avoid problems with rust and additive corrosion.

Rust-colored fuel

This comes from prolonged exposure to water. The gas tank should be replaced or recoated with an approved gas tank sealer. Rust particles are the enemy of electric fuel pumps and fuel injectors.

Metal particles

Metal particles are usually a sign that the fuel pump is about to fail. Some types of high-pressure fuel pumps utilize metal rollers that pressurize the fuel. Tiny slivers of metal come from disintegration of the plating on the outside of these rollers, which indicates impending pump failure.

Changing Filters

When it comes to this very important service on your vehicle, it's not always the best idea to have someone else do it for you. If you do it yourself, you can do several "extra" procedures that are beneficial for your vehicle. Most mechanics are in a hurry and don't want to bother with additional steps and procedures — even though they know that they're important. If you do it yourself, you can do it right — every time!

Oil filters

Always change your oil filter when you change the oil. Not all filters are alike. Factory filters are of excellent quality, as are some brand names (Hastings, Atlas, and Purolator, for example). Call the dealer and ask for a price break on a case. Filters used at some "el cheapo" places are substandard, don't adequately filter oil, and leave engines unprotected against harmful contamination. If you frequent chain stores or quick-change shops, take your own filter with you.

Air filters

Typically, air filters are replaced unnecessarily. While the owner's manual is a good guide, you should take a look at the filter before routinely changing it.

You should service your own air filter, checking to see if it's so dirty that you can't see light through it. Once a month, tap it against the ground to dislodge dirt. Also, rinsing it with a garden hose can extend its life two to three times.

Air filters get dirty faster where there is sand, dust, or other airborne debris. Beware of cheap filters, which don't fit well and allow dirt to enter.

Fuel filters

Some car-makers don't recommend fuel filter changes. They don't want the cost of this important service to be considered when their vehicle is rated against competitors vehicles in terms of maintenance costs. Just by changing the fuel filter regularly, you can prevent costly fuel-system problems. To save money, change it as part of your regular tune-up.

Oil Change Procedures

There are many ways to change motor oil. Follow these steps to make this procedure as faultless as possible.

1. **Make sure that the engine is *hot*.**

   Oil has dispersants in its additive package. These chemicals are there to keep dirt in suspension in the oil so that dirt leaves the engine when the oil is drained. Ideally, the oil should be hot so that the dispersants can do their job. Run the engine for at least 20 minutes at highway speeds to insure the oil is hot.

2. **Raise or park the vehicle in such a way so that the drain plug is at the lowest point of the oil pan.**

   This may require making one wheel higher than the other. Chock the wheels, set the parking brake, and place the transmission in gear (manual transmission) or in Park (automatic transmission).

3. **Open the hood and pull the dipstick out of the dipstick tube.**

   Pull the dipstick out far enough to make it easy to spot. This step is important because the protruding dipstick will remind you that the oil is being changed and that there is no oil in the motor. It can also serve as a reminder to secure the drain plug before adding oil.

4. **Remove the oil filter _before_ draining the oil.**

   Some cars have an air lock that holds several ounces of dirty oil in the oil filter housing, channels, and ducts. This trapped oil will drain out with the dirty oil if you remove the filter first.

    Be sure that the drain pan is ready to catch oil from the filter. If the filter is mounted straight up, use an ice pick and punch a hole in it to drain the filter before you remove it. This helps to prevent a mess.

    Be sure that the oil filter seal comes off with the filter can. If not, be sure to remove it from the engine before installing the new filter. Sometimes the sealing washer sticks to the engine block and remains there after the old filter is removed. If it is allowed to remain in place and the new filter is screwed on top of it, you might not notice it. This allows the oil filter to be "double gasketed," quickly destroying your engine! The extra sealing gasket pops out and creates a leak when the engine is running at a higher rpm, probably when you are on the highway. Suddenly all the engine oil gushes out the leak, and by the time the oil pressure warning light comes on, you will have lost an engine from running without oil pressure!

5. **Remove the drain plug.**

   The drain pan should be positioned so that it can catch the stream of oil. Use a box-end wrench or a closed wrench to avoid stripping the plug. A socket works okay, too. The drain pan should be positioned so that it will catch any drips of oil from both the drain hole and the oil filter.

6. **Examine the drain plug for the presence of a sealing washer.**

   Some car-makers (Toyota, Mercedes Benz, and Isuzu) require that the drain plug sealing washer be replaced at every oil change. When in doubt, check with the local dealership and find out what they recommend.

   Important precautions include the following:

   - Poor centering of the drain plug washer can cause oil leaks at the plug.

   - Tighten the drain plug by hand until the washer contacts the oil pan squarely. This helps to center the sealing washer. Then tighten it with the box wrench.

   - Be careful if the drain plug seal has a raised portion. The plug will leak if the raised portion is not placed securely against the oil pan.

   - Be sure to remove all traces of the old drain plug gasket or sealing washer before installing a new one. If any pieces of the old gasket remain, the new gasket won't seal and you will have a new leak.

7. **Install the oil filter.**

   If the filter mounts with the threaded end upward, fill the filter with fresh oil before installing it. Wipe the engine mounting flange (the round place against which the filter mounts) clean and wipe the filter rubber sealing ring with fresh oil. Follow the directions on the filter about hand-tightening torque. In general, the filter should be tight enough to properly seal but not so tight that the metal filter canister comes in contact with the mounting flange.

8. Add the necessary amount of oil to the motor.

In general, most engines take either four or five quarts. It is generally safe to start with four quarts and add the last quart if needed. Check the owner's manual for recommended fill amounts.

9. Prime the motor before starting it.

This step requires cranking the engine over several times without allowing it to start. Observe the proper procedure for your car:

- **Carbureted vehicles:** Unplug the ignition coil or disconnect and ground the high-tension coil wire to disable the ignition. After the oil pressure light on the dash goes out, enable the ignition and start the motor.

- **Fuel-injected cars:** Crank the engine over (like you're trying to get it to start) while holding the gas pedal on the floor. This puts the motor in Clear Flood Mode, and the computer shuts off fuel to the injectors, preventing the engine from starting. After the oil pressure light goes out, release the pedal to let the motor start and idle.

10. While the motor is idling, look underneath for oil leaks. Turn off the motor, reinsert the dipstick, and check the oil level.

 Some oil will "hang up" in the engine for as long as 20 minutes. For this reason, the dipstick may read slightly low. Keep this in mind before deciding to "top off" the oil level to make the dipstick read totally full. Put a sticker on the door post or under the hood indicating the mileage of the oil change.

Motor Oil: Engine Life-Blood

Should you add fresh oil to dirty oil if the car's oil level is low? Probably not. If the oil level is down a quart or more, it is usually a good indication that the useful life of the oil is over and it's time for an oil change.

However, if your car is a leaker, you should keep adding oil as needed to keep it from dropping below a quart low.

 If there are over 2,000 miles on the oil or more than three months have passed since your last oil change and the level is down a quart or more, have the oil changed right away. Adding fresh oil to old, burned oil does not help the engine because the remaining oil is practically useless anyway. If the oil level in your engine is low, here's what may be happening to your engine as a result:

- **Oil breakdown:** One of the most important jobs of motor oil is to help cool the engine. A certain amount of oil is needed to carry heat away from the hot internal parts of the engine. When the oil level drops, the remaining oil becomes hotter and begins to break down. The oil molecules form long chains of hydrocarbons, causing some of the oil to turn into tar and stick to the bottom of the engine, and the oil becomes useless. Without a good supply of cool oil, engine wear is accelerated.

- **Heat loss:** When motor oil becomes hot, it loses its capability to lubricate the hot parts of the engine. Just like hot oil in a hot frying pan, the oil forms into beads and runs off the hot metal where it is needed the most. Without oil on the sliding surfaces inside the engine, engine wear is accelerated.

If you get stuck in traffic for any length of time in really hot weather, consider how your motor oil is affected. A couple of bad cases of gridlock and your oil could really be fried.

✔ **Additive losses:** When oil level drops, the remaining oil does not have enough detergent additives to properly keep the inside of the engine clean. A low oil level causes sludge to form inside the engine, clogging up oil passages and starving critical parts of much-needed oil.

✔ **Driveway spots:** Pay attention to your parking spot. Does your vehicle leave suspicious stains on the ground? These stains can be tip-offs to problems.

Lay a flattened-out cardboard box in your parking place, and park your car over it after driving some distance. ***Important:*** Make sure that the cardboard is flat and not near a hot muffler.

The next day, move the car and examine the cardboard for spots. If you see any, make a mental note of where on the car the spot came from. Cut out the soiled piece of cardboard and take it to your mechanic for further diagnosis.

Reacting to the Red Light: What to Do with No Oil Pressure

You are driving merrily along one fine day and suddenly your red oil pressure or engine light comes on. You don't hear any knocking and have no idea what can possibly be causing the problem. What do you do?

A. Drive to the next exit, pull into a service station, and have the oil level checked.

B. Drive to your destination and have the problem checked at your convenience.

C. Reach under the dash and remove the offending bulb.

D. Immediately pull off the road and check your oil level. Add oil as necessary.

Surprising as it may seem, the answer is D. (Would you believe that a significant number of people choose answer A?)

Usually, the oil light comes on when there is a leak and the engine oil level is low. But what if the engine is full of oil and the light comes on?

There are several possible reasons for the oil pressure light to come on:

✔ **You are low on oil.** For whatever reason, you should get more oil in the engine and get the oil loss problem checked. In order for the light to come on, no oil will be showing on the dipstick. You will find that the engine is at least two quarts low.

✔ **There has been a catastrophic loss of oil pressure.** When this happens, the engine usually begins to knock and rattle within a few minutes of the light coming on. (Technically speaking, as the lifters are deprived of oil pressure and bleed down, they start to go clickety-click. The rod bearings begin to make low-end knocking noises as they lose oil pressure.)

This cacophony of horrible engine noises increases in amplitude until the engine either seizes up or throws a connecting rod through the side of the block! In either case, the end result is the total demise of your engine.

If you think that the engine has lost oil pressure, don't try to tough it out unless you are hell-bent on replacing the engine. If you are in a tight spot and really have to get further down the road, add a couple extra quarts of oil to the engine. Drive as if you have an egg under your foot, giving the engine as little gas as possible. Keep the engine rpms as low as you possibly can and don't go over 35 mph.

✔ **The hole leading into the oil pressure switch has been plugged, fooling it into believing that there is no oil pressure.** If you don't hear noises and the engine purrs just as nicely as always, there is a chance that you have nothing immediate to worry about. Nonetheless, be sure to have the oil pressure checked as soon as possible.

If your engine has enough sludge to plug up the switch, you have a serious sludge problem. Sludge can also prevent oil from lubricating important parts inside the engine and, in extreme cases, can starve the engine of oil.

✔ **The oil pressure sending unit has failed.** Technically speaking, the circuit is nothing more than a switch that completes a ground for the oil light. When the engine develops enough oil pressure, the resistance of a spring opens the switch. It is possible for the switch to short internally. Even though there is oil pressure, the switch remains grounded. In other words, the switch is defective.

✔ **The wire connecting the sending unit to the dash gauge has somehow been grounded** (shorted to ground or shorted out). If you suspect this to be the case, unplug the oil pressure sender. If the light stays on, the wire is grounded. If the light goes out, there may still be a problem with the sending unit.

If the oil light comes on at idle or low speeds and then goes off at higher engine rpms, there is almost always a loss of oil pressure, but this loss is not bad enough to cause the engine to seize up and destroy itself. You are living on borrowed time, and engine replacement looms in your immediate future.

 People employ several tricks of the trade in order to get a little more borrowed time before the engine goes out to lunch:

✔ **Add 2 – 3 cans of STP Oil Treatment to the engine or change the oil to straight 50-weight oil.** The thicker oil temporarily causes the oil light to stay off but buys only a little time before you face inevitable engine failure. *Note:* This used-car-lot trick has been around for many years and is used to thicken the oil just enough to keep the warning light from coming on.

✔ **Replace the oil pump.** Because the pump generates oil pressure, this fix can actually last for a while. However, the pump usually wears out with the engine bearings. Replacing the pump helps to restore the pressure, but rest assured that the bearings will soon fail.

 ✔ **Dump the oil and use 100 percent synthetic oil.** I personally have employed this tactic on my own 1980 Chrysler 225 engine. The engine has been knocking for a long time yet is still going strong after 30 – 40,000 miles. Synthetic oil does such a good job of lubricating the bearings that it pretty much eliminates further wear.

✔ **Remove the oil pan and replace the worn-out bearings.** Since the crankshaft is probably ruined (it has been worn out-of-round and can't be repaired), the bearings won't last long. Remove the crankshaft and replace it along with all the bearings. One trick is to remove the oil pan and replace the worn-out bearing shells.

✔ Some used-car lot salespeople have actually installed pieces of leather in place of bearings for a temporary fix. This fix is good only for a few minutes.

One fellow installed leather in place of a spun bearing and towed the car to within a few blocks of a used-car lot. He started the car and drove it onto the used car lot. Then he traded it in for another used car, making a killing on the deal. By the time the car lot found the ruse, the sly customer was long gone. This time someone actually pulled a reverse scam on a used-car lot!

Determining Oil Pressure

How do you know whether you have enough oil pressure? What if your car came equipped with an oil pressure gauge? Can you trust it? When do you start making plans for a new engine or new car? Can your oil pressure tell you when things are about to start coming apart inside your engine? Is there such a thing as too much oil pressure? Is too much oil pressure harmful? These are some commonly asked questions regarding oil pressure.

 In order to accurately determine engine oil pressure, you should fit a mechanical gauge to the engine oil pressure port. Usually the oil pressure sending unit is removed and an analog gauge is plumbed into the passageway. This type of gauge doesn't rely on the electrical circuitry used by the engine sending unit and dash gauge cluster. Dash gauges are not accurate and should be used only to monitor changes in the pressure in relation to typical readings.

Before making oil pressure readings, the engine oil should be changed. The oil may be diluted with gasoline, throwing off the readings. Also, used oil may have lost its foam inhibitors. Foam also causes low readings.

Next, thoroughly heat up the oil. The oil on the dipstick should be almost too hot to touch. This takes 20 minutes or more, depending on the ambient temperature. Failure to allow oil to reach operating temperature results in artificially high pressure readings!

Rule of thumb: There should be one pound of oil pressure (1 psi) for every 100 rpms of engine speed. If the engine is idling at 650 rpms, for example, there should be at least 6 $^1/_2$ pounds of oil pressure. At 3,000 rpms, there should be at least 30 psi of oil pressure.

Most oil pressure sending units are set to close their internal contacts and illuminate the oil pressure warning light at 3 – 5 psi of oil pressure. This is considered the minimum amount of oil pressure for an engine at idle.

If your engine is running at the minimum level of pressure, it is time to think about a rebuilt engine or another vehicle. Usually the oil light will start coming on at idle after you drive for some distance. This means that the oil has heated up and thinned out — and the pump is incapable of making enough pressure to turn off the oil pressure switch.

Most oil pumps have internal pressure relief valves that limit engine oil pressure to no more than 70 – 80 psi. When an engine is cold and the oil is thick, the pressure can easily reach that high. If the oil pressure relief valve doesn't open and bleed off the excess oil pressure, the oil filter may rupture. The oil pump can easily produce more than 100 psi of oil pressure if the oil pressure relief valve sticks shut.

While good oil filters are made to withstand this kind of pressure, cheap ones are not. For example, a Hastings oil filter is rated to hold 300 psi of oil pressure. A cheap brand filter can only handle 60 – 80 psi of pressure before the can splits open at the seam or separates from the base.

Be a Dipstick Detective

EGAD, HOLMES !

When was the last time you considered your oil level dipstick a diagnostic tool? As simple as it seems, a thorough examination of your dipstick can give you valuable information about the health of your engine. Everyone who checks his or her own oil should become familiar with the trouble signs that can show up on the end of a dipstick.

Pull the dipstick and carefully examine the oil on the end. Do so *before* changing the oil, or you will miss the story. If you wait until the oil is clean, all the evidence will be gone.

Goopy scuzz

If the end of the dipstick looks like it was used to stir a chocolate milkshake, you have problems. Here are several possible causes:

- ✔ **Short-distance driving:** People who don't drive very far never warm their oil enough to boil off any contaminants. (Short trips are ten miles or less per trip per direction.) This causes moisture build-up inside the engine, resulting in a whitish film on the dipstick. When you see such a film, it is time for an oil change. Short-distance drivers should change their oil more frequently than the recommended intervals.

- ✔ **Bad thermostat:** Sometimes cooling system thermostats fail to close completely and the engine never gets hot. The results are the same as in the preceding situation, even for long-distance drivers.

- ✔ **Blown seal:** Commonly resulting from a blown head gasket, this kind of dipstick goop signals the need for some expensive repairs. If you detect it in time, you are in for a head gasket replacement with some additional machine shop costs. If not, the scuzz will neutralize the oil on the cylinder walls, and the piston rings will scrape the walls without lubricating oil. Then you'll need a new engine.

Slimy sand

Now grab a bit of the stuff right off the end of the stick and squeeze it between your fingers. This is not a job for the faint of heart — that oil can be slimy, gross, and sometimes really hot! Does it seem gritty? If so, your engine is in jeopardy of the sandman. Fine grit or sand is getting in somehow and is about to cost you a motor. Sand quickly infiltrates and destroys engine bearings unless you take immediate steps. The time to start is right now.

Used oil can cause cancer if left on your skin for prolonged periods. Be sure to clean it off completely with warm soap and water.

Begin by checking for every possible source that would allow sand to leak into the engine. Don't stop until you have fixed the leak. Also, change the oil, oil filter, and air filter immediately. Possible "sand doors" include the following:

- Poor air filter seal or air filter canister seal, including possible holes in the air ductwork and seals connecting the filter to the throttle body

- Leaking crankcase ventilation system, grommets, PCV valve hoses, or vent filter

- Leaking oil filter cap seal, gasket, or rubber sealing grommet

- Leaking valve cover gasket or valve cover end seals

- Leaking front or rear engine seals

Smelly stew

Let your nose play detective. Sniff the end of the oil dipstick. If it smells something like old turpentine, the oil is polluted with unburned gasoline. After smelling enough oil, you can easily identify this condition with your nose.

Another test is to place a drop of the suspicious oil on a piece of white copy paper. Watch how the oil soaks in and spreads. If it soaks right into the paper and quickly spreads into a big stain, it is gas contaminated. If you still aren't sure, try testing oil from several other cars as well as some fresh oil.

If the oil is contaminated, your engine is leaking fuel into the oil, and your duty is to track down the source. It is important to check this out because you have a fire hazard under the hood. If you don't find the fuel leak, the engine can blow up. Furthermore, the piston rings and cylinder walls may become damaged if you don't do something.

Start by checking the following:

- Leaking carburetors or injectors allow fuel to run into the oil pan when the engine is not running.

- Leaking rubber diaphragm on the fuel pump (carbureted vehicles) or fuel pressure regulator (fuel-injected vehicles) may be contaminating the oil.

- The Charcoal Evaporative Emission Canister may not be doing its job. If the activated charcoal can't hold gas fumes from the fuel tank because the charcoal is deactivated, the engine will be filled with gas fumes. Also, be suspicious of the plumbing and valves to the canister. On occasion, the canister venting system allows fuel from an over-filled gas tank to be routed into the intake manifold, filling the engine.

Black blot

If the dipstick is so dark that you can't even see the metal marks under the blackened oil, you are overdue for a change. While engine oil normally blackens with age, it should not be like tar.

After changing the oil, keep checking the dipstick. If the oil seems to darken quickly, be suspicious. Blackened oil usually means that the oil contains burned carbon particles (soot). Soot is getting into your engine, and the oil is suffering because soot causes the detergents to break down and the oil to thicken. *Note:* Diesel engines are an exception because their oil is normally black.

The oil should be changed immediately, and you should consider the reason for contamination in the first place. Here are some of the more common causes:

✔ Oil change intervals may be too far apart for your driving conditions. You are probably running the engine hard, revving it too high, or otherwise stressing it.

✔ Your engine is running too hot due to malfunction of one or more other systems. Anything that causes engine overheating can cause the oil to burn and darken quickly.

✔ Combustion by-products are polluting the oil. Sources of combustion by-products in the oil include worn piston rings and excessive blowby caused by poor crankcase ventilation when the engine is under load.

✔ Using the wrong grade of oil can cause oil breakdown. Oils marked 5W-30 and 10W-40 are likely culprits when they are pushed past their limits. These thinner oils don't hold up to sustained high-speed driving or hot weather operation.

With practice, you will be able to diagnose most major problems with a glance, a sniff, a touch, and some hand soap. Avoid a lot of wasted time, money, and grief by regularly inspecting your dipstick.

Zen Dipsticks

When, where, why, and how are some of the questions people have about car maintenance. A car owner's manual plainly details the factory recommended service intervals. But what about the in-between time? Do you simply leave the hood closed between required service visits? This section gives you some tips about what you can do to maintain your car with minimal effort. For the sake of preventative maintenance, it is a good idea to get involved with your vehicle.

Zen is the practice of doing a great deal with little effort. It also refers to carrying out a duty without any thinking needed to complete the work. Think of this as an exercise in Zen: A little effort carrying out the necessary steps for maintaining your car produces benefits of huge proportions, especially in saving money. The idea is to achieve maximum results by doing the bare minimum, just like Zen.

When? Most people purchase fuel every week. While this may seem an ideal time to check your vehicle, the liquid levels in the engine cooling system and oil are best checked when the engine is cold, before you run it. A weekly check, perhaps one morning, is generally the best.

Where? If you have no idea what the oil level should be or where the dipstick or fill indicator mark is, consult your owner's manual or stop by the shop and find out where to look.

Why bother? Because you want to develop a relationship with your car, like a Zen master and student. Don't be intimidated. You are your car's master. Your vehicle is in your charge. You must monitor its progress as it gets old, or you run the risk of surprise repairs down the road. You can avoid many repairs if you follow a good preventative maintenance program. You have to put a little bit of energy into the relationship to gain the benefits of a trouble-free car.

Who? Face it; somebody has to do it. Who do you trust: the corner gas station attendant or yourself? Yes, you are the best person to carefully monitor the situation under your hood. By using the methods outlined in Chapter 4 and with a little practice, you can learn a lot about your engine.

Chapter 2
Batteries and Brakes

● ●

In This Chapter

▶ Extending the life of your battery

▶ Knowing when your battery is about to die

▶ First aid for ailing batteries

▶ Reviving a really dead battery

▶ Slaying "dragon" brakes

▶ Breaking in new brakes

● ●

*W*ithout the battery in your car, you have nothing! No lights, no radio, and even more importantly, no starting power. When was the last time you took a look at your battery or gave it some care? This chapter passes on some tips that will make you a battery expert — or at least imparts some expert advice. Also, I'll explain some ways to revive a battery that appears dead and bring it back from the great beyond. Finally, you'll learn how to spot and deal with the brakes failing to release and how to break in new brakes so that they will last much longer.

Making Your Battery Last

Always wear protective eyewear when working with batteries.

The life span of your battery depends on you. Proper attention can extend its life, and poor treatment can shorten it. This section gives you some practical advice to help you get the most from your battery.

You must begin with the right battery. Select one with a minimum Cold Cranking Amp (CCA) capacity of at least 1 CCA per cubic inch of engine displacement, 1.5 CCA per cubic inch for reliable subzero starting, and 2 CCA per cubic inch for diesel engines.

Tap water is poisonous to batteries. If you have a battery that allows water to be added, do not let garage mechanics add tap water — it contains minerals that are harmful to the battery. Always use distilled water in your battery.

Heat is harmful to batteries as well. Modern cars have higher engine compartment heat because of downsizing. In addition, smaller front grilles and lower hoodlines allow less air into the engine area. As a result, engines run hotter than ever.

Air space around a battery is important, and the engine area should have a cooling duct directing air flow toward the battery. Heat can cause the internal battery plates to warp. Warped plates can touch, shorting out the battery, so do not remove the battery cooling duct or case.

Make sure that the battery is securely mounted. Vibration shakes off the chemical coating on the battery plates inside, ruining the battery. Pounding on a battery clamp with a hammer has the same effect and can also break the battery case. A loosely secured battery can be jarred hard enough to hit the hood and short out; therefore, make sure that the battery is securely mounted. Also, vibration damage from road shocks can cause separations between plates, resulting in dead cells and premature battery failure.

> TIP
>
> Clean the battery and its tray regularly, especially in areas where road salt is used. The accumulation of dirt and grime on the battery top will cause it to discharge itself in short order. This accumulation makes the alternator work harder, too.

Please keep in mind that improper handling can cause permanent damage to internal battery connections. Do not lift the battery by the posts. Also, use caution when connecting battery cables, and don't overtighten the connections because the terminals may break away.

Recognizing Signs of Impending Battery Doom

Winter plays havoc with batteries, especially in the Snowbelt. Even loose or corroded battery connecting terminals and cables can cause a no-start condition. Batteries don't suddenly quit. If your battery dies one cold, dark morning, the truth is that it has been terminally ill for some time.

By the time your battery shows symptoms of a problem, it's usually beyond help. You may have to buy another one, pay tow charges, and possibly shell out for a new alternator. While there is little or nothing you can do to repair a battery, it is possible to predict its imminent failure. Here are some telltale signs of trouble:

- **Wet on top:** This usually means that the battery system is overcharging, but it may also mean that the battery is incapable of accepting a charge. As the internal plates wear out, their capability to accept and retain a charge diminishes. As a result, the remaining active portion of the battery plates does all the work but is overcharged by the alternator. The overheated portion of the plates boils the battery acid electrolyte, making the battery wet on top.

- **Fuzzy terminals:** When the battery heats up and gases are released, acid from the electrolyte is carried out the vents and attacks the terminals and battery posts. As a result, the terminals become covered with corrosion.

  A healthy battery doesn't need to have the terminals cleaned.

- **Thirsty:** Does the battery level keep going down, constantly needing water added? The battery electrolyte level drops, and the cells require additional water as a result. After the battery starts to use water, it is almost certain to fail within 12 months. Refilling the battery with tap water hastens its death.

✔ **One fuzzy terminal:** This is the sign of a cracked battery case. The crack may be invisible to the eye, but it's there. Usually it's near the edge where the metal post meets the battery top. Movement of the vehicle causes the electrolyte to splash onto the post where it enters the underside of the battery top. The acid wicks up the post to the terminal, causing the terminal to corrode and creating excessive resistance in the battery circuit.

Excessive resistance makes the alternator work harder to keep the battery charged. This condition quickly ruins the alternator as it overworks to charge the battery through a corroded terminal. Acid may also leak onto the battery tray, ruining it and any other nearby electrical connections.

✔ **Bulge:** A bulging battery case means that the end is near. Excessive internal heat build-up caused by an aging battery makes the metal plates expand and push outward on the battery case. Conversely, a battery case may bulge if it is frozen. The electrolyte turns to ice, expands, and pushes outward on the battery.

✔ **Meter reader:** The dash ammeter shows that the battery is charging constantly. If your car has an ammeter, it should show a charge condition (positive or higher readings) only after you start the car and while you are using the lights and accessories. Otherwise, the battery is weak and the alternator is working overtime to keep it charged. If the meter registers full charge immediately after you start the vehicle, the battery is very weak.

Allowed to continue, this condition may cause the alternator to quit before the battery dies, making it seem as though the alternator is at fault. Your mechanic will probably replace the alternator and charge the battery, which will then weaken the new alternator and so on. The battery will finally refuse to accept a charge and will be replaced. By then, the battery may have destroyed several alternators.

Beating the Battery Blues

Nothing ruins a day like getting into your car or truck, turning the key, and...nothing. Don't let the battery blues get you down. Know your battery's enemies and how to fight them off so that you don't get left in the dark.

Undercharging

Average battery life is about 48 months, depending on type, size, and internal construction. Many batteries fail earlier because of deep discharging or chronic undercharging.

Excessively cranking over the engine or leaving the lights on completely discharges the battery. Letting the car sit for long periods without using it also discharges the battery. As a result, *sulphation* occurs: Sulfur permanently attaches to the metal plates in the battery, preventing it from fully recovering when recharged. Sulfur on the plates slows the chemical reaction that produces electrical current.

Chronic undercharging can be caused by too many short trips, excessive cranking, a defective voltage regulator, a weak alternator, a slipping fan belt, or undetected excessive voltage drain resulting from an electrical short or trunk light that stays on. It takes about 30 minutes of driving to restore the current used in just two minutes of cranking.

In general, a sulphated battery is junk and must be replaced. However, you can easily and cheaply employ several tricks that will sometimes bring a dead, sulphated battery back from the boneyard.

Restoring sulfated batteries

Slow charging at 6–8 amps for up to 24 hours may bring a dead battery back to life. If a battery does not accept a "trickle charge" (1–2 amps) after two hours, it's probably beyond hope. A trickle charger can be employed; the battery charger set on the lowest setting also works.

 If a dead battery will not accept a charge, connect the dead battery in parallel (positive to positive, negative to negative) with a good battery and then connect both batteries to a charger.

Note: Some battery chargers are specifically designed to break through the sulfate layer by applying a higher charging voltage of 18–20 volts.

Overcharging

If your alternator is overcharging your battery, your battery can fail from plate damage or loss of electrolyte. A low electrolyte level (low liquid level inside the battery) or frequent light bulb replacement are symptoms of an alternator that is overcharging. Have a shop test your alternator's output and compare your results to the specifications. If output is high, first check the voltage regulator connections and its ground, which are likely sources of alternator overcharging problems.

Reviving a Really Dead Battery

If you go away for a while, leave your car lights on, and run the battery dead flat, is it possible to revive it? Long sitting without charging also runs down the battery. Can it be revived after you come back and want to use it? The answer is *sometimes* — but it is worth the effort to try anyway. When a battery goes totally flat, the acid goes into the lead plates, leaving the electrolyte composed of mostly water. This is why a battery that is low on charge can freeze in cold weather. A charged battery contains a liquid that is mostly acid. A dead one contains water that will easily freeze and crack the battery case.

Before attempting to revive a dead battery, check the condition of the battery posts. If they are loose, the battery is junk. Now, gently pry off the top of the battery and check the level of the electrolyte. Look inside the battery and see whether the liquid electrolyte is up to the top of the filler hole liquid-level-mark. If the top is sealed, inspect it closely. In many cases, the seal can be cut open so that the cover can be removed.

 Do not attempt to charge a battery that is low on electrolyte — it might overheat and explode! Also, be sure to add only distilled water.

Sometimes the battery is so dead that it needs a very high initial charge to shock it back to life. Your mechanic can use a boost charger placed on the highest setting (at least 30 amps) to give the battery a boost for about 30 minutes to get the charge started. Now the battery is ready for a lower charge for at least eight hours.

If the battery has been discharged too many times, some of the sulfuric acid becomes permanently bonded to the lead plates. This condition (called *sulphation*) can result in a charging voltage of more than 16 volts because the cells are only taking a very surface charge. Even after a two-day charge, a sulfated battery may only come to 60–80 percent of capacity.

Sometimes a mildly sulfated battery can be cycled and brought back to near 100 percent capacity. To do this, the battery needs to be discharged to about 50 percent state of charge and recharged through several charging and discharging cycles. If the battery fails to come up on subsequent charges, it is junk. Remember, a slightly sulfated battery will cause the vehicle's alternator to run all the time — costing gas mileage and eventually killing the alternator!

A battery below 11.6 volts is considered to be heavily sulfated and in a low state of charge and needs special charging. It should be placed on a very long, slow state of charge for a minimum of two days, preferably three to four days.

Because the sulfuric acid is tied up and stratified into the plates, the acid needs a sufficient overcharge to get back into solution.

Even after the battery comes up to a full state of charge, it is a good idea to give it an additional 1 amp charge for another day to "freshen it up." Do this after a one-day cooling-off period.

Batteries showing from 11.6 to 12.1 volts also need extra time to reach full charging capacity. It is also a good idea to freshen the battery up with a 1 amp charge for another day. With any low voltage battery, it is always wise to give it a second charge after letting it cool down for a day.

Looking for internal shorts in the battery

Checking a battery's specific gravity is a good way to tell whether the battery has internal problems. Use a quality hydrometer ($5 to $15) and avoid using one that has floating balls that have been saturated with battery acid, or it may be inaccurate. If there is any question, compare your hydrometer with a known good one. Also, beware of bubbles sticking to the float(s) and compensate for ambient temperature as shown on the hydrometer. If the hydrometer doesn't have a built-in temperature chart, consult a battery charging chart or ask a battery store for the correct number for the ambient temperature in your area.

A battery with specific gravity readings between cells differing more than 30 points are suspect and may harbor potential problems down the road. Batteries showing more than 50 points difference between cells in gravity are junk. Ditto for two or more "floating balls" when using a hydrometer.

When checking the voltage levels on the battery, first check the voltage with the battery connected to the charger and then again after the battery has been at rest for about an hour. A sulfated battery shows very high initial voltage level, which drops off as soon as the charger is turned off.

Beware of a battery that is below 11.6 volts and is shorted between the lead plates. Lead sulfate in the separator will form a shunt across the positive and negative plates, and the battery will self-discharge quickly. Also, if a standard charger is used with a maximum voltage of 14.8 volts, beware of a battery that gets really hot to the touch when charging. This is another sign of internal shorts.

 Always wear safety goggles when working around batteries and never make a spark in the region of the battery when it is charging or after it has been charged. Treat it with respect. A sulfated or shorted battery can explode without warning while being charged! Sulfuric acid causes severe skin burns, damages a car's paint, and corrodes metal parts. Always protect your hands and eyes when handling a battery.

An easy tip-off is the smell of burning friction material. To some people, this is the smell of burning plastic or Bakelight. If you have ever left a pot on the stove and burned the Bakelight handles, you know the smell. Get out of the car and give each wheel a sniff. Smell hot? Now, carefully do the touch test. Find the hot one?

Blasting batteries

Imagine the force of an explosion from a quarter of a stick of dynamite. The hydrogen in your car battery would have that much force if it exploded. Heed the following advice to avoid a blasted battery:

✔ Never charge a battery while it is connected to the car.

✔ Make sure that the vent caps are tight, and cover with a damp cloth if possible.

✔ Never disconnect a car battery while the car is running or while the ignition is on.

✔ Always connect the negative jumper cable clamp last and disconnect it first. Never connect to fuel line tubing or moving parts. Don't allow the positive clamps to touch any metal other than the battery cables.

✔ Always fully recharge any battery before installing it or driving. Installing a dead battery or jump-starting a car with a dead battery and letting the alternator charge the dead battery may overtax the alternator, causing system failure and an unexpected breakdown.

✔ Never use a 24-volt truck charger on a 12-volt automotive system. Doing so can damage sensitive components, which can then fail.

✔ Never attempt to jump-start or recharge a frozen battery or a battery with a low electrolyte level.

✔ Always wear safety glasses and stand back before starting the disabled car.

Slaying Dragon Brakes

One common cause of poor fuel mileage is dragging brakes. Dragging brakes also cause car owners to frequently replace brake pads or shoes. Many vehicles have this problem, and the owners have no idea that something is wrong. It's like driving with one foot on the gas and the other pushing the brake pedal. Your car is trying to go and stop at the same time. What a waste of gas and brake material!

Spotting dragon brakes

One of the simplest ways to determine whether your brakes are dragging is to do a coast test. Simply put the gear selector in neutral and see how far the car will coast. Does it feel like the vehicle is free-wheeling, or does it seem like the brakes are slowing you down? This type of brake drag is especially noticeable just before the vehicle comes to a rest.

Dragging brakes also generate friction and heat up the brake assembly, including the wheel. One way to catch a dragging brake is to carefully feel the hub of the wheel. If you have driven for some distance and coast to a stop, the hub should be cool to the touch under nondragging conditions. If it is hot, the brakes are dragging. Careful! The hub can be really hot and burn your hand.

As the brake friction material heats up, mechanics say in technical jargon that "its coefficient of friction will change." In other words, as the friction material and rotor (drum) get hot, they become more grabby. At some point, the friction material gets so hot that it loses its coefficient of friction and begins to fade. Overheated brakes will either be too sticky or will react poorly when you press the pedal, causing the brakes to fade.

Testing the mechanical way

Here are some neat, quick tests to determine the mechanical cause of dragging brakes.

Bleed and squirt

If you suspect that a certain wheel is not fully releasing, break open the bleeder on that wheel. If opening the bleeder screw results in a healthy squirt of brake fluid, that wheel's brakes are being held under brake fluid pressure.

This test works even better when the wheels are off the ground. If the wheel is hard to turn before you open the bleeder and turns freely after the bleeder is opened, there is a fluid restriction somewhere upstream.

Crack and drip

Crack the master cylinder connecting lines (where the lines come out from the vehicle and join to the master cylinder) about one-half turn. If the master cylinder is fully released, the fluid will be able to seep past the internal seals and drip out of the loosened fittings. If there is pressure on the master cylinder pushrod, the internal seals will cover up the fluid reservoir, preventing fluid from dripping out.

If there are no drips, pull up on the brake pedal and see whether the fluid starts dripping. Sometimes it may be necessary to unbolt the master cylinder from its mount in order to make it drip. These conditions mean that the master cylinder pushrod is being held in a slightly applied position by a binding brake pedal, stop lamp switch, or faulty power booster.

Turn and rock

In some rare cases, loose wheel bearings or suspension components allow the brakes to drag. To find this kind of problem, remove the cover from the master cylinder. Turn the wheel completely from lock to lock and watch for a spurt of liquid on the surface of the master cylinder as you reach the end of the turn in each direction. Repeat the test while pushing and pulling on the front end, rocking it from side to side. If there is a spurt, the wheel bearing or ball joint is loose, allowing the brake rotor to move against the brake pad.

Pump and squirt

If air is trapped in the brake system, the brakes may drag when the air expands as it is heated by the brake fluid. To quickly identify trapped air, pump the brakes vigorously several times. Remove the master cylinder cover and quickly release the brake pedal. If air is trapped, there will be a *huge* squirt of fluid from the reservoir when the air pushes back against the fluid. Be careful not to allow the fluid to get on the paint or in your eyes!

Mechanical testing

A mechanical device that uses hydraulic pressure and a very high reading pressure gauge actually measures the amount of physical pressure that is put upon a sensing pad. The device can be used to measure residual pressure on each brake caliper. These devices are not common, so you may have to ask a professional to do this for you. Using this device will pinpoint a sticking brake component without question.

Why is it happening?

The list of reasons for brake drag is a long one. Start at the top of the list and work your way down. The causes are generally written in most likely to least likely order.

The typical reason for brake drag is linkage binding. Another common cause is the brake-light-pedal switch getting out of adjustment. Sometimes, pulling up on the brake pedal provides temporary relief, but the brake light switch is usually faulty. A weak brake pedal return spring could also be at fault.

Lubricating the brakes with WD-40 may be all that is necessary to cure binding linkage. The brake light switch, mounted at the top of the brake pedal arm, usually must be replaced or at least repositioned. Lastly, the spring, also located at the top of the brake pedal, must be replaced if it is too weak.

Another common cause for brake drag is a restricted hydraulic line (hoses that act as check valves) where the inside of the hose lining comes loose where you can't see it. When mechanics do brake work, they often use brake hose pliers (or vice-grips) to pinch off brake lines. As a result, the internal walls of the hose become damaged and come loose. The brake fluid is forced into the brake wheel caliper or cylinder but can't get back to the master cylinder when the brake is released. This is because the hose lets the fluid come from the master cylinder but acts like a check-valve and doesn't let it return. The end result is that the brakes are held applied by the fluid pressure build-up.

Corrosion of the brake hardware can cause brake drag. Most common is corrosion of the brake caliper slides, mounts, and other sliding hardware.

 Corroded caliper slides are typically the cause of one front brake wearing out faster than the other.

Parking brake cable corrosion, linkage, or adjusting hardware cause rapid rear brake wear because the parking brake cable attaches to the rear wheels. When it binds, only the rear brakes drag.

Dirty work habits can cause premature brake failure. After a rotor or brake drum is machined (as in turning the rotors), the metal shavings need to be cleaned out of the part. The rotor or brake drum is supposed to be cleaned with hot, soapy water. Most mechanics don't bother cleaning the part, leaving fine metal dust impregnated in the friction surface. These metal shavings are caught up by the brake friction material and become abrasive, causing the brake pad material to wear out quickly.

Machining brake drums and rotors is a normal part of every brake job. The components are mounted in a lathe and machined until they are *trued*, or flat, again. After the machining operation is completed, it's a nuisance for the mechanic to stop and take the time to properly clean off the shavings. There is really nothing you can do about this practice unless you do your own brake work. In this case, you can clean the drums and/or rotors yourself before you install them.

Why does one brake job seem to last twice as long as another? Why do the original brakes that came with the car last so much longer than the replacement brake linings? Where does the brake pad and brake shoe friction material go? How long a brake job lasts depends on the type of lining chosen for the replacement brake shoes and/or pads. The friction material goes into the dust alongside the highway (as well as all over your wheels).

If the wrong grade, type of friction material, or cheap brake linings are chosen by the mechanic for your particular brake job, the pads or shoes won't last long (for example, semimetallic material may be the standard equipment, but cheaper organic material is used instead). Also, brake lining friction material is graded using letter codes to represent the coefficient of friction. The grade AA is very soft, and the grade FF is very hard. If the friction material is supposed to be an FF, type EE will be too soft for the design. You'll be back for another brake job in record time!

If the brake friction material chosen is too hard, you will have difficulty pressing the brake pedal (excessive effort) and the brakes will squeal like a stuck pig every time you use them (very annoying and embarrassing). If you want to determine the correct coefficient grade for your vehicle, stop by the dealer parts department and examine the edge code on a new set of linings.

Faulty shoe adjustment is responsible for the rear shoes not doing their share of stopping the vehicle. The fronts have to do all the work and quickly wear out. Improper rear shoe/pad adjustment is typically caused by your not using reverse gear or the parking brake often enough. Using the reverse gear and/or the parking brake automatically adjusts the rear brakes.

Two-footed drivers are another common cause of excessive brake wear. Have you ever driven behind someone who keeps pressing the brake and the brake lights flash on and off as they drive along. Most people who rest their left foot on the brake pedal are unaware of this condition and merrily press on the brakes as they simultaneously press on the gas pedal. You can't stop and go at the same time! The brakes really take a beating when you drive with two feet — because you don't know it when you are causing the brakes to apply.

 Other less likely causes include a rough, corroded master cylinder; swollen rubber cups in the system; loose or worn front wheel bearings; bent linings; loose or distorted backing plate; weak or broken shoe return springs; faulty power brake booster (leaky valves, weak reaction springs binding); overfilled master cylinder (with a diaphragm-type cover gasket); defective master cylinder quick-take-up valve; or aftermarket wheels or wheel covers that cause the brakes to overheat.

Breaking in New Brakes

The world's biggest auto-maker recently published a new procedure for breaking in new brakes. The procedure was published in a technical service bulletin for GM technicians to follow when replacing brake pads and is applicable to all brands of brakes on all types of vehicles. Following GM, several aftermarket companies have come out with their versions of the procedure. I feel it is important enough for you to know about it.

If you are a technician, you probably don't have time to leave your repair bay and drive the vehicle for half an hour in order to properly break in (burnish) the new brake pads. Make a copy of the procedure and give it to your customers to follow. If you are not a mechanic and you get a new set of brake pads installed, consider following this procedure in order to get the best results from your brakes.

When a new set of pads are installed in a disc brake system, the pads must form a proper seat against the brake rotor. It takes a number of stops before the friction material is able to grind down enough to conform to the surface of the brake rotor. Until this happens, only a small part of the brake pad is able to make contact with the spinning brake rotor.

This process is called *burnishing the pads*. If the brake pads are not properly burnished, the friction material can be subjected to a great deal of excessive heat during the time the pads are seating themselves. This heat causes the brake bonding resins in the brake pad to crystallize, turning the friction material into a very hard substance.

Crystallized pads cause poor brake performance, a hard brake pedal, and brake noise. Brake pads that are crystallized and too hard squeal, grind, or groan when you apply the brakes. The rotors also suffer from excessive scoring and accelerated wear by the pads.

While it is not necessary to go out and do the burnish procedure in a parking lot, you can carry it out by paying attention to your braking and making sure that you don't overheat the brakes. In fact, it may take you days or even weeks to complete the procedure on your own. Here's the burnish procedure:

1. **From 40 mph, take 6 seconds to stop.**

   Keep rotors cool by driving half a mile between stops.

2. – 11. **From 50 mph, take 5 seconds to stop.**

   In other words, for the next 10 stops, take 5 seconds to stop. Remember to drive half a mile between stops to cool the rotors.

12. **From 40 mph, take 6 seconds to stop.**

13. **Finally, cool the brakes by driving 3 – 4 miles without applying the brakes.**

Chapter 3
Tires and Other Important Parts

● ●

In This Chapter

▶ Understanding the hype about tire rotation

▶ Maximizing the life of your tires

▶ Changing your spark plugs

▶ Squashing squeaks inside your car

▶ Cleaning and "de-squeaking" your windshield wipers

▶ Unlocking vapor lock

● ●

*W*hy should you rotate your tires? What can you do to get the most from your tires? What is the proper way to change spark plugs? How can you get rid of squeaks, and what are the best ways of loosening rusty nuts and bolts? How do you make those noisy wiper blades shut up? What is vapor lock, and how do you deal with it when it attacks your engine? This chapter answers all these questions and more.

Tires Rotation Pros and Cons

To rotate or not to rotate, that is the question — and a controversial one at that. To some, it is simply a matter of economics. To others, it is a safety concern. One way of looking at it only involves short-term consideration, and another way takes into account the big picture. One school of thought says never rotate tires — just replace them as they wear out. The other side says that tire rotation causes all four tires to wear evenly and replacement involves installing a set of four new tires all at once.

The debate gets hotter. Because of a fleet management magazine article dealing with ways to avoid over-maintaining vehicles, fleet managers believe that rotating tires is a waste of time and money. The article describes the tire rotating procedures concerning several thousand leased Buick Century cars. The finds were that tire rotation did nothing to improve tire life and was only an expense. Instead of rotating the tires, this fleet manager replaced the front tires at about 30,000 miles. The rears were left in place until the cars were turned in after three years of use or 60,000 miles, whichever came first. Because the cars were used by traveling salespeople, mileage was the deciding factor. The vehicles usually racked up the mileage in about two years.

The author claims to have saved $204,000 from not replacing the rear tires. This article made the rounds in the automotive maintenance trade circles, and now the advocates for not rotating are jubilant.

Arguments against rotation

The "non-rotators" give the following reasons for leaving the tires alone:

✔ By replacing tires in pairs, two tires on the car are always in fairly good shape. Rotating the tires means that the four tires have dangerously low tread patterns just before they are replaced.

✏️ When you factor in the cost of having the tires removed and reinstalled, the price outweighs any value gained by rotation.

What about it? Good idea? Actually, the issue is much more involved. The following section gives the rebuttal for this issue.

Arguments for rotation

Rotating the tires allows the mechanic the opportunity to make a visual check of the tires and brake system for wear of the brake pads and tire wear abnormalities. Spotting a thin brake pad can save the life of a brake rotor, and uncovering an alignment problem by recognizing uneven tire wear patterns can save the life of a perfectly good tire.

Vehicle designers engineer the suspension, steering, and brake system around four matched tires, all with equal tread. Operating a car with two of the tires always worn more or less than the other two creates a dangerous imbalance in the handling characteristics of the vehicle. The front or rear will have more aggressive tire treads, which can contribute to the loss of control in a panic situation or in inclement weather. On the other hand, if all four tires are rotated regularly, their traction capabilities always are comparable.

Replacing all four tires doesn't mean that the tread patterns are dangerously low. The Department of Transportation (DOT) requires all tiremakers to put built-in wear indicators (called *wear-bars*) on all tires sold in the US. When the first tire exhibits a wear bar, it has only enough tread to go a short while longer before it becomes unsafe. The other three usually are replaced as a matter of course, even though their wear bars aren't showing. According to the DOT, all tires are safe right down to the wear bar, leaving $1/32$" tread depth for a safety margin.

Front-wheel-drive cars have vastly different wear patterns. The front tires tend to wear on the shoulders (the part on the side where the tire curves). The rear tires tend to wear in the centers. Rotating them tends to even out those wear patterns, producing maximum tire life from all four. Instead of getting 30,000 miles on the front tires, rotation can make them last 40 – 60,000 miles.

Racking up a lot of miles on a vehicle in a short time may result in only the front tires wearing enough to require replacement. The cost savings comes out of the pocket of the next owner, who usually has to replace all four. When someone buys a car and half the tires are worn, the typical response is to get rid of all the tires because nothing is known about their history. And it is human nature to want to start out with four "known-good" tires.

Failure to rotate the rear tires makes for a very noisy ride. Anyone who drives rental cars often has experienced the howling sound of cupped rear tires. (Cupped tires have scalloped places in the tread area — like someone took a knife and carved out parts of the tread all around the tire.) A fleet manager may be able to force all the drivers to live with this noise because the car is provided as part of the job. But most car owners find the sound of poorly maintained rear tires unacceptable, replacing them long before the wear indicators show up.

If you are a fleet manager and are trying to squeeze the maintenance dollar as hard as you can, tire rotation is not for you. But if you want the maximum safety and comfort from your tires and are unwilling to put up with tire noise, read the next section to learn the proper method for rotating tires.

Maintaining Maximum Tire Life

Don't rob your tires of a long life. You can achieve the maximum life for your set of tires by following the P-R-A-B rule: *Pressure, Rotate, Align,* and *Balance.*

Pressure

Incorrect tire pressure is one of the main causes of premature tire wear and is the easiest to correct. The less pressure a tire has, the hotter it runs. Heat is the enemy of tire rubber. Low pressure also costs in fuel economy and handling. Too much air pressure causes the middle of the tire to contact the road more than the sides, resulting in poor traction and reduced emergency avoidance capability. Over-inflation also causes a harsh ride. Both over- and under-inflation cause uneven tire wear.

Note: Changes in temperature can result in low tire pressure. One pound of pressure is lost for every ten degrees of temperature drop. Tires with perfect air pressure in the summer can easily lose ten pounds of air pressure when the thermometer drops. Conversely, tires correctly inflated in the winter months can become grossly overinflated in the summer.

Check tire pressure when the tires are cold, before you drive that day. If necessary, wait at least two hours after use for the tires to cool before checking pressure. Use your own gauge; the ones on the air hoses at gas stations are grossly inaccurate. Check your tires every month or at least when the seasons change.

Using a tire gauge

First, purchase an accurate gauge. Never use one that is attached to an air hose because these gauges are terribly inaccurate. Find the label on the glove box or door post telling you the correct air pressure for your car. If you can't find the label, stop by a tire store that sells your brand of tires and inquire about the correct pressure for your car. The local dealer also should have this information. Press the tire gauge firmly against the valve stem until the tire gauge gets a good reading of the tire pressure.

Rotate

The front and rear tires wear differently. The drive axle of the car always wears more evenly than the non-drive axle. This means that the rear tires of a front-wheel-drive car wear unevenly; for a rear-wheel-drive car, the front tires wear unevenly.

The general rule of thumb is to rotate the tires every 7,500 miles. Stop-and-go city driving calls for more frequent rotation. If you drive long distances and seldom stop along the way, rotate the tires less often. *Note:* Rotate unidirectional tires only front to rear.

Four-wheel-drive exception: Do not cross the tires from one side to the other unless you see directional wear of the tire, called *heel-toe* wear. Using the palm of your hand, feel around the circumference of the tire. If it feels rough in one direction and smooth in the other, there is heel-toe wear. In this case, cross the tires.

Alignment

Poor alignment costs in two ways: premature tire failure and poor gas mileage. Poor alignment can also rob your car of steering and handling capability. Alignments should be done only by a shop with modern equipment, using the latest technology to measure *thrust angle*, which determines whether all four wheels are going in the same direction. Just measuring the front wheels is not adequate for modern cars, especially front- and four-wheel-drive cars.

Front-wheel alignment problems are usually easy to spot. If your car has a problem with rear-end alignment, however, you may not even know it unless someone tells you that your car is "dog-tracking."

Balance

Unbalanced tires wear unevenly and make your vehicle shake. In the process of balancing, tire technicians add small weights to the edges of the wheels. If you feel vibration through the steering wheel, check your wheels for missing weights. (Look for a clean spot where the weight used to be. If you have any doubt, have the tires rechecked for proper balance.) To prolong the life of your tires and suspension, have your tire balance checked every 30,000 miles — more frequently for stop-and-go drivers.

Rules for rotating

 The rotation procedure rule is this: Swap the tires front to rear and rear to front. Now switch the tires side to side on the drive axle (the axle that powers the wheels). On a front-wheel-drive car, the drive axle is the front axle, and vice versa for a rear-wheel-drive car. The old rule for radial tires, "Never cross radials," is outdated and no longer true.

Measuring tread depth

 Use a tread depth measuring gauge to keep track of tread loss. Uneven tread depth means that you need to rotate the tires. Purchase a tread depth gauge (about $10) and measure the tread in the center and sides of the tire. Keep a record to pinpoint uneven wear.

Sparky spark plug

Quick! Name a part of your car that has a 136-year history. No, it's not the sandwich that your kids left under the seat. The answer is your spark plugs.

It all began in 1860 with Etienne Lenoir, a Frenchman, who invented a hollow brass bolt with a center-mounted porcelain insulator. The spark arced across a gap between two platinum wires. The bolt was threaded into the combustion chamber and the wires projected from the end.

The next big breakthrough was the resistor spark plug. Contrary to popular belief, these were not made to suppress radio static. (Car radios were rare at the time of the resistor plug invention.) Rather, they were created to diminish rapid wear of the electrode due to spark surges. The resistor prevents the current from sparking more than once. Non-resistor plugs tend to generate several sparks before the voltage is quenched. Resistor plugs first appeared in 1948 Chryslers.

Projected tip designs came next, with the dual advantage of being both cooler and self-cleaning. Copper electrodes made them cooler still.

Precious metal electrodes followed. By replacing steel electrodes with a precious metal such as gold, platinum, and palladium, plug life can double or even triple. Platinum does not erode in the combustion chamber.

Modern engines equipped with platinum spark plugs can easily go 100,000 miles between spark plug changes.

Installing New Spark Plugs

Modern tune-ups require little more than the replacement of spark plugs. Many people elect to do this job themselves. Some techniques make the job easier, and other techniques lead to the early demise of the replacement plug. Here are spark plug installation techniques and mistakes to avoid.

Getting the plug torque correct

Proper tightening specifications are especially important for today's engines. Too much *torque,* or tightening, can result in the following problems:

- The electrode spreads farther apart, increasing the plug gap and required firing voltage.

- The plug shell can become distorted and damage the seal, causing the center electrode to blow out.

- The threads seize in place and damage the cylinder head.

Too little torque can result in the following problems:

- The plug comes loose and leaks compression, allowing the threads to fill with carbon and compression blow-by.

- The plug runs hot, causing engine ping.

- The center electrode overheats and melts.

 Generally, you achieve proper plug torque by using an inch/pound torque wrench. In reality, most mechanics use air ratchets or impact tools to install spark plugs and do not heed proper torque specifications.

As an alternative, you can tighten plugs by using the "angle method." There are two types of spark plug designs: the older gasket seal type and the tapered seat design. (When you remove the old plugs, you can see what type you have. When you purchase new ones, the type should be apparent when you look at them.) Here are the procedures for each type:

- **Gasketed plugs:** Tighten $1/4$ to $1/2$ turn after the gasket meets the cylinder head, depending upon application. New engines require a half turn, and older engines require less assuming that you're using a new sealing gasket.

- **Tapered plugs:** Tighten $1/16$ turn after the seat touches the head.

Doing it right

Installation of a new set of plugs may be the most important service that your engine receives. How you install the plugs can make a terrific difference in the life of the plugs and the life of the engine. Here are some tips:

- Wait for the engine to cool completely before you remove the plugs. If you don't, the plug threads are more likely to seize and strip out the threads.

- Don't yank on the spark plug wires. This mistake can be an expensive one. Instead, rotate the spark plug boot (the part that covers the spark plug), gently twisting and pulling until it comes free. The plug boots have a tendency to stick to the spark plugs and will tear if you yank on the wire. Gently turning and twisting the boot helps to free it up so that it doesn't tear.

- Before you remove the old plugs, remove any traces of dirt lodged in the spark plug area. When the plugs are removed, that crud can fall into the engine and damage the piston rings. Use compressed air or spray solvent to clean the area before you remove the plugs.

✔ Unscrew the plug by using a hand ratchet, not an air impact tool. If the plug starts to seize, *stop.* Spray some penetrating oil into the plug thread area and let it soak for a few minutes. Gently screw the plug into the cylinder head and back out again several times while soaking the threads with penetrating oil.

✔ Compare the part number and the physical size and shape of the old plug with a new one. Be sure to check with the dealer for any updates on part numbers. Ongoing changes in technology can sometimes provide a new or different spark plug to solve some types of drivability concerns.

✔ *Lightly* coat the threads with anti-seize compound. Don't overdo it! Too much can make the compound leak onto the electrode and cause a short.

✔ Always start screwing in the plugs by hand. This step is very important because you can cross-thread the plug if you aren't careful. If the spark plug threads go into the engine threads wrong, the spark plug will not screw in all the way and the threads will be mucked up. Screw in the plug as far as you can to feel for burrs or damaged threads. If the plugs don't screw in properly, chase the threads with a tap.

✔ If you do damage the threads and they don't clean up with a spark plug thread tap, you can always repair the plug hole with new threads. Repair kits are available that allow you to install new threads in the engine plug hole.

Squashing Squeaks

Few automotive problems are as pesky and irritating as a persistent squeak inside your car. Modern cars are generally very quiet due to aerodynamics advances, better assembly techniques, and new sound absorption materials, which makes the occasional "car cricket" even more bothersome.

Squeaks are generally caused by two materials rubbing against each other. Usually, they are two different materials, such as plastic and steel or similar materials with different coefficients of friction. As the two surfaces alternately catch and let go, the energy released causes the high-pitched vibration that I call a squeak. This is known as the *slip-stick effect.*

To correct a squeak, you must first locate it. Car interiors reflect sound because of all the glass, so finding the squeak may not be as simple as it seems. To safely pinpoint the spot, have a friend drive down a bumpy road while you listen for sounds. Confirm that you've found the offending area by pressing down on the spot to see whether the sound is interrupted. Still having trouble finding the squeak? Put one end of a small piece of rubber hose to your ear and use the other end as a stethoscope.

After you've cornered the gremlin, you can use any of several techniques. First, make sure that the squeak is not from a loose fastener. Even new cars can have loose fasteners; vibrations inherent in driving often cause screws to back off. When dealing with a dashboard squeak, you can use a piece of polyurethane foam to separate the panels. Polyurethane foam is preferable to a metal shim or a penny because shims can fall into a fan motor or short across two electrical connectors.

If separating the surfaces is not appropriate, try a silicone spray. Although effective, it often does not provide a lasting fix. After the lubricant dries up, the surfaces will squeak again.

Avoid treating squeaky ashtray cover springs or hinges with these materials. Because the lighter is usually nearby, the electricity and heat can ignite the flammable oils and cause a fire. Instead, try using one of the following substances:

✓ **Drylubes:** Powdered graphite is excellent for friction reduction, coats the surface well, lasts a long time, and will not ignite. It can be messy to use, so place a cloth or newspaper to catch any overspray. Sprays with lithium, Teflon, or moly compounds are also effective anti-squeak agents. Because the aerosol uses an oil-based carrier, be careful around electrical connections and upholstery. It may be safer to disconnect the battery's ground cable, reconnecting only after the carrier evaporates and leaves a dry film.

✓ **Lithium grease:** This surface lubricant is often overlooked but very effective. Lithium grease is slippery and provides a tenacious, long-lasting fix. This aerosol is easy to use, especially with the thin tube plastic extension usually provided. Be careful not to overspray onto fabrics because lithium lubes are hard to remove. Take the same precautions you would for any combustible. Lithium grease is great for panels, springs, lock cylinders, and hinges.

✓ **Talcum:** This substance is similar to graphite in its properties, especially for coating large areas. Talcum works great for quieting sounds from the leather or rubber boot covering the gear shift lever on manual transmission cars or anywhere leather, vinyl, or rubber comes in contact.

Squawking sway bar bushings

One of the most common complaints in the colder winter months is noisy sway bar bushings. The rubber becomes hard and brittle and makes lots of noise when going over bumps. Lubricating the rubber bushings is futile and can even make things worse as the lubricant attacks the rubber.

✓ First check whether the manufacturer has made updated versions of the sway bar bushings. Some have issued Teflon-coated bushings.

✓ If there is no new, updated bushing, you may want to replace the old ones anyway, especially if they are cracked or worn.

✓ If all else fails, try lubricating the rubber part of the bushing with a grease containing a solid lubricant, such as graphite, molybdenum, lithium, or Teflon. Be sure to thoroughly clean the surface of the roll bar until the metal is rust free and perfectly smooth. If the bar is pitted, it may need to be replaced for a lasting fix.

Squeaky dashboards

One of the most vexing problems with modern cars is a squeaky dash. Somewhere down in the guts of the console or dash hides the elusive squeak gremlin. Just how do you catch it?

✓ While someone else drives the car, push and pull on various parts of the dash until you isolate the noise.

✓ If the source of the noise is impossible to isolate, remove the dash pad and dash front fascia one at a time. If removing the pad or fascia makes the noise go away, insulate the offending part and use one of the trick cures that follow.

✓ Removing the fascia and pad gives you access to the innards of the dash. Have someone drive the car once again and try to isolate.

Try one of the following tricks to get rid of the noise:

✓ Remove the sheet metal screws and coat the threads with silicone RTV. The RTV will work in a few hours and help to stop the vibration.

✓ If the sheet metal screws are too small, use larger screws.

- ✔ Insulate the dash or fascia plate by using mechanic's "dum-dum," which is equivalent to air conditioning insulation compound.

- ✔ Whittle small wood wedges and jam them into the spaces where the noise is occurring.

Squeaky body parts

Does your seat squeak? Is an elusive squeak gremlin loose somewhere inside the car? Is body panel or piece of sheet metal full of chirping birds? Here are some tips for locating and curing those annoying noises:

- ✔ Have someone else drive the vehicle over bumpy roads while you ride in the back seat, trunk, or even on the hood. Doing so will help you isolate the part of the car where the noise is coming from.

- ✔ Put a sand bag on the fender, hood, trunk, and bumper. Does the noise stop? If so, try tightening the mounting bolts. If the bolts are tight, try spraying one of the "trick cure" substances into the offending area.

- ✔ Use a long piece of hose to find the source of the noise. Tape the hose onto the body and leave the end terminating at the suspected source. Do you hear the noise when you put the other end to your ear?

- ✔ Use a solid particulate lubricating spray on the various areas where the squeak is occurring.

One of the following trick cures may help to get rid of that annoying chirp:

- ✔ Graphite powder or spray gets into tight spots well. The powder can be "puffed" into tight spots and will work into the squeak, making it go away after a little while. The graphite eventually works into the squeak, coating the surface and killing the squeak.

- ✔ Teflon-based sprays are excellent for lubricating squeaking rubber and plastic panels. Teflon is a great sliding surface lubricant.

- ✔ Lithium-based sprays are great for spraying into squeaking hinges, sliding surfaces, and any metal-to-metal assembly. (Lithium is also known as "white grease.")

- ✔ Baby powder is great for interior squeaks and chirps. Liberally coat the area until the noise goes away and repeat as necessary. Talcum powder also works well.

Wind noise

Noise made by the wind passing over, around, and through various body panels can drive you crazy. Here are some tips to cure those "ghostly" moans, screeches, and howls.

- ✔ Have someone else drive the vehicle while you hang out the window. Listen to the sound from the outside of the car. Is it coming from the front, top, or rear of the vehicle?

- ✔ Place large pieces of masking tape over the windshield trim. Cover only one side at a time until the noise goes away. After you locate the source of the noise, remove and reinstall the windshield trim using butyl rubber sealer to fill the cracks and stop the noise.

- ✔ Place large pieces of masking tape over the front and side trim. Cover only one side at a time until the noise goes away. After you locate the source of the noise, remove and reinstall the trim by using butyl rubber sealer to fill the cracks and stop the noise.

- ✔ If the roof-mounted rack is the source of the noise, remove the rack when you're not using it.

when you're not using it.

✔ If you cannot fill the cracks, try deflecting the wind by installing a hood-mounted wind deflector. A front-end body-bra is another possible cure.

Recipe for Rusty Nuts

Here are some of the time-honored concoctions, chemicals, and elixirs that have proven invaluable in curing a multitude of vehicular ills. In the event that you don't have any penetrating oil handy, you can use any of the following items to help free up a rusty fastener:

✔ Oil of wintergreen from a drugstore acts like a penetrating oil.

✔ Remove the dipstick and use it to apply some engine oil on the stuck part. Add a drop or two of gasoline to make it penetrate.

✔ Use a crayon, candle, or, even better, beeswax as a lubricant. Heat the frozen part with a propane torch and let the wax flow between the threads.

✔ A sharp rap with the ball end of a ball-peen hammer will usually shake things loose. If possible, use a pneumatic chisel to vibrate the fastener loose.

✔ Slowly tighten the fastener just a smidgen and then slightly loosen it. Keep up the back and forth movement, all the while soaking it with oil.

✔ Use the heat wrench. An oxy-acetylene torch is a great tool for removing stuck parts. If necessary, use dry ice to cool off the part in the middle after heating the part on the outside.

✔ Use a reverse-fluted drill. These twist drills have counterclockwise flutes. When you use them in a reverse drill, the force of the drill bit turning counterclockwise will back out the frozen bolt.

Windshield Wiper First Aid

Do your windshield wipers wipe out your nerves? Do they screech like someone scraping their fingernails across a chalkboard? Have hope! You can cure your car from the wiper woes. First, thoroughly clean your windshield. Get the glass really clean.

A grease-free windshield cures most problems. Squeaks are usually caused by oil and grease build-up on the windshield and wiper blades. Follow these steps for a squeaky-clean, but screechless, windshield:

1. **Clean the windshield with ammonia and wadded up newspapers.**

2. **Clean the wiper blades with rubbing alcohol or straight windshield washer fluid.**

3. **If steps 1 and 2 fail to cure the problem, replace the wiper blades.**

The rubber wiper insert is supposed to flip freely back and forth as the wiper goes across the glass. After time, the rubber stays flipped to the side where it always stops.

Imagine a push broom for a moment. The bristles are angled or set in the direction the broom is supposed to go. When you push the broom, it glides smoothly across the floor, but when you pull back on the handle, it hops back toward you. This is exactly what happens with your wiper blades when they take a set, and that's why replacing them can cure the problem. After the blades are permanently bent to one side or another, they are not repairable or cleanable. Just like an old push broom with the bristles permanently bent in one direction, the rubber is permanently bent and will not recover.

Wiper mortis

What can you do if your windshield wiper motor quits, it's pouring rain, and you must drive? Head into the kitchen for an onion. Cut it in half and rub onion juice on the outside of the glass. The oil in the onion juice will cause rain to roll off the glass in beads, usually improving vision enough to safely drive the car — preferably to a repair shop!

Have you seen those ads for "lifetime" wiper blades, so tough that they never wear out? Don't fall for it! When you buy those expensive wipers, you have to pay a hefty shipping and handling charge to exchange them. And they still wear out — maybe not as fast as normal wiper blades, but by the time you pay for the wipers, shipping, handling, and postage to return them, you are better off buying name-brand replacement blades from your local parts store.

 Be careful when you change wiper blades! After you remove the blade from the spring-loaded arm, don't leave the spring-loaded arm standing out away from the windshield; it can snap back against the glass with enough force to crack the glass. After you remove the blade, return the arm gently against the glass while you replace the blade insert.

Okay, you cleaned the glass and replaced the blades. Still got a problem? Here's the fix for those really stubborn cases:

1. **Turn on the ignition and turn on the wipers.**

2. **Turn off the ignition when the wiper is halfway across the windshield.**

3. **Carefully lift the wiper off of the windshield and slowly lower it back onto the windshield. Observe the edge of the wiper blade when you do so.**

   The wiper blade should come in contact with the glass at a 90-degree angle. If the blade is tilted to either side, you must bend the wiper arm.

4. **Look at the blade and determine which way the arm needs to be bent.**

5. **Using a pair of pliers, carefully bend the wiper arm a small amount in the direction that will make the wiper blade perpendicular to the glass.**

If this procedure still doesn't cure the problem, you should consider replacing the wiper arms, which contain a spring that is calibrated for your windshield. As the wiper arm gets old, the spring loses its tension, causing the blade to skip across the glass or make noise.

Unlocking Vapor Lock

Many owners of carbureted cars experience problems with vapor lock. The problem usually manifests itself as hard starting after the car has been driven and shut off. The car has to cool for a time ranging from a few minutes to a few hours. Fuel-injected cars are less prone to vapor lock but still can suffer from the problem.

Vapor lock is often caused by high fuel volatility, which is measured by *Reid vapor pressure*. Reid vapor pressure refers to the expandable (volatile) capacity of gasoline when exposed to increased temperatures. In general, high-octane fuel is more volatile than regular grades.

High volatility fuel problems

Fuel volatility is the capability of the fuel to turn from a liquid to a vapor while inside the engine. The problem is that winter-grade fuels are sometimes too volatile and summer grades are not volatile enough. This situation causes a plethora of drivability conditions that are difficult to understand and impossible to fix. Sometimes just changing brands of fuel cures hard-starting or hesitation problems — something a tune-up cannot address.

Carburetor flooding

When fuel in the carburetor float bowl evaporates after shutdown, hot soak of the engine compartment occurs. (See the following sidebar for a definition of hot soaking.)

Hot soaking can cause excessively long cranking times, even after the car has been sitting overnight. Does your engine crank and crank before catching and firing up? The reason could be that the carburetor is dry and has to be filled with gas before the car will start. Modern fuel has major problems with being too volatile, causing carburetors to empty themselves of fuel and making starting difficult.

Charcoal canister saturation

The charcoal inside the canister holds fuel vapors from the fuel tank and carburetor. If the fuel is too volatile, it foams out of the fuel tank and saturates the activated charcoal, causing the charcoal to become deactivated. The canister ceases to store fuel vapors and routes the fumes right into the carburetor, flooding the engine.

Vehicle fires

 Saturated canisters can dump fuel into the engine compartment. Combine this condition with one small spark from the alternator, and your car has an engine fire.

Flying gas caps

Excessive pressure buildup in the gas tank can cause the gas cap to pop out of your hand when you loosen it.

Fuel dribbling

Hot soak can cause expansion in the fuel line between the fuel pump and the carburetor, resulting in high pressure at the needle and seat of the carburetor. This condition can cause the needle to unseat and additional fuel to enter the float bowl, causing flooding.

Using winterized fuel blends during warm weather can cause problems. Winter fuel is blended to be more volatile so that it ignites easily in freezing weather. If the car still has winterized fuel during a warm snap, the fuel may boil and create a vapor-lock problem.

Hot soak defined

Hot soak happens when an engine is shut off after reaching operating temperature. Latent heat from the combustion chamber and exhaust manifold continue to heat the engine block. Underhood temperatures soar. The engine block actually boils the coolant in critical passages in the cylinder head. All the fuel in the engine compartment is hot soaked and tends to boil, creating vapor lock.

Mechanical causes

Hot air problems: If you have a stuck heat riser or thermal air door, remove the top of the air cleaner. Does the problem go away? If so, the thermally heated air intake system (called *Thermac* or *EFE*) may be working overtime. This system is only supposed to route warm air into the intake of the throttle housing when the temperature drops below 60° F. Problem: Hot air at other times can cause the fuel to superheat. Removing the air cleaner will pinpoint the problem because it allows the engine to draw in unheated fresh air.

Carburetor base gasket or spacer problems: The omission of the insulator under the carburetor, or an old, hardened spacer, can allow the carburetor to overheat when the engine is shut down. Some manufacturers incorporate metal or phenolic spacers under the carburetor to insulate it from heat transmission through the intake manifold. Two car-makers use phenolic resin float bowls to lower fuel temperature on high heat applications.

Thermostat problems: If the engine runs too hot, try running a cooler thermostat in the system. Cooling system scale can prevent engine heat from radiating into the cooling system and can cause hot soak problems. Too much coolant mixed with too little water can also cause overheating.

Exhaust leak problems: Hot exhaust gas leaking under the hood can cause the underhood temperatures to soar. Also, exhaust gas leaks can dilute the air charge into the engine and cause lean mixtures, which make the engine run even hotter.

Simple solutions

Change fuel brands. Not all fuels have the same Reid vapor pressure. In general, the more alcohol in the fuel, the more it tends to boil. Try different brands and compare their drivability. *Note:* Oxygenated fuel can contain more alcohol and can be much more volatile. Ditto for premium grades.

Pop the hood. On excessively hot days, pop open the hood and let out the heat before it has a chance to boil the fuel.

Cool the fuel. For carbureted cars, place a wet wash rag on the mechanical fuel pump to cool it. For fuel-injected cars, cool the entire fuel system with a garden hose.

Insulate the fuel line. Be sure that the fuel line is away from all heat sources. Wrap suspect hoses or pipes located near hot engine parts with fiberglass insulation, aluminum foil, or silver duct tape. Do not substitute rubber hose for metal line, or you might cause vapor lock.

Install an underhood fan. Installing an underhood fan can cool things a bit. Purchase the kind that mounts on the radiator and pushes extra air into the engine compartment. Be sure to get an adjustable thermostatic control so that you can set the temperature and set the fan to run for a few minutes after shutdown to cool the underhood area. Installing a fan to blow directly on the carburetor can also help.

Complex solutions

Cool the air ducts. Installing an auxiliary air duct from the front of the car to the carburetor will help keep it cool. You can rig up an add-on air duct to bring cool fresh air into the area of the carburetor or fuel injectors.

Make pressure modifications. Because fuel under pressure resists boiling, raising pressure from the tank to the carburetor can help. Install an electric fuel pump as close to the tank as possible. Install a pressure regulator as close to the carburetor as possible. The fuel pump will raise the pressure to about 6 psi and the regulator will lower it back to about 2 psi. Follow the instructions that come with the pump for installation help.

Insulate the fuel tank. Install heat shields between the muffler/exhaust system and the gas tank to keep the exhaust heat from boiling the fuel in the tank. A muffler shop will be helpful here.

Insulate the carburetor. Adding an asbestos plate or layer of fiberglass insulation between the manifold and carburetor can help keep the carburetor cool. Consult a local carburetor specialist for help here.

Make design changes. Later fuel system designs allow fuel to return to the tank, preventing excessive pressure from developing in the fuel lines. Internal bleeds in the fuel pump or an additional metering port on the filter or pump allow high pressure and vapors to escape back to the fuel tank. This keeps the fuel cool by constantly circulating the fuel between the fuel tank and pump. Retrofitting these systems (known as a *three-line fuel filter* or *three-line fuel pump*) requires fitting a return line back to the fuel tank. This solution is complex and may require the assistance of a mechanic.

Chapter 4

In the A.M., Do the P.M.: Preventative Maintenance

● ●

In This Chapter

▶ Pay now or pay a bunch more later

▶ When to service which specific parts

▶ Generic maintenance intervals

▶ How to get the most from your car: mechanics' tips

▶ How to care for and remove stains from your car's upholstery

▶ Who to go to get what done and how to save money in the process

▶ What to look for when selecting a car wash

● ●

*H*ow many times have you heard, "You can pay me now or pay me *much* more later"? Is there any truth to beating the game in maintaining your own car? Do dealers provide the best service? What about chain stores and quick lube places? Is there any reason why you should go one place and not another?

When it comes to maintaining your car, *you* are the one who decides what should be done. Which repair shop you pick can make a big difference in the outcome. Some people spend money needlessly, paying for work that's not necessary or done prematurely. With economics being so tight, most people want to get away with the bare minimum in order to stretch their dollars. How can you do the least yet make the most of your car?

Doing routine preventative maintenance can add years to the life of your car. Follow these guidelines, and I guarantee that your car will run more smoothly and spend much less time at the repair shop.

 One big money-saving tip is to find a shop that will do several maintenance items at the same time. This is called doing *overlapping repairs*. For example, when having the hoses changed, get the coolant flushed. When changing the timing belt, replace the water pump. If the shop doesn't want to overlap repairs, go somewhere else!

Now it's time to dive in under the hood and get started with your P.M. Remember, preventative maintenance is the best way to save money on your car repairs.

Checking Fluid Levels

It is best to check your oil level every week before you start the car for the first time in the morning. It only takes a moment. You don't even need to wipe off the dipstick. This one basic preventative maintenance measure is fundamental to long engine life. The most important liquid in your vehicle is the oil in your engine and drive-train (which includes the transmission, transaxle, and/or differential). For more information about where to go for oil changes, see the section "Liquids and lubricants" that follows.

In most cases, it is best to have your mechanic check the level and condition of the drive-train oil when you have the motor oil changed. This is because accessing and checking are usually difficult and may require that the vehicle be up in the air on a lift. However, *you* must monitor the level of oil in your engine.

For accuracy, it is best to check your engine oil level with the vehicle on a flat surface. With the engine off and cold, have a look around the engine bay. Become familiar with the general layout of your engine compartment. While you may not know what everything is, become familiar with the layout in general. Since you are doing the job normally done by a service station attendant, you must also assume his or her duties in looking for things amiss under the hood. The idea is to be acquainted with the way things are. Then if something frays, tears, breaks, or leaks, you will be able to spot it. If *you* don't check around and look for problems, who will?

Be sure to check the hoses connecting the motor to the rest of the car. Are they cracked or bulging, or are there any leaks? Using a flashlight, carefully examine the condition of the fan belt or belts.

If needed, consult your owner's manual for help in identifying the items under the hood. It is important to know the location of the following items: oil dipstick, transmission dipstick, coolant reservoir, brake fluid reservoir, and windshield washer reservoir. Many modern cars have see-through liquid containers that allow you to check the fluid levels without touching anything. Are the brake fluid, coolant, and windshield washer reservoirs made of translucent plastic, allowing you to visually observe the fluid level? If so, you should be able to determine whether they are low at a glance.

Over time, the windshield washer fluid level should be the only level that goes down. If any other fluid level drops, there may be a leak; have your mechanic take a look. Leaking coolant or brake fluid can be a real disaster! Hopefully you will be able to spot dropping fluid levels during your weekly under-the-hood inspections.

Tuning Up

In the old days, you could tell that your car needed a tune-up because the engine became hard to start. Modern cars don't act like they need a tune-up. If you miss your service interval, the ignition module might fail due to worn spark plugs, wires, cap, or rotor. Some ignition modules cost $400!

 Because some cars require valve adjustments and special equipment to properly set the mixture and timing, tune-ups are best done by a mechanic who specializes in your car make or by your dealer. Using a cheap tune-up place can really cost you! In some cases, those mechanics are in too much of a hurry to get on to the next job and can carelessly create more problems.

Servicing Belts and Hoses

Careless installation of drive belts, timing belts, and hoses can cost you in other ways. While these jobs may seem simple, sloppy or incorrect installation causes the parts to fail prematurely and in some cases, damages other parts (if a belt is tightened too much, the water pump or alternator will soon fail). Not all belts and hoses are the same quality, and cheaper ones and don't last as long as good brand-name parts, such as Goodyear, Dayco, and Gates.

Caring for Tires

Rotating tires and checking alignment is necessary to get your money's worth from your tires. Find a local tire dealer willing to make a deal that includes periodic rotation, balancing, and alignment. Also, some shops give free alignment checks by driving your car over a metal plate. (See Chapter 3 for more information about tire rotation and alignment.)

Cleaning Injectors

Many late model cars don't benefit from injector cleaning; new injector designs don't get dirty. The cleaning solvents can shorten the life of injectors; don't fall for this ruse. Consult your owner's manual, contact your dealer, or call the manufacturer's customer service hotline and ask whether your engine's injectors should be cleaned and whether cleaning solvent will damage them.

 Just because your local car dealership makes it a practice to clean injectors doesn't mean that doing so is a good idea. Some unscrupulous dealerships are cleaning injectors even though the car-maker says not to. The dealer's service department is making extra money on a service that is not needed as well as shortening the life of your injectors!

Replacing Shocks and Struts

Shock absorbers and MacPhaerson struts (depending on which kind your car has) are important in handling and preventing certain kinds of tire wear. Replacing them is a judgment call, and many times they are replaced needlessly. Get more than one opinion before having your shock absorbers and/or struts replaced. Also be aware that many different companies are making shocks and struts. Some companies offer better handling, some offer a smoother ride, some offer lifetime guarantees, and some offer the cheapest price. Be sure to ask about these concerns because you may be buying a cheap shock or strut that will not perform in the manner you're used to: Your car may not have the same ride quality that it had before the shocks or struts were replaced.

Maintenance Intervals

In general, your owner's manual is the best source of maintenance interval information. But what if you don't have a manual? Also, you should know that the maintenance manual does not list all the items to be maintained. Some are left out by the manufacturer in order to get a better rating in car operating cost comparisons. So, in general, take the recommendations in your maintenance manual with a grain of salt. If you have any doubts, follow the advice in this chapter.

To keep your car running smoothly and to prolong its life, you need to keep it well lubricated and make sure that each type of filter is operating properly and not getting plugged up. Also, each part needs service after a certain number of miles or years. The following sections tell you when each service should be performed.

Liquids and lubricants

Motor oil: Change every 3,000 miles or 3 months (whichever comes first). *Exception:* Synthetic oil can easily last 7,500 miles or more.

The most important service is an oil change. In general, oil in quart containers is better quality than bulk oil dispensed from storage tanks. When it's on sale, stock up on good oil (like Castrol, Valvoline, or Mobil). Bring your own oil and ask for a discount for supplying your own parts. Take advantage of advertised oil change specials.

Automatic transmission: Modern front-wheel-drive cars, especially automatics, have *very* expensive transmissions. Because of the low hood profiles used today, these units run hot and need more service. It's much cheaper to have the transmission serviced than to have it fixed, with repair costs ranging from $2,000 to $3,000!

Service the automatic transmission every 25,000 miles for most front-wheel-drive cars — shorter intervals are recommended for city driving. Rear-wheel-drive vehicles can go 50,000 miles between changes. This service usually involves changing the fluid, pan gasket, and transmission filter. The transmission linkage and transmission bands (if your vehicle has them) should also be checked at this time. Some shops call this a *transmission tune-up*.

Many automatic transmissions have transmission filters, which should be replaced when the transmission is serviced. However, some cars don't require transmission filter replacement but instead have filters that are merely cleaned and reused. Find out which type your vehicle has by asking the dealer's parts department whether it cleans and reuses the transmission filters. Don't pay for a filter replacement if the filter is supposed to be reused and don't let the mechanic reuse the old filter if it should be replaced!

The best place to go is a transmission specialist or dealership. Manual transmissions and differentials require much less maintenance and can withstand more abuse. Also, they don't have filters to replace. Both manual and automatic transmissions benefit from the installation of synthetic oil instead of the usual petroleum lubricant. Synthetic oil costs more but protects this very expensive part of your car better than petroleum oil.

Manual transmission, rear/axle, differential: Change every 50,000 miles. Manual transmissions on front-wheel-drive cars also have an integral differential located in the front axle, which is called a *transaxle*. Rear-wheel-drive vehicles have separate differentials, located in the rear axle. Don't forget to have the differential or transaxle serviced, too.

Power steering fluid: Change every 30,000 miles (includes the power steering filter when applicable). Some car-makers don't call for power steering fluid changes, but dirty fluid can cause power steering failure. Power steering repairs are very expensive, but power steering fluid changes are cheap insurance against major problems later on. Also, some cars (Volvo and Mercedes-Benz, for example) have power steering filters.

Brakes: Flush the fluid and inspect the brakes every 30,000 miles or 2 years (whichever comes first).

Brake fluid service is very important. You need your brakes! Having the fluid changed may prevent expensive brake repairs or catastrophic brake failure. Some anti-lock brake parts are easily ruined by old brake fluid and cost about $2,000 to replace. Save money by having your brakes inspected when they're being flushed.

Antifreeze/Coolant: Change every 2 years or 25,000 miles, whichever comes first. (*Note:* Antifreeze and coolant are different names for the same thing.)

Modern engines use a great deal of aluminum, which requires a proper mixture of coolant and additives to prevent aluminum corrosion and acid build-up. If you skimp on periodic changes, you increase your chances of a blown head gasket and/or ruined cylinder head. Coolant turns acidic from combustion gases leaking into the cooling system. The more you drive, the more frequently you should have the coolant changed.

This service should be done by the dealer or someone experienced with your type of car. If it is done improperly, an air bubble can become trapped and cause a blown headgasket. Also, it is important to frequent a shop that recycles coolant rather than dumps it into the environment (it contains toxic heavy metals).

There is a new type of coolant on the market called *propylene glycol.* It differs from the traditional ethylene glycol coolant in several ways — mainly, it is much less toxic. It doesn't taste sweet like ethylene glycol and doesn't poison pets that might wander by your car and drink some. If your vehicle leaks coolant and you are concerned that it might harm your pets, you may want to use propylene glycol. Be sure to check with your car's manufacturer about using it, as the use of some such substances voids the warranty.

Filters

Oil filter: Replace at every oil change, or every 6 months if you're using synthetic oil.

Air filter: Replace every 30,000 miles (more often in dirty areas where there is a great deal of sand and dust on the road).

Fuel filter: Change at the tune-up. (There will be an extra charge for this service above and beyond the cost of the tune-up.)

Services

Tune-up: Follow your owner's manual — typically every 30,000 miles. Note that some newer cars can go 60,000 and even 100,000 miles between tune-ups. If you own one of these cars, be sure to have the other things (like fuel filters and transmission services) done at the recommended intervals. If you wait until the tune-up to have these important services done, you have waited too long and may damage your vehicle.

Belts and hoses: Check the condition of the belts and hoses annually and replace every 5 years or 60,000 miles. Replace the timing belt typically at 60,000–90,000 miles.

Many modern engines have timing belts that *must* be replaced at 60,000–90,000-mile intervals. On many cars, especially Asian imports, extensive engine damage can occur if you fail to change the timing belt and it breaks. Consult the dealer for the proper service interval for your engine and ask whether your engine will be damaged if the timing belt breaks. If the belt breaking won't damage the engine, the worst thing you risk by skimping on this service and driving until it breaks is having to get towed. Your choice!

Tires: Rotate every 7,500 miles. Have them inspected for nails or cuts and check proper air pressure at every oil change. Check the alignment and balance when having a tune-up. You have to pay extra, but this is a good time to have this service done.

Generic intervals for parts replacement

If you don't have a service manual and wonder what to do when, I have compiled a handy-dandy table of what repairs to expect next. Table 4-1 lists other car parts and when you should have them serviced or replaced. This table is handy for knowing whether you are being sold a bill of goods for replacement of some item that really doesn't need to be replaced! Remember, this is a generic chart. If the manufacturer calls for more frequent intervals, follow that recommendation.

The type of driving you do has the biggest effect on how often to carry out the services listed in Table 4-1. If you drive less than ten miles per trip per direction, follow the more frequent intervals. If you drive mostly long distances (50 miles or more per trip), follow the longer intervals.

Table 4-1	What to Expect Next
Part	*When It Will Need to Be Serviced or Replaced*
Shocks and struts	25 – 75,000 miles
Suspension, tie-rods, and ball joints	50 – 150,000 miles
Tires	30 – 60,000 miles
Muffler and pipes	60 – 150,000 miles
Belts and hoses	60 – 150,000 miles
Front brakes	24 – 50,000 miles
Rear brakes	40 – 100,000 miles
Headlight bulbs	3 – 8 years, or 50 – 150,000 miles
Windshield wiper blades	1 – 3 years
Radiator	100 – 200,000 miles or 10 – 12 years
Water pump	100 – 175,000 miles
Battery	2 – 6 years
Timing belt	60 – 90,000 miles
Timing chain	100 – 150,000 miles
Clutch (manual transmission)	80 – 150,000 miles
CV joints	80 – 150,000 miles
Universal joints	150 – 250,000 miles
Fuel injectors and fuel pump	100 – 200,000 miles

Getting More Bang for the Buck

Here are some mechanics' tips for making your car last longer and for getting the most from your car:

Buy the biggest and best battery that will fit in the battery tray. Long-life batteries hold a charge better, tax the alternator less, and power the starter better — making the alternator and starter last longer. Replace the battery six months before its warranty expires — an old battery causes the alternator to charge all the time, shortening its life.

Buy paint protection when your purchase a new car. Then apply a coating of silicone-type paint protection every six months (three months in polluted areas). Doing so makes your paint job last longer and helps to prevent acid-rain damage. If you want to do it yourself, you can buy the same paint protection from an automotive paint supply store and apply it at home — at a considerable savings.

 Use synthetic oil in your engine and transmission. Longer engine life and better gas mileage more than compensate for the extra expense. While petroleum oil must be changed every 3,000 miles, synthetic oils last 7,500 miles or more. I like the Redline Synthetic Oil best.

If there is room under the hood, install a bypass oil filter. Bypass filters really clean the oil and remove all contamination, making the engine last much longer.

Have your oil analyzed every year. Lube oil analysis can detect potential problems long before they cause major engine damage.

Install a reusable lifetime air filter. These filters can be cleaned and reused indefinitely and do a better job of filtering the air.

Annually, treat all the rubber weather-stripping on your car with a coating of silicone grease. The rubber won't split, crack, or tear, and silicone prevents cracking from summer heat and splitting from freezing rain.

If you park outside, use a car cover. The sun's rays and environmental fallout really age a car. If you can't garage it, cover it!

Invest in an inexpensive, simple-to-use torque wrench. Mechanics use air-driven impact guns and overtorque the lugnuts, which can warp the brake rotors and permanently damage them. Retorque (retighten) your own lugnuts anytime the wheels are off.

Don't forget your mechanic during the holidays. The little you spend on your mechanic now will pay off in the years to come.

Fighting Stains

Many people treasure their car's upholstery but don't know how to keep it clean and stain free. The Car Care Council found that extra-clean cars can bring as much as 50 percent more value when traded in or sold than a not-so-clean car with comparable mileage and equipment. Keeping it clean means higher resale value. Here are some general cleaning suggestions:

- ✔ **Nylon and polyester seats, interior, and carpeting:** Use mild household cleaners made specifically for this purpose. Dip a soft cloth in the cleaner and wring it out. Don't use solvents, gasoline, acetone, naphtha, dry-cleaning solvent, paint reducer, or laundry detergent unless they are specifically called for.

- ✔ **Leather upholstery:** Prevent leather from cracking by polishing it regularly with a cream made of one part vinegar and two parts linseed oil. Clean with a damp cloth and saddle soap. Seasonal cleaning is a good idea. Rub a damp washcloth in the saddle soap until you create a lather. Shampoo the area one panel at a time. Finish with a cloth dipped in warm, clear water. Be sure to get all the pleats, folds, crevices, and seams.

- ✔ **Vinyl upholstery:** Never oil vinyl; doing so makes it hard, and it's almost impossible to soften again. For cleaning, try sprinkling baking soda or vinegar on a rough, damp cloth. Then wash with a mild dishwashing detergent.

Cleaning techniques

Work fast. Stains set with time and heat, making them harder to remove. Some items, like fruit juice and soft drinks, may turn yellow with heat and age. In a pinch, clean spills by squirting the spot with shaving cream to help lift the spill. Rinse with cold water.

To remove lingering odors, sponge the area with a solution of baking soda and water (1 teaspoon to 1 cup). Shaklee Basic-G works well.

If the dirty spot is only slightly dirty, you can clean it with cornmeal. Use a stiff brush to work the cornmeal into the rug or seat fabric. Then simply vacuum it out.

Rub soiled cotton fabric with an art gum eraser (purchase at a stationery store).

Quick and thorough drying is the key to ring prevention. Use a hair dryer, heat lamp (don't scorch the upholstery!), or air hose. If a ring forms anyway, redo the entire area. Use small amounts and avoid saturating the area. Try to wet only the cover, not the padding underneath.

Rub gently from the outside of the stain toward the center. Repeat until it is removed. Finish with a damp cloth dipped in warm water and wrung out.

Cleaning specific stains

Use the following tips to remove specific stains from your car. If one type of cleaner isn't available, use the other one(s) suggested.

Alcoholic beverages: Immediately sponge with cold water and then with cold water and glycerin (available at drugstores). Rinse with vinegar for a few seconds if the stain remains. These stains may brown with age. If a wine stain remains, rub it with concentrated detergent, wait 15 minutes, and rinse. Repeat if necessary. Rinse again with plenty of warm water.

Ballpoint pen ink: Apply slightly warmed glycerin (available from a drugstore). Blot frequently with paper towels, keeping the stain moist with more glycerin while working. Finish up with cleaning solvent. Other possible cleaners include denatured alcohol and petroleum jelly.

Blood: Rub off as much as you can first. Then take a cloth soaked in cold water and wet the spot. Immediately sponge it off with cold water, wiping as you go, to keep it from setting. In 2 quarts of warm water, mix 2 tablespoons of dish detergent with $1/4$ cup sudsy ammonia. Using a sponge, wet the stain, rub gently, and blot with paper towels. Repeat as needed. Rinse it right away with cold water. If the stain remains, work in detergent, using bleach that is safe for the fabric.

Candle wax: Use a dull knife to scrape off as much as possible. Try to blot as much as possible into a piece of fabric or brown paper bag by pressing a warm iron over the blotting fabric or paper. Remove a colored stain by using dry-cleaning solvent. Finish by washing with detergent and rinsing with cool water.

Chewing gum: Freeze the gum with an ice cube and carefully scrape the gum off using a dull knife. If needed, use some dry-cleaning solvent. Sponge the area with water to remove any sugar stain left behind.

Chocolate and cocoa: First, wipe it up with a napkin or paper towel. Then wipe with soapy water followed by cool water. Remove grease stains with dry-cleaning solvent. If color remains, sponge the area with hydrogen peroxide and wash again.

Crayon: Remove melted remains with the ice treatment for chewing gum. Finish the job with the lipstick-removal procedure that follows.

Deodorant: Sponge the area with vinegar. If the stain remains, soak it with denatured alcohol. Wash with detergent and hot water and rinse completely.

Dog stains: Blot up excess moisture with paper towel. Pour club soda on the spot and continue blotting. Lay a towel over the spot and set a heavy object on top in order to absorb all the moisture.

Egg: Scrape with dull blade. Soak with cold water for at least 30 minutes. Remove the remaining grease with dry-cleaning solvent. Finish with detergent and warm water and rinse completely.

Fruits and fruit drinks: Sponge with cold water. Soap may set the stain, so start with cool water until all traces are gone. Then use soapy water followed with a plain water rinse. If color remains, wash with detergent and bleach that is safe for fabric.

Glue: Try loosening it by saturating the spot with a cloth soaked with vinegar. Consult the glue container for solvent instructions. You can remove cement glue by rubbing it with cold cream, peanut butter, or salad oil.

Grease or oil: First, use kitty litter or cornmeal as an absorbent. Soak up as much as possible and vacuum the absorbent away. Pretreat with detergent or cleaning solvent. Brake cleaning spray (available from auto parts stores) works well, too. Because cleaning solvents dissolve the stain and cause it to bleed into unaffected areas, use them sparingly. Start at the outside and work inward, using plenty of cleaner. Change the cloth often. Use dry-cleaning solvents (such as trichloroethylene) only in a well-ventilated area. In a pinch, pour salt, talcum, or facial powder onto the grease to soak it up.

Lipstick and other cosmetics: Carefully wipe from the outside toward the center with dry-cleaning solvent to loosen the stain. Remove any remaining stain with a mild household cleaner, rubbing in the detergent until the outline of the stain is gone. Wash with warm water, detergent, and bleach that is safe for fabric until the area is clean.

Mildew: Pretreat as soon as possible with detergent. Wash thoroughly with hot water, detergent, and bleach that is safe for fabric. If any stain remains, sponge with lemon juice and salt. Allow the area to dry in the sun. Note that mildew is very hard to remove, so treat promptly!

Milk, cream, and ice cream: Sponge or soak with cold water as soon as possible for 30 minutes. Wash with detergent. Remove cream grease stains with dry-cleaning solvent and wash again.

Mustard: Allow to dry and then scrape off as much as possible. Sponge with mild detergent.

Nail polish: Sponge with polish remover or banana oil. Wash. If stain remains, sponge with denatured alcohol to which a few drops of ammonia have been added. Wash again. Note that some fabrics (acetates and triacetates) react with nail polish remover. First, try the polish remover on an out-of-sight place to see how it reacts. Other solvents to try include carburetor cleaner and degreaser, acetone, paint remover, and dry-cleaning solvent.

Paint: *Oil based:* Sponge stains with turpentine, cleaning fluid, or paint remover. Follow with sponge and hot water. For older stains, sponge with banana oil and then with dry-cleaning solvent. Wash again. *Water based:* Scrape off paint with a dull blade. Wash with detergent and hot water. Rinse with cool water.

Perspiration: Sponge fresh stains with ammonia, old stains with vinegar. Soak with warm water and rinse. Wash in hot water. If fabric is yellowed, use bleach sparingly. If stain remains, dampen and sprinkle with meat tenderizer or pepsin. Let stand for one hour. Brush off and wash. For persistent odor, sponge with colorless mouthwash.

Road tar: Carefully scrape off as much as possible. Gently wipe toward the center of the stain with a cleaning solvent.

Rust: Soak in lemon juice and salt or oxalic acid solution (3 tablespoons oxalic acid to 1 pint warm water). You can use a commercial rust remover.

 Handle poisonous rust removers carefully and keep them out of the reach of children. Never use oxalic acid or other rust removers around paint, as they can damage it.

Soft drinks: Sponge off immediately with cold water and alcohol. Follow up with soapy water and rinse with plain water. Note that heat and detergent may set the stain.

Urine: Clean with soapy water after neutralizing with a little ammonia and water.

White water rings and spots: Dampen a soft cloth with water and put a dab of toothpaste on it or apply a paste of salad oil and salt. Let stand briefly. Rinse and blot with a dry cloth.

Vomit: Scrape up as much as possible. Follow with a solution of $1/2$ cup of salt to 2 quarts of water. Rinse with plain water. Wash with soap and water and rinse again with plain water.

Caring for your car's upholstery

Making these habits part of your daily routine can add to the life of your car's interior and increase the resale value of your car:

- ✔ Park your car so that it faces a different direction every day. Doing so prevents the sun from repeatedly bleaching the same area of upholstery.

- ✔ Keep the sunroof or windows cracked slightly open during hot days. This saves the interior from damage caused by the heat loosening bonding adhesives and cracking vinyl.

- ✔ Use a dashboard cover or cardboard shield to protect the interior.

- ✔ Vacuum seats, carpets, and interior regularly to prevent dirt, dust, and food crumbs from being ground into the upholstery. Once a spill combines with food, it can be very hard to remove.

- ✔ Avoid using pointed vacuum cleaner attachments that can tear the upholstery.

- ✔ Spray fabric upholstery and carpets with a good fabric protector to repel stains.

Choosing the Right Car Wash

Caring for the outside of your car is just as important as caring for the inside. Salt and road ashes can destroy your car's finish and age your car prematurely. Dirt is an enemy because it attracts and holds moisture, which turns painted surfaces rusty. A little time and money spent on regular service will pay off in the long run. You will enjoy a clean car much more, and it will have a higher resale value when you decide to get rid of it. And everyone knows that a clean car runs better!

Deciphering car wash buzzwords

Is there such a thing as a totally safe, non-hazardous, automatic car wash? It depends. If you own a new car, especially one that has a clear-coat finish, you want to frequent a frictionless or "touchless" car wash. If your car is older, the best bang for your buck may be one of the brushless types. If your car is a clunker and all you want is the bare minimum (probably free with a fill-up), you will probably be happy with a car wash that uses spinning brushes. I'll take a look at the advantages and disadvantages of each type.

Miters

These are the parts of the automatic washing machine that come in contact with your car. Miters can be made of plastic, nylon, cloth, or synthetic chamois.

Spinning brushes

This is the cheapest type of car wash, usually given away free with a fill-up. Those spinning cylinders covered with plastic bristle brushes do an excellent job of removing built-up and caked-on dirt. At the same time, the plastic bristles get embedded with pieces of sand from those who went before you. That sand leaves millions of swirl marks on a good finish. Spinning brushes are really terrible for cars with new or clear-coat finishes. They leave swirl and scratch marks all across the car that usually cannot be removed.

Brushless

These are nothing more than spinning strips of cloth called cloth miters. They are better than plastic bristles in that the cloth is not as likely to get pieces of sand embedded in it, but this can still happen, especially if a number of dirty cars have come before you. Also, the type of dirt found in your vicinity has a great deal to do with the tendency of the miters to become contaminated.

Dancing miter curtains

Overall, this is probably the best type of automatic car wash. Here, huge curtains of chamois-like material "dance" across the car. Because there are no fast-spinning parts and the miters move only a short distance, this type of car wash is the safest for delicate finishes. Dancing miters are not likely to snag antennas, rearview mirrors, or the trim.

Touch-free or frictionless

These systems use high-pressure water spray to remove dirt. To accomplish this effect, the jets produce up to 1,000 pounds of pressure. This type of wash is the most modern of all and does the least damage — with a couple of exceptions. If there is salt on the car, the high-pressure spray can drive the salt crystals deep into cracks and crevices (like under weather stripping) that wouldn't normally be contaminated. Also, if the car has peeling paint, watch out! The high-pressure spray will make it peel even more. Many frictionless car washes are actually hybrids; they use high-pressure sprayers along with miter curtains.

Find a good car wash: points to ponder

This hunt can be a chore, but you can look out for several things that will steer you away from places that are likely to damage your car. Here are some points to ponder when searching for a good car wash:

Is there a hand-drying crew? Better car washes employ a staff to finish the drying job and clean the windows. Otherwise, bring along some paper towels and do this job yourself as soon as you exit.

Do you see damaged junk in the pit? Before surrendering your car, ask to inspect the inside. Walk along the track and look for pieces of trim and other objects that may have been torn from previous customers. Do you see hubcaps, license plates, and sideview mirrors lying around? Bad sign!

Does the place have obviously old or worn-looking equipment? Car wash equipment must be adjusted constantly. If not, it can damage your car.

Is the car wash clean? A dirty car wash cannot produce clean cars! This also tells you how well the management maintains the place.

Are warning signs posted? Look out for signs disclaiming responsibility for any damage caused to your car by the establishment. These can indicate a place that has terrible equipment that destroys antennas and rearview mirrors. Look out!

Call consumer protection and the Better Business Bureau. These agencies maintain files that contain complaints about businesses. Ask how many complaints have been made. In some cases, there will be both a complaint and an unresolved complaint number. Look out for places with more than one or two unresolved complaints.

Getting good results

To get the best car wash possible, make sure that you do the following:

Spray your wheels with cleaner first. Before going through the machine, use a heavy-duty wheel cleaner and spray your wheels. Doing so softens the build-up of brake dust and helps get the wheels cleaner.

Hold the carnauba wax! Don't purchase the wax job. It is dispensed via spray and gets all over everything, including your windows. The next time you drive at night, you'll think that you're in a dream with everything surrounded by halos and swirls of light. The fun really starts when you try to get the stuff off! (If you want to clean your windshield from carnauba wax, see the section in Chapter 3 on cleaning the windshield.)

Get fresh water. Go early in the morning. Most car washes recycle their water, and as the day or week goes on, the water gets more minerals in it. In some areas where there are water shortages, the water may not be changed very often. Ask the management when the water is changed and plan your visit around this time.

Check your car for damage before leaving. If you are missing a wheel cover or hubcap, you should find out before you get very far. Ditto for any other damage caused by the machine. In particular, check the operation of your wipers and automatic antenna.

Part II
On the Open Road

In this part...

 his part tells you what to do when you're out on the highway and freeway, including driving safety tips.

Chapter 5

Hot Tips for Road Trips

• •

In This Chapter

▶ Preparing for your trip

▶ Staying awake and alert

▶ Choosing the right sunglasses

▶ Eating on the road

▶ Traveling smart

▶ Choosing a motel

▶ Knowing what to take with you

• •

*B*eing on the road can be a happy or disastrous event. Seasoned travelers have long since learned the pitfalls of travel by car and know what to do to prepare themselves as well as to handle bad situations. In this chapter, I will pass on a hundred years' worth of travelers' experiences.

Getting the Car Ready for a Long Trip

When getting ready to spend more than a day or two driving, there are some things you should do to reduce your odds of breaking down on the trip:

✔ **Don't have any work done on your car at the last minute.** If something wasn't fixed correctly or completely, you'll find out within a few hundred miles or so — far enough away from home that you won't know a mechanic you can trust. If your car needs a tune-up, have it done at least 30 days in advance.

✔ **Start your trip with fresh oil and a new oil filter.** Use high-quality oil. *Best:* Use synthetic oil to keep your engine oil temperature lower and to lengthen your change intervals. If the transmission and transaxle haven't had a fluid change in the last year or last 30,000 miles, it's time to change the fluid.

✔ **If the air filter and fuel filter are over 12 months or 10,000 miles old, have them changed.**

✔ **Have all four wheels pulled so that the brakes, tires, and suspension can be inspected carefully.** Check the spare, too. Now is a good time to seriously consider new tires.

✔ **If the brake fluid is more than a year old, have it flushed.** When you're going down a mountain, old brake fluid can boil, resulting in dangerous brake fade. Has your brake pedal ever become mushy and gone to the floor? Pretty scary! Replacing the brake fluid in the master cylinder reservoir isn't enough. Flushing the old fluid out of the entire brake system and replacing it with new fluid is a must.

✔ **If the wiper blades are over six months old, install a new set.**

✔ **Have the headlights aimed with the car fully loaded with luggage and passengers.** If your car doesn't have halogen bulbs, have a set installed. You will gain substantially better dusk-to-dawn visibility.

✔ **Have the coolant serviced if your last service date was more than one year or 12,000 miles ago.** Be sure that the shop uses a 50-50 mix of coolant and distilled water.

✔ **Keep your own breakdown kit in the trunk.** Stock it with six or more flares, a sturdy flashlight, spare fan belt, pliers, an adjustable wrench, a multipurpose screwdriver, some waterless hand cleaner, and a roll of paper towels. Also, take along a jug of water and an approved container full of fuel. (See Chapter 15 for a complete list of what to take along in your emergency road kit.)

Keeping Yourself Awake, Alert, and Alive

Long road trips can be uncomfortable and boring. Boredom can lead to sleepiness, which can lead to sudden death. Here are some tips from experienced long-distance drivers that can help to make your trip more enjoyable:

✔ **Purchase a pair of clear-lens glasses.** Very lightly tinted sunglasses will do in a pinch. Wearing the glasses keeps your eyes from drying out in your car's ventilation draft. One of the biggest problems with night driving is sore eyes. Dry eyes become red eyes and hurt. This tip came from a friend who used clear lenses so that he could continue wearing his contact lenses while driving at night. It works very well for anyone, whether or not you wear contact lenses.

✔ **Buy the best sunglasses you can afford.** Defects and anomalies in cheap sunglasses can quickly tire your eyes. High quality shades provide maximum UV protection for your eyes and keep them fresh longer. Better sunglasses cut haze and can reduce blindness from snow, fog, or dust. (See the following section, "Choosing a Pair of Sunglasses," for more information.)

✔ **Keep your car windows clean inside and out.** Dirty windows cause excessive eye strain.

✔ **Take Mom's advice: Don't slouch!** Good posture can prevent back pain and improve alertness. Keep your head up and shoulders down.

 Reclined seats are both sleep inducing and unsafe. A slight tilt may improve comfort, but overreclined seats defeat the purpose of seatbelts. In an accident, you'll slide underneath!

✔ **A CB radio can be a great help on the road, both for staying alert and getting the latest traffic reports.** You might choose to leave it off when driving with children, however. Trucker language is often R-rated.

✔ **Books-on-tape are great, especially if you are driving by yourself.** Listening to a story can keep you awake as well as make the long hours seem shorter. If you find yourself struggling to follow the plot, either it's time to stop and rest or you accidentally selected something by James Michener. Just kidding!

✔ **Chewing gum — preferably sugarless — can help keep you awake and alert.** Avoid sugared gum and candy because it will make you thirsty. Don't like gum? Chewing ginseng can give you a lift that's better than caffeine and doesn't make you irritable. Check local health food stores.

- ✔ **Stuff your ears with soft, self-forming earplugs, generally available at pharmacies.** Prolonged exposure to road noise is tiring; these plugs cut the decibels but still let you hear horns and sirens. Tired? Pull them out. The sudden rise in noise level increases alertness.

- ✔ **Keep the car's interior as cold as you can stand it.** Heat encourages sleepiness. Every so often, lower the windows and circulate some fresh air. Put a damp washcloth in a plastic bag and keep it in your cooler for a wet wake-up.

- ✔ **Track a truck.** If you have a hard time keeping a good pace and need to make time, find an 18-wheeler that is going at about the speed you want to travel. Get five to ten car lengths behind the truck and stay put. The big trucks contact truckers going the other way and get reports about any speed traps or road hazards ahead. You can benefit by tagging along. In addition, tagging along gives you something to concentrate on and helps you stay alert.

- ✔ **Take breaks every two to three hours, even before you feel the need.** Have a light snack, do calisthenics, stretch your legs with a short walk, or even take a shower (many truck stops offer showers for a nominal fee). If nothing seems to wake you up, take a nap! Never mind the lost time; you may be preventing an accident. Which one would you rather be: "Mr. Smith, who arrived late" or "The late Mr. Smith"?

Only pull over in rest areas where there are other cars around or in a well-lit area where you feel safe. In a pinch, try the restaurant parking lot at a truck stop. Church parking lots are pretty safe bets, too.

For more information about driver fatigue, see Chapter 6.

Choosing a Pair of Sunglasses

Many people will never buy a decent pair of sunglasses simply because they are afraid to lose them. In reality, they are going cheap in a critical area where there should be no compromise. You cannot replace your eyes once they are damaged — and the sun can do permanent damage to your eyes if you don't properly protect them.

There are two kinds of damaging sunlight radiation, both in the form of ultraviolet rays. Long wavelength ultraviolet ray A (UVA) is considered the aging ultraviolet ray. UVA is the main component in snow blindness and excessive outdoor activity eye soreness. Symptoms include redness of the eyelids, excessive tearing, light sensitivity, and a feeling of grit in the eyes. The symptoms can take several hours to a couple of days to go away.

Intermediate wavelength ultraviolet ray B (UVB) can cause permanent damage to the retina, resulting in age-related cataracts, sunburn, skin wrinkles, and skin cancer.

The American National Standards Institute (ANSI) and Sunglasses Association of America call for 99 percent filtration of all UVB rays and 60 percent filtration of UVA rays. A quality pair of sunglasses should provide close to 100 percent filtration of both harmful types of UV radiation.

Before buying a pair of sunglasses, find out how much protection they provide. Some brands say that they provide UV protection but not how much. These are misleading and should be avoided. The ANSI Standard Z80.3 means that the sunglasses meet the minimum filtration requirements.

What about colored lenses? Some sunglasses are designed for use under driving conditions, where it is necessary to be highly aware of the color of road signs and traffic signals. When the glasses incorporate spectral filters to filter out certain light wavelengths, the glasses are said to be better for driving. These types of glasses cause the primary colors to appear brighter, making red and yellow lights even more visible.

Some sunglasses offer enhanced blue-light filtration. Since blue light is more scattered than the rest of the spectrum, blue filtration limits the hazing effect that tends to partially obscure your vision. Some offer gradient lenses with more filtration on the top to reduce light from the sky in much the same way that the darkened strip across the top of the car windshield does. There are even double-gradient lenses with more filtration on both the top and the bottom — ideal for lifeguards and people who are around the water, where glare also reflects off the water.

Sunglasses facts and fallacies

Fallacy: The darker the sunglass lenses, the more protection they afford.

Fact: It is possible to have a very high level of UV protection even though the lens may be very light. Read the label carefully for the degree of UV light protection. If you are not sure, get a new pair.

Fallacy: If you can see your eyes, the sunglass lenses are not dark enough.

Fact: Even if the lenses are jet black, they will not protect your eyes from harmful UV rays without the protective coating. In fact, dark lenses without adequate UV protection are downright dangerous. Unprotected dark lenses send a message to the pupil of the eye to admit more light. Not only is the unfiltered light absorbed by the eye; in the long term, it may be a source of eye damage.

Fallacy: Light-colored eyes need more protection from the sun.

Fact: Whether your eyes are light or dark, the amount of protection they need is the same — 99 percent UVB inhibitors. However, people with light-colored eyes may be more sensitive to light and may be more comfortable with darker lenses.

Fallacy: On cloudy days, the cloud cover filters the sun, so you don't need sunglasses for protection.

Fact: Harmful ultraviolet rays UVA and UVB are present even on cloudy days, and you should wear sunglasses anytime you are driving for an extended period of time.

Eating and driving do mix

What do you like to eat when you drive along? Here are some suggestions.

Good choices

Try unsalted or lightly salted popcorn, walnuts, cashews, peanuts, cheese, peanut butter on crackers, chocolate-covered raisins, yogurt-covered almonds, rice cakes, puffed corn cakes, granola bars, trail mix, yogurt, pudding, fresh fruits, or dried fruit/fruit leather. If you choose a variety of nuts, make sure that they are unsalted.

Generally, you want good, bite-sized foods that are neat to eat, interesting in texture, and complex in flavor. Mix shredded wheat, unsalted pretzels, unsalted wheat crackers, and unsalted dry-roasted peanuts in a container, and the miles roll away in a healthy and satisfying manner.

For drinks, try two-percent milk (chocolate or plain), individual "sippin' pack" juices (freeze first), or lemonade. But water is best because it always quenches thirst.

Bad choices

Try to avoid the following foods, which are messy and may make you more thirsty:

- **Sticky:** Marshmallows and gummy bears

- **Greasy:** French fries, potato chips, BBQ, pizza, and fried chicken

- **Crumbly:** Cookies and pretzels

- **Sweet:** Soda pop, punch, and candy (These contain too much sugar and increase thirst. The end result? Extra pit stops.)

- **Salty:** Tomato juice and prepopped or prepackaged or popcorn

Becoming a Travel-Wise Traveler

Planning on doing some traveling this summer or winter vacation? Here are some timely tips to make things easier.

Getting the cheapest and best gas

To find the best prices on gasoline when traveling, pay attention to roadside billboards advertising off-brand, cut-rate fuel. Take that exit even if you don't want to use that brand. Cut-rate gas stations are usually surrounded by a number of brand-name stations also offering low prices on fuel. If you use high-test, one station will typically offer cheap high-test fuel as a loss leader.

If you use only one particular brand of gas, plan ahead and get a list of gas stations on the way that carry your brand of gas. You can secure such a list by writing the oil company. In general, all name-brand stations are pretty much the same when it comes to open-highway engine performance. The differences in brands are usually apparent only when doing local stop-and-go driving.

Take a minute to drive around, checking out all the stations in the exit area until you find the cheapest fuel of the octane and brand you like.

Be sure to save the gas receipt from each purchase. If you buy a tank full of bad fuel and break down because of the fuel, you will need proof of your purchase. It costs only a little extra time and may be the only thing that you have to prove that you got a load of "Robbie's Rotgut Watered-Down Gas!"

Saving gas while using the air conditioner

Run the air conditioner at the warmest setting with the fan on high. This keeps the compressor cycling at a minimum. Also, choose the setting that has air coming out of the upper register vents. Because cool air normally falls, upper vents put cool air in the upper part of the car where it is needed most.

Missing your exit

Don't get flustered. As soon as you realize that you have passed your exit, start looking for the next exit with an on-ramp going in the opposite direction. Form a mental picture of where you want to go. Pay special attention to the place you want to exit when going in the opposite direction. Usually, you need to look back behind you at the exit signs facing the other way.

Driving defensively

 Beware of the number of people who are now running traffic lights in the bigger cities that you may visit. Because of the downsizing of police departments, there are fewer traffic cops enforcing these traffic laws. More and more people are running red lights, creating a new national safety concern.

Be especially careful at intersections, even when the light is in your favor. **Worst places:** Washington, D.C. and New York City.

Preventing back pain

If you get back pain after driving for a long distance, vibrations from the car may be causing it. Chiropractors have found that these vibrations are close to the frequency at which the human spine vibrates, and lengthy exposure can hurt your spine. This is the most plausible explanation I have ever heard for the problems that drivers have with back pain after long trips.

 Sit with an inflatable pillow against your spine to help dampen the vibrations, and take short walking breaks every few hours.

Combating dehydration

If you plan on traveling to a high-altitude region, beware of dehydration. Your lungs exhale more water in high, dry, oxygen-scarce air; your thirst mechanism is also suppressed. Symptoms of dehydration include dark yellow urine, headaches, and muscle soreness.

 Drink at least 12 cups of water a day regardless of how thirsty you are. Gatorade is good, too.

Wearing a hat

Bring along a baseball-type cap and wear it when driving. You'll look like a local resident. Women should tuck their hair up inside the hat to give them a male profile when driving at night and in bad parts of town.

Practicing car safety in strange places

When in a strange city, don't rent a car that has a bumper sticker or other displays of the rental car company. Crooks know that you are from out of town and are probably a good mark. Always take your valuables with you, knowing that someone can easily steal the rental car while you are away. Also, avoid checking a map while sitting at an intersection, which is an invitation for a carjacking. Plan on traveling in a strange city during the day so that you are safely in your hotel by dark. You don't want to be traveling on unfamiliar roads in the dark.

 Rent a car from an agency near the hotel and use the hotel shuttle to travel to and from the airport. Off-airport rental agencies are usually cheaper. Also, most car rental companies usually have a free shuttle to and from the hotel. Talk with the hotel concierge or desk clerk and ask the name of a local and cheap rental company — maybe one that offers discounts for guests of that hotel.

Parking to stop crime

While in a roadside restaurant, always park your car in plain sight of the window. Ask for a table near the window so that you can keep an eye on your car while you eat. At a motel, ask the clerk to assign you a room overlooking the parking lot where you can easily see your car.

At a rest stop, be wary of anyone hanging around the rest room or parking lot. Take a moment to scan the area for loiterers before you leave your car or enter the rest room. Stay with your travel companions if possible. Avoid parking next to vans because they are the perfect hiding place for thieves and muggers.

Avoiding hotel room lockout

When leaving a hotel room without the key, remember that the door is spring loaded. Prop open the door securely using a chair or, in some cases, the door dead bolt.

Best advice: Never leave your hotel room without your key or your pants, even if it is only a trip to the candy or ice machine. Each time you leave your room, ask yourself: "Am I presentable to the people in the lobby as I am dressed?"

Heeding the travel guide book warning

Don't rely on a travel guide or tour guidebook, especially if it is an old one. Remember that restaurants, hotels, bed and breakfasts, and inns often change management, cooks, and menus. Your outdated guidebook may list a particular restaurant as being a nice, friendly place. Now, a couple of years later, it's the place where Mr. Ripp U. Off works!

 Find a current travel guide, read the local newspaper's restaurant reviews, or ask local people for suggestions. Other good sources of advice: the hotel concierge, taxi driver, gas station attendant, or car rental agent.

Taking risks with airport security

Don't trust your computers or software with airport x-ray machines. While it is true that a majority of the machines will not damage computer floppy disks, don't trust them. Also, some metal detectors in walk-through gates are much stronger than others, and a power surge will permanently damage your data.

 Leave a backup disk at home and have airport security hand-check your computer and disks.

Getting TB from airplane passengers

What if someone on the airplane has tuberculosis? Your chances of catching this very contagious disease from shared air are pretty low, according to the Centers for Disease Control in Atlanta. TB-infected people breathe out only a very small number of bacteria, which must then make it past your efficient respiratory tract defenses. Usually, contracting TB requires prolonged exposure to a contagious person. Try not to sit next to someone who has a persistent cough. Turn on the fresh air nozzle and be sure to drink plenty of water to keep from becoming dehydrated on a long flight. Dehydration allows mucous membranes to become more susceptible to airborne disease.

Buying overseas

If you plan on making purchases with your credit card while traveling overseas, beware that exchange rate fluctuations can make the items you purchase much more expensive than you thought by the time the credit card company processes the paperwork. It takes about one week for most purchases to clear.

 Make purchases by credit card only if the US dollar is rising or if the transaction is completed via electronic means immediately. Use cash when the dollar is falling.

Swatting sand flies

If you plan on going south of the border to visit Mexico or Central or South America, take along protection against the horrible sand flies that inhabit these regions. They may transmit leishmaniasis, a parasitic infection that develops into itchy, painful sores that can take months to heal. These small flies have a painless bite, but the sores develop a matter of days (or perhaps months) later. Protect yourself by wearing long pants, socks, and shoes or be sure to use an insect repellent. Dusk to dawn is the worst time, so stay indoors during this period and sleep under some fine mesh mosquito netting.

Practicing rental car safety

Before leaving the rental car lot, be sure to do a "bulb check" on all the dash warning lamps. Turn the key and don't start the car until you have familiarized yourself with all the dash warning indicator lights. If you don't know what a certain lamp means, ask the lot attendant to explain it before you leave. That way, if a warning lamp comes on while you are driving the car, you will know the cause. Also, doing this tells you whether the car is equipped with anti-lock brakes (ABS), air bags (SIR), and traction control (TRAC).

Avoiding car rental insurance traps

If you plan on using a credit card to pay for rental car insurance, be aware that it may automatically include coverage for collision insurance. Many credit cards and corporate cards, including American Express, lack collision insurance coverage for cardholders.

 If you rent cars often and your personal vehicle coverage won't cover a rental car (possibly because your car is still being used while you are away), consider getting a credit card that offers this service. The cost of Collision Damage Waivers (CDWs) with rental companies can run as high as 50 percent of the daily rental rate.

No Tell Which Motel

When traveling in a strange city, you often face the problem of choosing a motel. No one wants to spend too much on a motel, but a really cheap motel may not be worth the savings if you can't get decent sleep. This section gives you some tips for finding a motel when on the road in a strange city.

Choosing a motel

Most motels are located on the way into or out of a city and at major interstate junctions. Don't stop at the ones on the way in or at the first one you see. Look them over and compare prices, which are usually posted on the outside in large letters. Get an idea of the price of motels in that locale. Typically, the closer you get to the center of town, the higher the prices are. Choose a motel on the way out of town that fits your budget and tastes. Don't be afraid to turn around and go back to the one that you saw and liked.

 Don't stay at the cheapest motels unless you like bad beds, noisy neighbors, all-night parties, faulty air conditioners, and rancid-smelling rooms. Also, beware of places that advertise weekly or monthly rates. These are usually so run down and roach infested that only vagabonds and roadside rogues will stay there — to keep company with the cockroaches!

 The best "bargain" motels are those that were once luxury motels and are now under a different name. They look like an old, big-name hotel without the usual name. The price listed on the sign may still be there, but with different lettering covering up the old sign.

Before you check in, always ask the price of the room. The price listed on the sign outside may be for only a few select rooms that are always taken. If one is available, it will most likely have a small bed and no shower and be inconveniently located. You may end up paying quite a bit more to get what you want, so ask first. Don't assume.

Always ask whether there are any special promotions, discounts, freebies, or specials available when checking in. You may find that by signing up for a free club membership, you get free breakfasts. Ask whether you get a discount for your company (business discounts) or your particular travel club or for being a senior citizen.

Selecting a room

Ask to look at your room before checking in. Check the air conditioner or heater to see whether it is reasonably quiet. Give the bed a try, too. You may find that it has no box spring or is a heated waterbed that is too hot. See if the TV works.

If you are a light sleeper, always try to stay on the top floor; then heavy-footed occupants above you won't awaken you. Try to pick a room at the end of the hall so you won't have occupants on both sides of you. Doing so reduces your chances of having a noisy neighbor by 50 percent.

Don't choose a room next to an elevator, staircase, or door leading to the outside. Elevators squeak, and doors to the stairs or the outside can become a noisy nuisance, opening and slamming all night long. Ditto for vending and ice machines.

If you find something about the room objectionable, complain immediately. If you wait, there may not be another room available. Ask for compensation in some way for your inconvenience, especially when changing rooms. Ask for a room upgrade, a free meal voucher, or a discount on the rate.

If you want a quiet room, ask for one. Alert the clerk to the fact that you need peace and quiet. If the room isn't quiet, ask for another room. If you don't get a good night's sleep because the room was not quiet, you can refuse to pay the bill.

 Avoid a room that has an adjoining room. The lock on the door leading to the other room is often inferior — someone could easily jimmy it open from the other side.

Choose a room facing away from the highway. The sound of trucks, sirens, and traffic can spoil your sleep. The same is true for airport hotels and the runway and large parking lots where car alarms can wail all night.

Hotel rooms facing the beach are usually not worth the extra cost. At night, the beach may be the scene of noisy parties. In the morning, many beaches have crews that groom the beach with loud tractors.

Lastly, always pay with a charge card. If a dispute about the bill arises, it is easier to file a complaint and get reimbursed if you charged the room cost.

Miscellaneous Items to Bring

Finally, bring along the following handy items to make your trip as trouble-free as possible:

- ✔ Moist towelettes and tissues or napkins for spills and quick cleanups
- ✔ Gloves to wear when pumping gas
- ✔ A cooler with a freezable, drinkable water pack in the lid, which saves on buying ice and provides drinking water
- ✔ An auto record book for keeping records of your car and travels (these are available at stationery stores)
- ✔ A funnel in a sealable plastic bag to use when adding oil to the engine
- ✔ A pillow from your own bed for better sleeping
- ✔ A hat with a sun visor to help when driving directly into the sun
- ✔ A pair of flip-flops for wearing in the shower and around the pool
- ✔ A small coffee pot or coffee maker to make coffee or tea in your room
- ✔ Vitamins, antacids, Dramamine, aspirin, and other common medications

Chapter 6

Highway Driving

. . . .

In This Chapter

▶ Driving around truckers

▶ Avoiding driver fatigue and sleepiness

▶ Dealing with deer hazards

▶ Deciding which type of drive to drive

. . . .

W hen it comes to getting behind the wheel of a vehicle, just about everyone learns by going to the school of hard knocks. The longer you drive, the more you pick up about those unwritten rules of the road. Sometimes tragedies occur in the process of learning the ropes. Wouldn't it be wonderful if someone with a great deal of driving experience would pass on some of those valuable driving tips so that you could avoid a calamity in order to learn for yourself — especially to entry-level young drivers?

Sure, a good driving course teaches you a great deal about safe driving. But there is so much more about being out there on the highway that no one ever tells you about. I have driven a truck coast-to-coast more than a dozen times and have driven in every type of driving condition there is. While on the road, I have collected a great deal of good information about the pitfalls of highway driving. Truck drivers log millions of miles and have to learn all the tricks of the road in order to survive. I learned a great deal from talking with them on the CB and in person and by observing their driving actions. In this chapter, I'll pass on some of the more important things I learned.

I highly recommend that parents make this chapter required reading for all young drivers in their family — especially the section on driving with big trucks. Big trucks are probably the most frightening things you encounter on a regular basis on the highway.

Superhighway Driving

Have you ever wondered where on the road is safest to drive? Do you always drive in the right lane? Middle lane? Fast lane? How about when driving with other cars on the road? Do you follow behind, stay to the side, or lead the pack? Here are some tips for driving on freeways, turnpikes, and interstates:

✔ **Stay in your lane.** Every time you change lanes, you risk hitting another vehicle that is in your blind spot.

✔ **When driving on a crowded highway with big trucks, watch which lane the trucks are in.** If you see them changing lanes and driving in a lane different from the traditional trucker's right-hand lane, a problem may lie in the road ahead. Truckers communicate with each other by CB radio and often know ahead of time that a problem is coming up. If all the trucks suddenly move into the passing lane, a lane closure may be ahead.

✔ **Watch out for "snake drivers," probably the most dangerous drivers on the road.** They snake though traffic, going from one lane to the next and cutting back and forth to speed ahead. If you see snake drivers coming up in your rearview mirror, get over and out of the way. Don't let these drivers sideswipe your car or cause you to make an emergency lane change to avoid hitting them as they fly by.

✔ **Be wary of driving alongside panel vans.** Panel or delivery vans are especially dangerous because the lack of windows creates a huge blind spot and the driver may not see you. If you are driving beside a panel truck or van, make sure that the driver can see you so that he or she doesn't decide to change lanes and suddenly pull right into you!

 A modern travel tip: When you're traveling with a purse, briefcase, or laptop computer, it's wise to put it on the floor. If you leave it on the seat, a panic stop can throw it violently onto the floor. If you must keep it on a seat, securely belt it in place with the seat belt. Securing it with a seat belt also makes it less likely that a thief can pop open the door, reach inside, and grab your valuable item when you're stopped.

Pack Driving

Due to the increased congestion of today's roads, it is almost impossible to avoid being a pack driver. In general, driving in a group of cars is safer if you do it properly. Here are some pack driving tips:

✔ **Avoid driving in another driver's blind spot.** If you can't see the other driver in his rearview mirror, he probably doesn't know you are there. In the event that the other driver wants to change lanes, you will be in a dangerous spot.

✔ **Avoid driving in the other driver's escape path.** This is the direction that the driver is most likely to go if there is suddenly a road hazard ahead. If you are driving in his escape path, he may not take the time to look to the left or right before making an emergency lane change — right into the side of your car.

✔ **Drive at the very front or very rear of the pack.** Try to stay out of the middle. The middle is the most likely place to become trapped by the other cars if you have to make an emergency lane change.

✔ **Stay in the outside lane.** If the pack is too big for you to maintain a position in the front or back, try to stay in the right-hand lane or, if you must, in the left-hand lane. As long as you are in an outside lane, you have an escape path.

✔ **Always plan an escape path so that you can make an emergency lane change.** If something suddenly pops up in the road in front of you, have a place to go.

✔ **Always give gap, take gap.** This is a way of being courteous to other drivers. If someone is trying to enter or exit the highway, either adjust your speed to open a place for the other driver or change lanes.

Is it better to go with the flow of traffic — even if that means breaking the speed limit with everyone else? This is a personal judgment call. Observing the speed limit only to have the whole world pass you by can become very annoying. If you find this happening and don't want to go faster, get over to the right and let the other drivers spring all the speed traps.

Sleepiness Kills

About 31 percent of the nearly 50,000 people killed on US highways every year die as a result of falling asleep at the wheel. This percentage is second only to that of people killed as a result of drunk driving accidents. Sleep-induced crashes can be exceptionally destructive because a sleepy driver may make no attempt to avert a collision.

It doesn't matter where you are going or how late you are; *no one* will give you an "A for Effort" if you die in the process of getting there. Driving tired isn't heroic; it's suicidal *and* homicidal. Look at the following sidebar and see if you've experienced any of these symptoms on the road. Then commit the avoidance procedures to memory.

Five signs of driver fatigue

Focusing difficulties: Reading the signs ahead becomes harder and harder. Your eyes are burning and feel strained. Frequent blinking increases until the blinks turn into closed eyes. Your head nods or you can't stop yawning.

Tracking difficulties: You have trouble steering in a straight line and begin to weave from side to side like a drunk.

Reduced reaction time: You catch yourself about to nod off. You're driving erratically or at abnormal speeds, drifting, tailgating, or missing traffic signs. Your thought process, from perception of danger to avoidance, is dramatically impaired.

For example, when a traffic light changes, drowsy drivers take far longer to react. This won't be a problem from red to green because someone will eventually honk. But if the change is from green to yellow to red, sleepy drivers may run the red light with potentially fatal results.

Tunnel vision: Locking onto the road ahead without checking the mirrors or scanning the roadside indicates deteriorating alertness. Even worse, staring at something along the side of the road can lead to disaster.

Time warp: You have wandering, disconnected thoughts. You suddenly realize that you don't know how far you have been driving or what has been happening for some period of time. This may include going miles past exits and turnoffs, so now you're both sleepy *and* lost!

Sleeping death avoidance procedures

Get a good night's sleep before driving. If you knew that staying up late was going to kill you the next day, how important would those "vital" last-minute details be?

Share the driving with another person if possible. You may not like to, but the alternative could be death or permanent disability for you and your passenger(s).

Eat smaller meals while on the road. A full stomach makes you drowsy. Snack if you need to, but avoid sugar-loaded candy and sodas because sugar makes your blood sugar go up and down like a roller coaster. Fruits and vegetables are better. Also try popcorn or beef jerky. (For a more complete listing of foods to eat on the road, see "Eating and driving do mix" in Chapter 5.)

Drink coffee or tea sparingly. Caffeine increases alertness but can't replace sleep. Avoid over-the-counter stimulants, both for health and legal reasons. Some contain such powerful decongestants that some states require prescriptions for them. All provide a temporary lift, but the lift comes at the expense of worn-out nerves. A jumpy driver can be just as dangerous as a sleepy one.

If you find yourself experiencing driver fatigue, find a safe place to pull over and rest. Good choices are rest stops and truck stop plazas. Look for places where you see big trucks resting. Staying alive takes precedence over staying on schedule. Remember, a brief rest period may keep you from killing both yourself and others on the road with you. Would you rather be "The Late Mr. Jones" or "Mr. Jones, who arrived late?"

Encountering Big Trucks Up Close

Truck drivers are some of the hardest working people in the world. Piloting huge tractor trailers (also called *18-wheelers*), they carry food and goods all over the country. The highway is their workplace, and their rig (truck) is their office. Big trucks are a handful, requiring a driver's constant attention. A pleasant commute for you is a road full of little four-wheeled hazards (also called *four-wheelers*) for them. Maybe that's why truck drivers are surprised and pleased when four-wheelers give them a little respect. The following sections give you some tips for driving safely around big rigs.

Stop depending on truckers' vision

Don't depend on truckers to see you. Many trucks have convex mirrors, which distort distances. It's hard to tell how far back your car really is. Also, if the truck engine is causing the mirrors to vibrate, the driver may not have a clear view of anything.

 The most dangerous place to drive is *beside* the truck, especially in the vicinity of the front fender. If the driver changes lanes suddenly, you may end up in a ditch or beneath those tires. So if your cruise control has you lounging alongside an 18-wheeler, either complete the pass or drop back until you can. In the daytime, look for the truck driver's silhouette in his rearview mirror. If you can see him, he can probably see you. With practice, you will have a good idea of whether you can be seen when you're driving at night.

Be extra careful while driving on the right-hand side of any truck. On the open road, truck drivers want to keep the right side clear, both for access to upcoming exits and in case they have to get off the road quickly. If they lose air pressure to their air brakes, which creates a serious brake pressure problem, they have only a few seconds to get off the road before the wheels lock up and the truck comes to a halt in the middle of the road.

In town, big trucks need to swing wide when making right-hand turns; otherwise, the trailer will run over the curb. Before you pull up on the right side of an 18-wheeler sitting in the left lane with his right turn signal on, think of how his right rear wheels will look planted in the middle of your trunk and back seat — or worse.

Get out of the way

When the truck's turn signals indicate that the driver wants to get in your lane — especially to the right — get out of the way! Truckers drive everywhere, often in areas that they don't know well. The driver may have just realized his exit is ahead and that you're in the lane he needs. A desperate trucker may be tempted to run you off the road. Either fade back or finish passing, whichever is safer.

Subconsciously, truckers are always looking for a clear path to the right. The driver knows that the mechanical spring brakes will apply if the rig suddenly loses air pressure to the brakes. Unlike cars, which use hydraulic pressure to *apply* the brakes, trucks use air pressure to *release* their brakes. If the air pressure is low, like if a hose breaks or a brake application device leaks air pressure, the brakes apply, causing the truck to stop dead in its tracks. The driver needs to get off the road immediately before the truck skids to a halt. If you follow too closely or linger to the right, you could end up underneath the truck.

Communicate on the road

Truck drivers are acutely aware of each other's visual limitations. Wise four-wheelers do the same. When truck drivers are passed by other trucks, they flash their headlights to tell the other drivers that the back end is clear of their cab. In the daytime, flashing your high beams is the easiest. Do so when the trailer is far enough ahead of you to safely enter your lane. Do not flash your high beams at night. Instead, turn your headlights off and on one time. Did the trucker see you? If so, you'll see the truck's running lights flash one or more times, saying "Thanks."

Avoid the blind spot

Don't drive directly behind a truck in the blind spot. Until rear-mounted video cameras become cost-effective, 18-wheelers will always have blind spots. If the truck driver knows that you're there, he or she may do some aggressive things to make you move. Oddly enough, truckers don't mind other trucks driving closely behind them. Almost all drivers have CB radios and communicate back and forth. But unless you are personally invited via CB radio to drop in among trucks in a group, *don't* do it.

Don't be the uninvited guest

Truckers like to run in caravans to *slipstream* — letting the lead truck cut wind resistance for the others. They also drive together to intimidate speed-trap enforcement or to just chat on their radios. If you drop in, they will likely try to squeeze you out. Worse yet, if you are between two big trucks when the truck in front has brake seizure problems, the truck in front of you and the truck behind you will do a "hammer and anvil" on your car that will leave it small enough to mail home in a shoe box.

Maintain your speed after you pass

Want to make a trucker angry? Pass the truck, pull back in front of it, and slow down. The trucker has to brake, check all the mirrors, look for the chance to downshift, and pass you again. Truckers hate passing because it involves a certain amount of risk. An unseen car may be in one of their blind spots. Truckers must build up great speed to pass, making them a perfect target for a speed trap. Passing also costs in fuel.

Be aware of trucks in your rearview mirror

About that truck radiator in your rearview mirror — chances are it was your fault . . . at least from the truck driver's viewpoint. Passing a truck and pulling back into the lane too quickly causes such an accident. Only crazed truckers will intentionally sit on the bumper of a four-wheeler; their insurance costs too much as it is. So when passing a truck, pull far ahead before reentering the truck's lane. It's best to wait until you can clearly see the truck's headlights in your rearview mirror.

Why do trucks pass on the right? Or, if you're in the right-hand lane, why do trucks sometimes loom up in the rearview mirror? In the truck driver's "winning formula," he or she must deal with one constant — the miles to cover — and two variables — time and fuel consumption.

Going up hill takes fuel and time. One of the ways truckers save fuel and precious minutes is to go fast on the downhill grade. If you're to the left and going slower, truckers will pass on the right. If you are in their lane doing your "civic duty" by driving 55, you become an obstacle.

It is not unusual to spend an hour or two in hilly country passing and being passed by the same truck, over and over. Flip on your CB radio and you will probably hear yourself described in unprintable terms.

If you see that big grill in your rearview mirror and the lane to your left is clear, get over and let the truck pass on the right. If you are already in the left-most lane, either speed up or move over to the right.

Keep glancing in the rearview mirror and if you see a truck beating down on you *without* his turn signal on, get out of his way. If his turn signal is on, stay where you are but keep an eye on him. Remember, the driver is busy trying to keep his mammoth vehicle on the road. Your most important consideration is giving that truck *lots* of room.

Let trucks pass

Most people speed up when someone tries to pass them. Doing so while a trucker is passing on the right is called the *Pushing Effect*. Drivers accelerate as if to say, "I was *not* driving slowly!" If you speed up while being passed on the left, you demonstrate what is called the *Towing Effect*. The higher speed of an adjacent vehicle encourages you to go faster as well. And other drivers out there just don't like to be passed.

If irritating the driver of a vehicle that outweighs yours by many thousands of pounds gives you a thrill, just don't let him pass you. Truckers hate it when a four-wheeler "camps out" in either the right or left lane, only to wake up and accelerate when the truck tries to pass. Do it often enough and the driver — or the driver's buddy in the next truck ahead — may just accidentally cut you off.

Stay clear of struggling trucks

Stay away from a line of trucks struggling up a hill. The trucks following the lead rig are slipstreaming to make their job easier — and a small vehicle between them ruins the effect. It may have taken all the truck's effort to get up to the speed it has achieved in order to get up the next hill. The trucker may have planned this move way back, maybe miles back. In some cases, the entire caravan of trucks may be working in concert in order to save time and fuel when dealing with a particular hill. If you decide to slip in the middle of the trucks for no apparent reason, you may wind up experiencing first hand "trucker's revenge," as described later in this chapter.

Avoid trucks in the rain

Stay away from big rigs in wet weather. Their wheel-splash will reduce your visibility to near zero, and the truckers may not see you for the same reason. Here's an interesting fact: Trucks can stop faster on wet roads than you can. Their front wheels squeeze out the water and their awesome weight improves traction. If they have to slam on the brakes and you are too close, the result may well be fatal. The same applies in snow or ice.

In general, trucks have better traction in the snow but can suddenly *jackknife* — folding where the tractor and trailer connect. Equally as deadly, you may lose traction and spin out while completing a pass, forcing the trucker to hit you or swerve off the road.

Watch your tail on entrance and exit ramps

Where is the most likely place for a tractor-trailer to crash? The answer is on an entrance or exit ramp leading to or from an interstate highway. The reason? The truckers do not reduce their speed enough for the ramp. Many ramps are designed with curves that are poorly banked or that are too tight. A study conducted by the University of Virginia suggests that most accidents occur as the trucks leave the interstates because they don't slow down enough for the ramp.

In most of the accidents that occurred, trucks ran into the rear end of a smaller vehicle. The study posed the possibility that ramp speed limits are set for cars, not big trucks. So when you are leaving the interstate and a big truck is on your tail, watch out! That truck may not be able to slow down quickly enough and may run over you.

In summary, the two keys to safe driving around trucks are to give them plenty of room and to stay visible. By the way, don't expect all truckers to act accordingly just because you show them respect. It may take them a while to recover from the shock.

Experiencing Trucker's Revenge

Truck drivers have some not-so-subtle ways of letting you know that they are displeased. You may be a little shocked by some of these methods, but after a few dozen sleepless hours behind the wheel of a big rig surrounded by little four-wheelers, you might become a little crazed, too. Here are truckers' favorite tricks:

✔ **Gravel Bath:** Here, the trucker pulls in front of you and eases onto the shoulder with his right tires. The trailer's wheels throw gravel and rocks, pelting your car. Say good-bye to your paint job and hello to a cracked windshield.

✔ **Brake Hiss:** The truck driver positions his or her truck so that the brake air release valve is right next to you. Then the trucker taps the brakes, causing the valve to emit a loud *hiss* noise that may frighten you and cause you to lose control of your vehicle.

✔ **Killer Trailer:** This stunt is exceedingly dangerous! The trucker pulls ahead of you until the back wheels of the trailer are right next to you. The trucker then cuts over into your lane, forcing you off the road.

✔ **Blockade:** Several truckers get together and form a "rolling road-block" of trucks, keeping you from driving by. They drive slower and slower and slower until you are really angry and try something stupid like passing on the shoulder.

✔ **Ramrodding:** The trucker drives close to your rear bumper and tries to scare you off the road via an exit or the shoulder. Given the longer stopping distances for trucks, this is extremely dangerous.

✔ **Tattletale:** The trucker uses his or her mobile phone to call 911 and gives a description of your car, saying that you are a drunk driver. Pretty soon, you're stopped by the county mounty — ruining your day.

Dealing with Deer Hazards

Each year, nearly 187,000 accidents involving vehicles and animals occur with an average of 1,700 people being injured or killed. Hitting a deer results in an average of $600 in property damage per accident — and the death of the deer. In Pennsylvania one year, the Game Commission recorded over 7,000 deer killings in January and February alone. In some states, the quantity of deer killed by cars easily exceeds those taken by hunters with permits.

Deer are a greater problem to drivers during spring and fall when they seek out new territory and cross the highways. Even though deer can accelerate from 0 to 30 mph in 1.5 seconds, their size prevents them from easily changing direction. Once a deer begins to run into the path of your car, it won't be able to avoid a collision and may even run right into the side of a stopped car in its path.

Deer like to forage in dense bushes alongside rural roads and are apparently oblivious to the sound of motor vehicles. In many cases, deer will stand right in the middle of the road and watch you run into them! Unless a deer has been hit by a car and lived from the experience, it has no fear of motor vehicles.

 One person will be killed by striking a deer while four others will die trying to avoid hitting one. Sometimes hitting the animal is a better choice than losing control of your vehicle. In addition, slamming on your brakes can lead to a rear-end collision.

Here are some tips for dealing with deer:

- ✔ **Use highbeams.** When traveling at night where deer are prevalent, keep your high beams on as much as possible and scan the roadside ahead. The glow of the deer's eyes may be all the warning you'll get.

- ✔ **Avoid the road edge.** Drive close to the center of the road as much as you can, assuming that there is no oncoming traffic.

- ✔ **Look out for deer crossing signs.** Highway departments place these signs where previous accidents with deer have occurred. Slow down and be on full alert. Deer are creatures of habit, crossing at the same place year after year. Attempts to install "Press Here to Cross" buttons at these locations have met with limited success. (Just kidding!)

- ✔ **Be extra alert during dawn and dusk.** Dawn and dusk are favorite times for deer to roam. These are also the times of least visibility for you.

- ✔ **Be wary of nice weather.** Deer are more likely to be on the roam during a nice evening immediately following a period of cold weather.

- ✔ **If you actually see a deer alongside the road or crossing the road ahead, slow to a crawl.** Deer are herd animals. Chances are good that more deer will soon follow the one you saw. Flick your lights from high to low beam and lightly tap the horn. Deer can become "hypnotized" by your lights, and flashing your lights can break the trance.

- ✔ **Plan an escape path.** When driving in traffic, always try to have a lane that you can swerve into if a deer suddenly jumps in front of you. If you see no "escape hatch," the best risk management may be to hit the animal.

Knowing Which Drive to Drive

Various configurations of wheel drive systems have been around since four wheels became powered by something other than a horse. The simplest system powered only one wheel, while more complex systems delivered torque to all four wheels at once. While this type of system is great for going in a straight line, the inner and outer wheels fight one another when you try to turn a corner, resulting in annoying wheel hop and loss of traction. In order to deal with this problem, the *differential* was invented (see the following sidebar for details).

The differential explained

By utilizing a differential located in the middle of the axle between the wheels, powering two wheels is uncomplicated and efficient. The differential couples the two wheels via a set of differential planetary gears. These gears remain locked together until one wheel starts to turn faster than another; then the differential springs into action, allowing the wheels to turn at different rates.

When you turn a corner in your car, the outer wheels must turn much faster than the inner wheels. How is this accomplished? By using a differential. This device has a set of gears that transfer power to both wheels all the time but at the same time allow the wheels to turn at different speeds when you're making a turn.

In the middle of the differential is what looks a little like the nucleus of an atom. Two planetary gears (called *pinions*) rotate around in a circle and are connected together by a common shaft. This "nucleus" is connected to the drive axles — one gear for each side of the vehicle. They are housed in such a way that the gears can move around one another, allowing the left and right axles to rotate at different speeds.

When you're going in a straight line, the pinion gears move together in the same direction. When you turn a corner and one wheel slows down while the other speeds up, the pinion gears rotate around the drive axle, allowing the left axle to turn at a different rate than the right axle. Both still receive power through the pinion gears, only at different amounts of torque, depending on which axle and wheel are being "geared down" by the pinion gears.

2WD versus 4WD

If powering two wheels is good, wouldn't powering four wheels be even better? Yes and no. Yes, when you need the added traction. No, when you don't — the extra weight of the two differentials, axles, and transfer case costs in fuel mileage. Many people wonder when purchasing a new car or truck whether they should get the four-wheel-drive (4WD) option. The answer depends on several important factors:

- ✔ Do you plan to operate the vehicle on slippery or slick roads very often?

- ✔ Do you drive where there is a great deal of sand, gravel, snow, or ice?

- ✔ Will you operate the vehicle off-road in the sand or mud or on rugged terrain?

- ✔ Is having good traction more important than getting good fuel mileage?

- ✔ Can you really afford the extra expense of purchasing, maintaining, and repairing a 4WD vehicle?

The more questions you answer yes to, the more it makes sense for you to own a 4WD vehicle.

Although 4WD provides much better traction, a big problem with 4WD arises when you make turns. The front and rear wheels of the vehicle must turn at different speeds when cornering. If the driveshafts are coupled together, one or more of the tires must slide or slip when turning a corner. The juddering and hopping of the wheels is very hard on the driveline — making driving on nonslippery surfaces very difficult.

On the other hand, 4WD vehicles stop better than 2WD vehicles because all four wheels are locked together, making braking more balanced. When one wheel starts to lock up before the others, it is "driven" by the axle connected to the other wheel — which also helps to slow down the wheels that are not locking up. In essence, the wheels with more stopping traction can share some of their traction with the wheels with less stopping traction. It's almost as good as having anti-lock brakes.

Part-time versus full-time 4WD

Remember the Eagle, that relic of the past made by American Motor Corporation? It was probably the first popular car with a part-time 4WD system. If you didn't know to look in the glove box, you would never know that the vehicle was capable of 4WD operation. Mounted inside the glove box was a rotary knob. Upon twisting the knob, the transfer case would lock and the front axle would be coupled to the rear axle. All four wheels were then powered.

This is considered a part-time system because the driver has to actively do something to make the vehicle 4WD. Most other forms of 4WD vehicles required that you stop the vehicle, get out, and manually lock the front wheels by turning the locking hubs at the ends of each front axle.

Full-time 4WD systems operate all four wheels all the time — which has its advantages as well as disadvantages. The biggest advantage is that you don't have to do anything to make the system work; it works all the time, powering all the wheels. This is great for trucks and off-road, heavy-duty vehicles, but for most people, full-time 4WD is not practical. The extra weight and drag on the engine costs a great deal in fuel mileage and wear and tear.

One exception is high-performance cars that need all the traction they can get to keep the wheels from spinning from all the power being delivered. The Dodge Stealth and Mitsubishi 3000GT are two examples.

4WD versus AWD

During the 1980s, it was discovered that the front and rear axles could be coupled by using *viscous coupling*. Viscous coupling connects the front and rear axles so that they can spin independently of one another until one axle's wheels start to lose traction. Then the viscous coupling locks both the front and rear axles together, giving the vehicle 4WD capabilities.

Viscous coupling involves a phenomenon that defies the laws of physics. As fluids heat up, the molecules get hot and the fluid becomes thinner. Not so for a new type of fluid made from silicone polymers. The hotter this liquid gets, the thicker it becomes, which makes it excellent for coupling things together.

This new polymer was first applied in motor oil. Called a *viscosity improver,* the liquid would make oil thicken as it heated up. This made multigrade oils (for example, 10W-40) possible. Next, it was used in viscous fan couplings. The fan could spin freely when the motor was cold or when going at road speeds. When the engine compartment heated up, the fan clutch locked the fan to the motor, making air move through the radiator.

Drive applications of viscous couplings use two sets of clutch discs that are placed very close together but not touching. The even-numbered discs are connected to the shaft coming in from the input side and the odd-numbered ones to the shaft going to the output side of the viscous coupling. When the even-numbered discs turn at the same speed as the odd-numbered ones, both the input and output shafts are turning at the same speed.

The entire assembly is bathed in viscous silicone polymeric fluid, which surrounds the discs. As long as both input and output shafts turn at the same speed, everything goes along for the ride without anything happening. When either the input or output shaft starts to rotate at a different speed, the clutch discs start to "churn" the viscous silicone liquid. This movement creates friction and heats up the liquid, which causes it to thicken instantly. The result is a transfer of power from the input to the output shafts via the viscous coupling.

The greater the difference in speed between the two shafts, the thicker the liquid becomes and the tighter it bonds the shafts together. When the two shafts start turning at speeds closer and closer to the same speed, the liquid cools and allows more and more slippage. After the liquid cools, the shafts are free to turn independent of one another again.

The result is a coupling that allows for small amounts of slippage, balancing traction and slippage as needed. The end result is a controlled transfer of power, so much so that the driver doesn't even notice it. Viscous coupling makes it unnecessary to shift anything, which is really convenient for most drivers. It's much better for traction on slippery roads and gives the driver much more confidence in the vehicle's capability to hold the road. The typical emergency situation requiring the presence of 4WD happens so fast that you don't have a chance to stop and shift into 4WD. AWD eliminates that worry.

Some cars have replaced positraction set-ups (read on for more information about this setup) with viscous couplings inside the rear axle. The typical viscous coupling is placed inside the transfer case, replacing the differential gears. Some examples of this application are the VW Vanagon and Chrysler's minivans.

For most daily lightweight applications, viscous couplings work well. They are lighter and much less complex than differentials, making them less heavy and bulky. AWD vehicles fitted with viscous couplings don't weigh as much as typical 4WD systems—a big plus on a high-performance vehicle where weight savings is very important. Some high-powered cars use viscous couplings in the transfer case and both front and rear differentials.

The downside of using viscous couplings is their inability to handle torque. In general, they are not very heavy-duty and don't hold up well in off-road use. You won't find them on Jeeps or trucks because they don't hold up to rigorous use.

Modern traction controls

If you have been shopping for a new car lately, you've seen a new type of drivetrain option called *traction control*. In some cars, especially higher-priced models, it even comes standard. Traction control (TC) prevents uncontrolled wheel spin during rapid acceleration or when driving on slippery road surfaces.

TC is really a spinoff of anti-lock brakes. It uses the ABS wheel speed sensors to detect when one drive wheel begins to spin faster than the other drive wheel. This information is already monitored by the *electronic brake control module* (EBCM) for anti-lock function, so adding TC requires only more sophisticated software.

Here's how TC operates: The wheel speed sensors detect a wheel beginning to spin out of control and send this information in terms of RPM pulses to the EBCM. The EBCM turns on the brake hydraulic modulator and begins to apply the brake on the wheel that has started to spin out of control. The ECBM continues to monitor the wheel spin and apply the brakes on the spinning wheel until the drive wheels are turning at matched speeds.

Some of the more sophisticated hybrid TC systems also electronically control the throttle or engine functions in addition to controlling the brakes. It is important to know which type of system a car is equipped with so that you are aware of its operating characteristics. In general, eliminating wheel spin when accelerating is very useful as a driving aid in those areas of the country where snow, ice, and wet roads are common.

Brake-only traction controls

The simplest way to give a car traction control is to use already existing hardware. With the use of additional programming in the ABS computer, the wheel sensors can be used to run the ABS system in reverse — applying the brakes when a sensor finds a wheel starting to spin *faster* than the other wheels.

This is nothing new. Savvy drivers have long since been lightly applying the parking brake to help the rear wheels keep from spinning helplessly. But this system can actually control each driving wheel separately from the rest, making it a big plus on 4WD vehicles.

The main disadvantage of this type of TC is that the brakes can overheat. They can wear out very quickly if traction control is overused. This system is programmed not to function at speeds over 25 – 35 mph and is useless at higher speeds.

The biggest advantage of this system is that it is inexpensive and requires no additional hardware to operate. An amber warning light on the dash comes on to tell the driver that the TC system is operating.

Power-limiting traction control

Another way to keep the wheels from spinning helplessly is to limit the engine's power. This is accomplished in one of two ways: mechanically and electronically. The mechanical method forces the throttle closed with a throttle-closing servo. The electronic method either retards the timing, shuts down one or more fuel injectors, or takes control of the transmission shifting, forcing it to either upshift or downshift.

The throttle control method is better than electronic controls because you feel the gas pedal stiffen or push back against your foot when it is working. This makes it unnecessary to watch the dash for the amber warning light.

The electronic method of control can also cause the engine to produce more emissions and even overheat the catalyst, depending on how it operates. Only those systems that selectively shut off the fuel injectors are immune to these problems. Another drawback of throttle control TC systems is that they regulate power going to both drive wheels, even though only one wheel is detected slipping. This can be a real problem if you are caught on ice and can't get going.

Because of the inherent limitations of throttle-only TC systems, they are always combined with a brake TC system to form a hybrid of the two. This provides traction control at all speeds, and both drive wheels can be regulated for best results.

Drivetrain differential traction control

By definition, any car with a limited slip differential (also known as *Positraction*) has a crude form of traction control. This type of system keeps some power going to both drive wheels, maintaining some torque to both wheels (even when one begins to slip) by using spring-loaded clutches located in the differential as part of the pinion gear set. When one drive wheel begins to turn faster than the wheel on the other end of the axle and the pinion gears want to begin rotating around one another, the clutches prevent this from happening — forcing power to be delivered to both wheels.

The latest version of Positraction uses what is called a *Torsen differential*. It controls power similarly to a limited slip differential, only it uses a complex set of gears. It can constantly maintain about 80 percent of engine power to the wheel with the most traction. The all-mechanically-geared Torsen differential is often used in combination with another type of TC. Unless you know that one is in operation, you never know that it's there.

Chapter 7

Weather and the Elements

• •

In This Chapter

✔ Defogging and defrosting your windshield

✔ Driving in snow and other bad weather conditions

✔ Getting unstuck from snow, mud, or sand

✔ Getting rid of those awful heater odors

✔ Protecting yourself from carbon monoxide poisoning

• •

*W*hen you are the pilot of your car, you must fend for yourself in less-than-ideal driving conditions. What you do with the steering wheel, gas pedal, and brakes may make the difference between a safe trip and a nightmare. Many hidden dangers lurk along the way. This chapter will help you deal with skids, snow driving, and getting unstuck, as well as other weather-related villains.

Defogging Windows

Your visibility can directly impact the safety of your vehicle. Because most accidents occur within a few miles of home, the proper functioning of the defroster is important in those first few minutes of driving.

Here are some defogging tips that will help keep your windshield clear:

✔ Always turn *off* the Recirculate option on the climate controls. Choose Fresh or Outside Air or turn the control to the setting that shows air coming in from outside the car. This step is critical for making the defroster function properly. While it seems that the contrary would be true, recirculating the air from inside the car makes it even harder for the defroster to remove moisture from the passenger compartment.

✔ Always use the High setting for the fan. This fan speed produces the most dramatic results in defogging the windows. Try cracking open a window to improve the speed of defrosting. In some models, doing so facilitates the operation of the blower.

✔ After the glass is clear, change to the proper mode selection for the air temperature that day. Turn off the defroster as soon as possible because this selection uses gasoline and forces the compressor to run all the time.

✔ If the glass starts to fog again, avoid the temptation to run the defroster continuously, which costs you in gas mileage. Instead, do the following: Increase blower speed; increase the amount of heat selected; crack open a window or two; and try to create a cross-breeze to carry moisture out of the car.

Most of the problem with window fogging comes from the moisture in your breath. If you can create enough of a draft to carry your moisture-laden breath out the window, you can easily solve the problem. Try keeping the windows on the left side of the vehicle cracked just a bit.

✔ If you have chronic problems with foggy car windows, check the evaporator drains for clogging. If the evaporator can't drain the moisture out the bottom of the car, the system functions poorly.

 In a pinch, you can defrost the glass by cutting a potato in half and rubbing it on the glass. The potato makes the glass give up moisture and can really help when the defroster doesn't work. Don't forget to wipe the inside of the rear window glass to defrost it, too.

Your car's heating, ventilation, and air conditioning system (HVAC)

The air compressor is the heart of the HVAC system. It is a small, round device about the size of a two-pound coffee can and is connected to the engine by a rubber drive belt — just like the other components, such as the water pump and alternator. The compressor compresses the refrigerant to very high pressures.

High-pressure refrigerant is very hot from being squished by the compressor. It is pumped to a special radiator, called the *condenser,* mounted in front of the cooling system radiator. The condenser looks just like the usual traditional radiator but is much thinner and is made from shiny aluminum. The high-pressure refrigerant gives up some of its heat to the outside air as the air passes through the condenser on its way into the engine compartment. This process makes the refrigerant ready to go inside and cool you!

The cooler refrigerant passes through another radiator located inside the passenger compartment, up under the dash. This radiator is called the *evaporator.* Inside the evaporator, the refrigerant is released from a very high state of pressure to a low state of pressure. When this happens, the refrigerant takes on heat from the air circulating in the passenger compartment and cools it. Now the low-pressure, warmed refrigerant is ready to be sucked back inside the compressor and be pressurized all over again.

Also located inside the passenger compartment, next to the evaporator, is a heater radiator. It warms the circulating air inside the passenger compartment and provides heat. When you choose defrost mode, the air conditioner evaporator first cools the air. The evaporator gets cold and pulls heat out of the air to cool the vehicle. As it cools the air, moisture condenses on the fins of the evaporator unit and drips out of the car through the evaporator drain. The cooled air is then warmed by the heater core on its way into the passenger compartment.

If the air conditioner compressor doesn't engage for some reason (low refrigerant, faulty compressor, and so on) or the car doesn't have air conditioning, the heater core alone must defrost the car. This is especially difficult because the heater has no way to remove moisture from the air. Moisture removal is very important because moisture fogs the windows. Note that cars not equipped with defrosters do a relatively poor job of defrosting windows.

Defrosting Frosty Windshields

When faced with a frosty, ice- or snow-covered windshield, be extremely careful not to damage the glass. Despite the urge to do so, *never* pour warm or hot water on the glass. In fact, just turning the windshield defroster on full blast can crack the glass if it is really cold or covered with ice and snow.

To prevent cracked glass, turn the heat on high with the blower speed on low. While it is gently warming the inside of the windshield, scrape the glass and clear the windows. If the glass is covered with a heavy coating of ice, start by scratching a tic-tac-toe in one corner to get through the ice. Now work your way to the center, clearing the rest of the glass.

Never scrape the ice off the windshield with any object that is harder than the glass, or you will scratch the surface. If you do not have an ice scraper handy, use a credit card or a plastic spatula that you would use in your Teflon frying pans.

If the windshield washer solvent is frozen and doesn't squirt, pour hot water on the spray nozzle and the hoses that connect the nozzle to the washer bottle (be careful not to get the hot water on the cold windshield). The solvent in the bottle usually doesn't freeze, but melted snow or ice can get into the nozzle or even the feed hoses and freeze there.

When you stop the vehicle for the night, turn on the windshield wipers and leave them up on the glass as you turn off the key. The wiper blades are now parked up on the glass and will be easy to free up and clean in the morning. (Some vehicles allow the wiper blades to be cocked and pulled away from the glass as well.)

 Most people don't realize that their windshield wipers have an automatic "parking" mechanism that lowers the wipers when you turn off the wiper switch. If snow or ice builds up in the cowl area of your car (just in front of the windshield) and you turn off the wipers, the buildup prevents the wipers from returning to home position.

Because the wiper motor remains engaged as long as the ignition is on, it will continue to strain, trying to return the wipers to their home position. If snow and ice are in the way, the wiper motor can't finish its job and will die trying — all while you are driving along unaware of the trouble. If you notice this situation occurring, leave the wipers running at a slow speed until you can safely pull over and scrape away the build-up so that the wipers can return to their home position.

Snow Driving for Life

A friend of mine from Maine laughed when he thought of southern drivers panicking at the slightest hint of snow and schools and businesses closing at the drop of a hat. Drivers from the North know from experience how to handle snow. Sunbelt drivers do not. They wait for the forecast and venture forth only to buy emergency provisions. Or they ignore the conditions altogether and drive foolishly. Instead, drivers should follow this game plan for best results.

Following in the tracks

If you are traveling before the roads have been plowed, look for tire ruts made by other vehicles and drive in them. Maintain a constant speed. Avoid sudden acceleration or sudden braking, allowing two to three times the normal driving distance between vehicles. Doing so allows you to travel at a reasonable speed while maintaining a safe stopping distance.

Think of driving in snow as slow motion — every action requires calculation, anticipation, and added time to execute safely. Remember, when on slippery surfaces, traction is greatest just before the wheels spin. If your wheels start to spin, ease off the gas pedal until traction returns.

If the road is getting too heavily covered with snow, pull into a truck stop and wait for a truck to leave. Simply follow in the ruts made by the truck. *Do not* follow too closely, however, since a heavy truck can stop much faster than you can in icy and snowy conditions.

Braking and steering

Stopping on ice and snow takes longer — much longer. Avoiding a collision may require all the extra space you've placed between your vehicle and the car ahead. Keep that buffer zone. It allows you better forward vision and longer reaction time. To stop on ice or snow, lightly pump the brakes, even if your vehicle has anti-lock brakes. (One person suggested pumping the brakes with the same amount of pressure that you would use to pet a puppy with your feet.) Try to keep the wheels rolling!

Snowy, ice-covered roads call for calculated, deliberate steering. When steering into a turn, make it gradual and smooth at a speed slow enough to avoid using the brakes. Should you skid, steer in the direction you want the car to go, usually opposite the way you are skidding. If you're turning with the brakes applied and you start to skid, immediately remove your foot from the brake while continuing the turn. The skid should discontinue. Reapply the brakes as necessary.

Getting Unstuck from Mud, Snow, or Sand

When it comes to going, all you have to do is push the gas pedal. But what happens if the wheels spin helplessly? You're stuck! If you make the wrong move, you may get stuck even further and even lose control and turn a sticky situation into a real-life tragedy.

Have you ever skidded out of control, getting yourself so stuck in the mud or snow that you've been unable to get out? The following sections come from real-life situations and represent some of the more common maladies that you may encounter yourself. In an emergency situation, quickly look over this material and find the subject heading that best describes your particular plight. You can read the other sections at your leisure — hopefully before you get stuck in the first place.

Stuck in Snow

First, turn the defroster and fan on low to defrost the windshield and warm the car interior while you dig yourself out from whatever you have sunk down into. Keep a lightweight snow shovel in your trunk for digging out. Driving forward and backward in the parking space to pack down the snow with the tires may work as well. Be sure to accelerate gradually so that the tires don't spin. Spinning your wheels wears an ever-deepening rut, which is even harder to get out of. Point the front wheels straight ahead to minimize resistance to rolling.

CAUTION

Never leave occupants inside a closed vehicle while the engine is running unless a window is cracked and they are safely belted in place. Never leave a child loose inside a running car, as the child may put it in gear. Ditto for a dog.

Increase your traction

You can use ashes, fertilizer, kitty litter, sand, or salt to increase the traction of the tire. Salt is the worst for the environment, followed by ashes and fertilizer. Ashes are useless if the earth is the least bit wet and should be used only when the temperature is below freezing. Fertilizer and salt help create a small amount of traction, but their biggest advantage is that they turn snow into slush by speeding up the melting process.

In the winter, carry around an unopened bag of kitty litter in your trunk. It doesn't weigh much and will be handy if you get stuck.

Cardboard, carpet, or even the vehicle's floor mats can help give the wheels some additional traction. Breaking down cardboard boxes works well, too, unless conditions are very wet or very muddy.

Carry several large cardboard boxes broken down flat in the trunk of your car. You can also lie on the cardboard when working on the car in wet conditions (changing a tire, installing snow chains, or changing the oil, for example).

In a pinch, a wheel cover or hub cap makes a handy shovel. In sandy, snowy, or muddy conditions, you can sacrifice the wheel cover to help keep the jack from sinking. Just set the jack on top of the wheel cover to help give the jack firmer footing. Wheel covers are also a handy holding place for lugnuts, tire chains, or the drain plug.

You can use any type of wooden object (see the following list) to make runways for the wheels. If you can, jack up the vehicle and place the end of the piece of wood under the drive wheels and then lower the vehicle onto one end of the piece of wood.

Some wooden things that you can use are as follows:

- ✓ Planks
- ✓ Sheet paneling
- ✓ Several 1 × 1s placed alongside each other
- ✓ Two 2 × 4s or one 2 × 8 per wheel
- ✓ Wooden lath
- ✓ Crates
- ✓ Wood chips or sawdust

Be sure to place enough wood under the tire so that the wood doesn't jack itself up into the undercarriage of the vehicle. If the wood does land in the undercarriage, it can damage the underbody or shatter as the wheel presses on the very edge.

Stand clear when the wheels begin to turn because the wooden piece can be thrown violently out at you!

If the ground is very soft and the wheels sink easily, jack up the vehicle and fill the space below the wheel with wooden branches, small logs, firewood, or cut saplings, building a wooden bridge. If the jack sinks when raising the vehicle, place cross pieces of wood under the jack or use a jacking platform such as a large, flat piece of wood. Eight feet of a 2 × 12 works well with most jacks. The only exception is truck jacks, which require an even larger piece of wood.

In cases of emergency and dire need, use an axe or saw and cut saplings 2 – 3" in diameter in 3 – 4' lengths. Lay them side by side and place the jack on top of them. If necessary, place another group of cut saplings across the first set at 90-degree angles. Keep building them up until the wheels are once again level with the road surface.

After you raise the vehicle, lay saplings down in the vehicle's path to prevent it from sinking again until you can get it on drier, higher ground.

Using tire chains

Whether you're dealing with mud, snow, or ice, tire chains are your very best weapon in fighting the traction war. Unfortunately, you don't always have a set when you need one and you have to improvise. Any type of chain will do, as long as you have enough of it to place around both drive wheels. *Note:* Wrapping a chain around one wheel is practically useless with most drive systems except for *true,* full-time, four-wheel-drive systems.

If the tire chains are too large, they can still be of service. Shorten the chains by hooking onto a link further up on the wheel, trapping the extra chains under the adjoining side. Be very careful: If the extra chain is left to flop around on the outside of the wheel, it can hit against the underside of the fender and damage the car!

If the tire chain set is too short, it is useful only if one extra chain set is used to lengthen the two short ones. You can do this procedure with a hack saw: Saw apart the extra pieces needed and add them to the short set, making it fit. If the only chain sets available are too small for your wheels, creating a longer set can be a real life-saver.

Here's an example of how this worked on my old Chrysler Cordoba: I was once stuck in the snow on my farm. I have a quarter-mile-long driveway that was covered with a three-inch layer of ice topped by several inches of snow. The only snow chains I had were too small. I hunted around the barn and found an old chain left behind in the barn and cut it up to add on to the chains I already had. In about an hour, I cut and fitted pieces of the extra chain onto the short ones. In a matter of minutes, I was able to drive the car out to the road and free my car after a month of being stuck.

If no tire chains are to be found, cut lengths of regular chain long enough to circle both the rim and tire and then bolt them together. *Note:* This operation may scratch or ding the rim's finish! If there is time and enough chain, cut as many pieces as there are spokes in the wheel — the more the better. This method still works even if you only have enough chain to circle each of the two main drive wheels only once. If the vehicle is 4WD, always put the chains on the front for the very best possible combination of traction and steering.

Here's another real-life example: When my truck was stuck in the mud alongside the Trinity River in Texas, I used a torch to cut my tow chain into two equal lengths. I wrapped each length around the truck's huge tandem rear wheels and tires and bolted the lengths tight — one on each side. The chains provided enough additional traction to get the truck moving up a slight grade to solid ground.

Using tow rope

While not as durable as chain, rope has advantages in that it usually doesn't damage the vehicle's rim or fenders and can be more easily fitted to the wheels. Its big disadvantage is durability — rope works well only for short distances. Just wrap the rope around the wheel and back through the opening in the spokes as many times as you have rope; tie a square knot after you're done.

One time I got my car stuck in the Florida sand and couldn't get enough traction to get out. All I had on hand was a tow rope. I cut it into equal lengths and used the two pieces to weave around the car's rear drive wheels. This trick gave me just enough traction to get out of the sand trap.

Using plants and weeds

You can employ local plants and weeds to add traction. Comb the area, looking for anything you can gather that will provide traction. Avoid using slippery objects like wet leaves or grass. Try to find things that are crunchy, like dry straw or hay, small dead shrubs, or weeds.

When my camper was stuck in the mud in the middle of the Painted Desert (it was the rainy season), I combed the empty desert and was able to gather dried weeds that looked a lot like small sagebrush. Within a few hours, I had gathered enough small, dead plants to build a path and get the camper unstuck and onto firm, higher ground.

Using other assets

Cat litter, sand, or fireplace ashes can get you out in a pinch. Apply about $1/4$ to $1/2$ inch layer in the direction you want the tires to go — being sure to apply it right up to the tire to get it moving. You need to put down only enough to cover the width of the tire. If continued application doesn't free the vehicle, try giving it a push from behind. Watch out for stones and gravel projected from spinning tires if you are standing behind the tires. Pushing forward and sideways on a rear quarter panel may free the tire from a rut.

Dig a runway

One of the most important things to get you unstuck is *momentum*. If you can't get the vehicle moving because of resistance in front of the wheels, you may have to dig out the area immediately in front and behind all four wheels. Hopefully, this added space will let you get the vehicle moving enough to get some momentum working on your side. Dig a "runway" in the sand, mud, or snow long enough for the wheels to get moving. Doing so allows the wheels to "climb out" more easily.

Dig out the underbody

Many times, the undercarriage of the vehicle comes to rest on the mud or snow as the wheels sink. Sometimes only a small bump or hill of mud, sand, or snow is interfering with the underbody and keeping the drive wheels from getting traction. You may have to crawl under the vehicle to dig out this material so that the drive wheels can get a foothold. Lie on carpet or cardboard to keep from coming in contact with the wet or cold terrain.

Practice pushing

If more than one person is in the car, have the weakest person get behind the steering wheel and aim the car straight (the easy job); have the other(s) help push it along. It may not seem like much, but even a small amount of pushing effort is sometimes enough to make the difference between go and no go. Usually, the most difficult part is finding a good foothold and something solid to push against. If necessary, dig footholds in the mud, ice, or snow. When pushing, let the vehicle rock backward and forward in the runway made by the wheels. Alternate pushing and pulling while the person behind the steering wheel gives it the gas when it is going forward (or backward, as the case may be). (See the section called "Rock and roll" for more information about this procedure.)

The person behind the wheel can be the team leader, calling out "push" and "pull" when rocking the car. If the car has an automatic transmission, the transmission can be shifted from forward to reverse to help the car rock back and forth. If the car is a stick shift, choosing second gear instead of first may help keep the wheels from spinning as easily while still giving gentle power to get it going again. Use your legs to push, as they are many times stronger than your arms. If possible, place your back against the vehicle and push your feet against the nearest object.

 Make sure that you are completely clear of the vehicle so that you don't get run over or crushed if it suddenly gains traction. The safest place to push is on the door frames. Roll down a window and push on the center or front door frame. Stay in the driver's line of sight so that the vehicle can be brought to an immediate halt if you slip and fall.

Slide sideways

If the surface you're stuck on is icy or too slippery and you have an assistant, push the vehicle sideways while the assistant spins the wheels by pressing the gas pedal. The spinning wheels act like ball bearings, allowing you to re-angle the vehicle in a better line of traction.

A friend of mine got her Acura stuck going down an icy driveway. Her car suddenly slid sideways and jammed itself at a sideways angle. I used this technique to get her unstuck, pushing her car sideways on the front fender while she spun the front drive wheels. The spinning wheels allowed the car to be easily moved back into a straight position in the driveway, getting her unstuck.

Rock and roll

The tried-and-true way to get unstuck involves rocking and rolling the vehicle until you have enough momentum to get free. While this is the best way, it can also be the most damaging to your transmission, transaxle, and/or differential. Attempt this maneuver with extreme care!

Sometimes you have to prime a pump with some water in order to get more water. Similarly, you sometimes must roll the vehicle backward in order to move forward. The alternating motion of going backward and immediately forward takes advantage of the reverse momentum generated when the vehicle has rolled as far in one direction as it will go and then starts moving the other way. The momentum is caused by the tires "ramping" up the end of the runway in one direction. Using this momentum can be like having another helper push you along.

In order for this method to work, you must change gears from forward to reverse in a hurry. Doing so is easy in an automatic transmission vehicle but more difficult with a stick shift. On the other hand, it is *very* easy to damage the automatic transmission (especially on Hondas). Manual shift vehicles are less likely to be damaged by this maneuver.

 When rocking an automatic transmission, beware that the transmission fluid overheats in just a few minutes. If you don't let the fluid cool, it will literally cook the friction devices inside the automatic transmission. Let the liquid rest with the engine idling for 10 – 15 minutes between every minute or two of rocking effort. Doing so allows the fluid to circulate and cool down.

Other tips

If your car is a rear-wheel-drive and the wheels are spinning helplessly, try applying the parking brake. Because of the way differentials work, lightly applying the parking brake can limit the spin of the wheel that has the least traction, giving enough traction to the other wheel to get you unstuck.

If your car has a stick shift, try starting out in second gear to limit the amount of power going to the wheels and keep the wheels from spinning too fast.

In a few words, *don't overspin your wheels!* It may be a great way to vent frustration, but it does nothing to get you unstuck. Rapidly spinning the wheels only serves to bury the tire even further and can cause major damage to the tire if you spin it too fast. Because of the way your vehicle's differential works, one wheel is actually spinning at twice the speed that the speedometer indicates when the other is stopped. If the speedometer says 70 mph, the tire is really going 140 mph. This speed can cause the tire to literally fly apart!

If the vehicle is a front-wheel-drive, it may be to your advantage to back up a hill. Backing up puts the drive wheels at the rear of the vehicle and puts more of the vehicle's weight on the drive tires. To back up a hill, you should open your door and look behind you in order to see where you are going. Note that using the rearview mirror or even looking over your right shoulder does not gain you enough rear view to safely back up this way.

Always remember that inertia is your best helper. Many people forget this fact, slow down too much, lose their momentum, and can't get moving again. If possible, always keep moving! Go! Go! Go! Be aggressive and don't relent. Remember, once you slow down, you lose precious momentum and can't go over small bumps or hills.

Other Bad-Weather Driving Dilemmas

What do you do if someone is stopped or crawling along in front of you? Quickly and carefully judge the situation. You may need to pass that stuck or slow vehicle up ahead in order to keep moving yourself. If the road is clear, get over and stabilize your vehicle in the oncoming traffic lane before you try to pass. Don't try to do both at once. Once you're stable, ease on the throttle and pass gently.

 Changing lanes is very dangerous in bad road conditions, so be especially careful. You may lose control when passing, so try to be as clear from the other vehicle as possible before you attempt this maneuver. Pass only at great risk, knowing full well that you may wind up in a ditch.

Rolling wheels are *always* better than no rolling wheels. If you lock the wheels, you won't be able to steer and the rear end of the vehicle can easily slide out and spin sideways. Don't lock the brakes. Press gently on the pedal. If you start to feel the wheels skid, pump the brake pedal rapidly — as fast as you can make your legs pump up and down. In many situations, slowing down and still being able to steer around an obstacle is better than trying to stop altogether and skidding into the object.

 If your vehicle already has ABS, *do not* pump the brakes — you reduce the effectiveness of the ABS system and can even cause the brakes to fail to function. In order for anti-lock brake systems to function, you must apply *firm*, steady pressure on the brake pedal.

Here's a life-threatening example of when ABS didn't help and I was almost in a terrible accident. I was coming down a steep, icy hill when I noticed that my anti-lock brakes were no longer slowing the car. Every time I pushed on them, all four wheels locked up and I started to slide. I tried to rub against the curb to brush off speed, but the curb was too ice-covered to do any good. The only choice was to aim down the hill and try to keep the car oriented straight ahead. Unfortunately, there were two vehicles in the roadway ahead, both coming my direction. At the bottom, a large van that slid against the curb was in my lane, and another car was slowly coming up the hill in the oncoming traffic lane.

There was just enough room to get behind the oncoming vehicle — if I could keep the car from spinning out of control on the way down! I kept pumping the brakes, even though they were doing nothing to slow the car. The pumping action kept the wheels rolling with just enough traction to keep the car under control. I wasn't able to slow down, but I did steer between the two vehicles — passing the van going about 50 mph!

Dealing with Mud

Mud is one of the hardest mediums to deal with because of its slippery nature. In addition, mud also tends to "suck" the wheels down into it, deeper and deeper. Mud is an especially big problem for rear-wheel-drive vehicles. After you create enough traction for the drive wheels, the front wheels often sink down into the mud like a plow.

While front-wheel-drive vehicles are not as prone to the front end digging in, they are more likely to lose steering, sliding helplessly out of control into a nearby fence, guardrail, or building. Because the front wheels are used for traction as well as steering, they also lose steering control when they break loose. Rear-wheel-drive vehicles don't have this problem.

But rear-wheel-drive vehicles suffer from the loss of power and just cannot climb a hill or sometimes even a small grade. Mud can contain a great deal of clay and is so slippery that even a four-wheel-drive vehicle will slip helplessly in the stuff. When the roads are slick as with snow or ice, slipping in mud can be a very big problem. At that point, only front-wheel-drive vehicles can make it up hills.

Getting Unstuck from Deep Sand

If you're ever brave (or just plain dumb) enough to drive on a beach, you face the possibility of sinking into soft sand and getting stuck. Even worse, if the tide comes in before you can get your vehicle away, you can lose everything! Be especially wary of the sand/shell mixtures next to the water. This "quicksand" surface is the most treacherous and should be avoided at all costs. If your Evel Kneivel days aren't quite over and you must drive on the beach, drive closer to the sand dunes when dealing with this kind of surface.

Here are some tips to help get you unstuck when you're up to your axles in the sand:

Deflate the tires until the tires bulge a great deal, dropping the pressure just enough to provide some support without going totally flat. The added traction may help overcome the sinking sand.

Keep the vehicle in a low gear, never in drive. Avoid overheating the automatic transmission by excessive rocking. Only rock the vehicle for a minute or two and then allow 2 – 3 minutes of rest so that the running engine can cool the transmission fluid. Excessive rocking can quickly fry the transmission. Also, avoid excessive tire spinning because the tire can fly into shreds and the differential can be destroyed.

Use the foot brake or parking brake to limit wheel spinning without traction. Applying the parking brake gently while moving the vehicle can cause the wheel with less traction to slow down, giving the other wheel some added traction.

If you find yourself sinking into a soft spot, floor the throttle and keep pouring it on until you get out (in low range or first gear). Don't worry about the tires spinning and sinking into the sand. If you let up for even a moment, you're stuck! The most important thing is to keep it moving — at all costs. Once you lose forward momentum, it will be very difficult to get going again.

Keep the steering wheel straight. Turning the steering wheel in either direction will just cause the tires to dig deeper into the sand and make it even harder for your vehicle to get the momentum it needs to get moving.

Use the wheel covers or a similar implement to dig ramps both in front of and behind the tires. Digging ramps gives you a good starting point to rock the vehicle and gain some momentum to escape.

 Dig out the underside of the vehicle to reduce the drag of the sand on the undercarriage. *Do not* place your body in a position where the vehicle can slip and crush you! Use the spare tire as a safety device, keeping it next to you at all times when you are under the vehicle. If the vehicle slips in the sand, that spare tire can save you from finding yourself pinned under a serious problem!

Once stuck, try to jack up the vehicle and put rocks, cardboard, boards, or other debris under the tires to give them added traction. Sometimes you can firm the sand by wetting it with ocean water. Look for dead brush, seaweed, or any plants that can be used to give the tires more traction. Install a set of tire chains or cables on the drive axle tires.

If you plan on venturing onto a beach, you may want to plan ahead and bring along some boards and tire chains just in case. Also, bring a cellular phone so that you can call for help in case you can't get unstuck!

Heater Odor Relief

The fall and winter months bring a variety of weather-related problems. Many drivers turn on their car heaters for the first time in months, only to be greeted with a weird locker-room odor of smelly socks.

Over the winter months, airborne microorganisms grow inside the car on the damp surfaces of the evaporator. During the warmer months, you can do several things to minimize the problem:

✔ Whenever possible, use the FRESH selection instead of recirculating the air. This setting corresponds to the MAX A/C or RECIRCULATE selection on many cars.

✔ Avoid parking under trees where leaves or pine needles are likely to fall on the car.

✔ Avoid dirty or dusty roads. When you have to drive on them, use the FRESH selection of the A/C unit.

✔ If the drive is to be a short one, avoid using the A/C at all.

✔ Make sure that the evaporator drain is not plugged up. If the evaporator is not draining out all the water, it becomes a fertile place for microorganisms to grow!

✔ On your approach to your driveway, say $1/2$ mile away, turn off the A/C, open the window, and turn on the heater with the blower on the high setting. This helps to dry out the A/C evaporator before you turn it off, making it more difficult for microorganisms to grow inside the HVAC system.

If your nose is already faced with this smelly problem, you may find that the mold, bacteria, and fungi are aggravating your allergies. The professional solution is to disinfect the car with Alcide, a chemical available from your local dealer or auto parts store. Alcide is a strong chemical disinfectant containing chlorine dioxide. It will kill just about anything, including you if you don't use it correctly.

An attractive alternative to using dangerous toxic chemicals is to mix a teaspoon of BASIC-G (sold by Shaklee dealers) and a pint of water in a spray bottle. With the car running, windows up, and defroster on high, spray the whole pint into the duct just in front of the windshield. Keep the windows closed, shut off the car, and let the solution soak in overnight (or for 12 hours). You're done! Repeat the treatment as often as needed, usually in the fall and again in the spring.

Recognizing CO Danger

One of the most deadly parts of winter driving is something that you can't see, smell, or touch. It is so insidious that it will snuff out your life and you may never know it exists. Even worse, as it starts to grab hold of you, your higher reasoning power is lost and you won't realize that it has you. This treacherous villain is *carbon monoxide (CO) poisoning*.

CO poisoning takes the lives of more drivers than we will ever know because it is hard to tell when CO has done its dirty work. This type of gas is especially deadly because the first thing it attacks is your logical reasoning. You just can't figure out what is happening. Your mind becomes foggy and you can't think clearly. Without ever knowing it, unconsciousness takes over, you lose control, and crash.

The biggest problem CO presents is that it dulls your thinking and you just can't react quickly enough to avoid a crash situation. With fuzzy thinking and slowed reflexes, you are unable to react in time to avoid the danger in the road ahead.

CO can get into the vehicle from a leaking trunk-rubber seal or exhaust gasket in the engine bay. In the earliest stages, CO makes you think you are getting the flu. Headaches, nausea, dizziness — all attributed to a virus — can actually be caused by the vehicle that we drive to work every day. Many people suffering from 10:00 headaches at work (thinking that it's the stress of their jobs) are actually victims of CO poisoning.

I almost lost my life to CO poisoning and know first hand how deadly it can really be. In an effort to help prevent people from being killed by this silent assassin, I offer you a life-saving Carbon Monoxide Detector for $5.00 (price includes postage and handling). The detector is credit-card sized and is designed for airplane pilots to stick on their instrument panel. It has a pink-colored patch of chemically treated material mounted in it. If the patch turns dark, you are in the presence of deadly CO gas! The detector is good for one year and can be used at home or anywhere you suspect CO gas poisoning. Call Nutz & Boltz at 800-888-0091 for more information.

Part III
In the
Breakdown Lane

In this part...

This part tells you what to do when you're stranded on the side of the road waiting for help — which may never come.

Chapter 8
Avoiding and Coping with Accidents

● ●

In This Chapter

▶ Keeping your cool in panic driving situations

▶ Dealing with unintended acceleration

▶ Knowing what to do if an accident occurs

● ●

*T*he moment an accident happens, the whole thing seems to be in slow motion. In other cases, the accident is over so fast that you never knew what happened. The problem is that you're in shock and don't know what to do after the accident occurs. This chapter gives you strategies for keeping your cool so that you can avoid accidents, and it also leads you though post-accident trauma, giving advice that may save you a great deal of trouble — and expense — later on.

Dealing with Panic Driving Situations

For this chapter, I interviewed an expert driving instructor, Miriam Shotland, who is an instructor for the Porsche Club and instructs the BSR Advanced Driver Training School. She also teaches high-performance driving and counterterrorism and knows a great deal about handling panic driving situations.

What to do if you skid

If you try to make a turn and your vehicle begins to skid and keeps going straight, what do you do? Actually, your wheels are turning; it's the mass of the car that's going straight. You go into a skid because you've asked your car to do more than it can do at one time. Obviously, you're going too fast.

When your car is going straight even though the wheels are turned, your tires aren't grabbing the road. In reality, you have zero steering control. The more you turn the wheel, the worse the skid gets. Instinctively, most people turn the wheel even more because the car stops responding. Then panic sets in, and you hit the brakes.

When you hit the brakes, you ask your car to turn as well as to brake. *Do not* hit the brakes! By doing so, you're just adding another item to your car's list of things to do. Ease off the gas and straighten the steering wheel. Do everything gently! Just straighten the wheel and be patient.

Rear-end skids

What if you start to turn and the rear end of the car starts to break loose and skid? First of all, you have to determine which way the rear end is skidding. In correcting a rear-end skid, the most important thing is to *look in the direction you want the car to go.* Next, you must figure out how much to turn the steering wheel. If you look where you want the car to go, you will automatically make the correct adjustments to the steering wheel to regain control of the car. You don't even have to think about it.

Two wheels off the road while turning

Suppose you're making a left-hand turn and the car starts sliding to the right. Your instinctive reaction is to try and keep the car on the road, but the wheels have gone off the road onto the soft shoulder. Those right-side wheels have no traction, and you've got the wheel turned in the opposite direction. Most likely, the two wheels off the road are going to give way. You're going to spin — generally into oncoming traffic!

In this situation, you've asked the car to do too much at once. Deal with the situation by asking the car to do less. By jerking the car back on the road, you're letting traction on one side of the car go, which almost always throws you into a spin.

Contrary to your natural instinctive reaction, take your feet off the gas and brakes: no brakes, no gas, no nothing. Straighten the wheel. Now, most importantly, *look in the direction you want the car to go*. After the car has slowed down, you can ease it back onto the road. But no matter what, don't deny that you're going off the road and try to keep the car on the road. This is where people lose control.

Collisions at intersections

Suppose you're coming into an intersection and a car runs a red light, coming right across your path. If possible, you don't want to broadside the car. When you do so, you transfer all the momentum from your vehicle to the car you hit.

The best diversion is to aim for the back end of the car, which causes you to spin the other car out of the way because you hit its lightest end. Don't hit the brakes. Coast into it — or even better, stay on the gas. Just like jumping out a window, it's not the fall that hurts you; it's the sudden stop! The same principal operates here.

Why would you want to stay on the gas? The safest thing to do is to transfer all the kinetic energy from your car to the rear of the other car so that no one gets hurt. You may think that pressing the accelerator would cause you to hit with more force than slowing down. But hitting the brakes, or even letting off the gas, increases your chances of suffering more bodily harm.

When you stop, you are actually thrown forward. What can hurt you is the transfer of your body weight. Not only is the mass of your car going to continue to go forward, but your body does also. When you stay on the gas, all the weight transfer goes to the rear of the other car, meaning that your body is not slammed forward very hard — if at all.

Both your car and your body are already moving in a forward direction as you slam on the brakes. When you hit the other car, your body has even less distance to go before coming to a stop. Your body has a greater deceleration rate and you are more likely to be hurt. As the laws of physics say, "A body at rest tends to stay at rest, and a body in motion tends to stay in motion."

T-Bone side crashes

If someone is about to run into the left side of your car at, say, 30 mph, what do you do? Your car is going to be pushed to the right. You, a loose object in the car, are going to be smashed back to the left at 30 mph. The laws of physics say that for every action there is an equal and opposite reaction. Your hitting the door at 30 mph is the "equal and opposite reaction."

That you are going to be hurt is almost a certainty. It's not the impact of the other vehicle hitting your car that's going to hurt you; it's the impact of your body being thrown over to the left side of your car. Your instincts usually cause you to lean over toward the passenger seat to try to escape the crash, which is the worst thing you can do. If you're being hit from the left, the car is going to move to the right.

The correct way to deal with this situation is to lean against the door being hit, which absorbs the energy of the car hitting you. Most certainly, you're going feel a bump. But you will not be hurt as much as if you were to lean over to the passenger seat and get backed against the door at 30 mph.

Unintended Acceleration

It was a hot, overcast Sunday morning. The scene began innocently as a grandmother left church with her two grandchildren. They got into her car; the girl tucked in beside grandma, and the boy hopped in the back seat. Suddenly, as Grandma started to pull out of the parking lot, unintended acceleration (UA) struck like lightning.

The car jumped into the street at full throttle. Terror froze Grandma at the wheel. She didn't understand what was happening; all she could do was hold the steering wheel as the car bolted into the street. Desperately, she yelled, "Whoa! Whoa!" She was panic stricken.

The car hit the median strip in the center of the road first and then roared past the median, catapulting over the curb on the far side and flattening a street sign. It continued across the lawn on the opposite side of the street. By the time the car struck a brick building head on, it was going about 45 mph. Eyewitnesses said that they never saw the brake lights come on. Apparently, it all happened too fast for the woman to react.

Understanding UA

Typically, the authorities blame such an incident on "a problem with pedal misapplication" — where you mean to press the brake pedal and instead press the gas pedal. Did a seasoned driver like Grandma misapply the pedal, or was this truly a case of UA?

Close scrutiny of the vehicle didn't turn up a single clue. If the woman had pushed the gas pedal instead of the brake, her foot would have driven the pedal into the floor, leaving "witness marks." There would have been a lasting imprint of where her foot drove the gas pedal into the carpet and sheet metal when the car hit the brick wall, but there were no marks. Very suspicious!

Examination of the car's throttle mechanism revealed nothing that might have caused it to jam. The throttle was found to be closed — not stuck in the open position. What, then, could have been responsible?

Could a supersonic transport plane (SST) taking off nearby turn on the car's cruise control, causing it to go haywire and opening the idle speed controller? This event would cause an engine to rev up. But how could the SST do that? Unseen forces of electromagnetic interference (EMI) come from certain radio transformers. The SST has a very powerful transmitter, often causing electrical disturbances in areas where it takes off and lands. The SST might be responsible, but no one can prove it.

Shortly after Grandma's accident, the vehicle manufacturer changed the design of the idle speed controller. Coincidence?

 This isn't the only case of radio EMI causing electrical problems with vehicles. When computers were married to cars, they gave birth to electronic poltergeists. In the 1970s, auto companies became aware of *electronic smog* in the air waves. Specially equipped trucks were sent to check the electronic environment. The amount of radio noise that they discovered, even in remote places, was amazing. This radio and microwave smog can cause the automotive fuel, ignition, speedometer, cruise control, and other onboard computer systems to "lose their minds," creating hidden goblins that can spring to life inside any computer.

Here's a classic example: A Chicago tour bus used to screech to a halt whenever it tried to cross a certain bridge. The culprit turned out to be a radio tower atop a nearby skyscraper. The steel bridge picked up the radio signal and reflected it into the bus's anti-lock brake control computer.

During certain times of the day, some microwave transmission towers can shut down any passing computer-controlled car. Local tow trucks just tow the car in and jump-start it. In addition, police cars experienced problems when CB radios were installed in computerized cars. As soon as the officer pressed the talk button, the car died.

Truckers who have beefed up their CBs with illegal linear amplifiers can electronically interfere with the cars next to them. And I bet you didn't know that traffic-sensing wires embedded in the road, used to activate traffic signals, can cause cars to stall. Also, improperly installed car phones, car alarms, CB radios, cruise controls, and sound systems can interfere with the normal operation of electronic fuel-management systems.

Reacting to UA

If your car suddenly accelerates, turn the key off and press the brake hard. *Do not* pump the brakes. Often, braking alone is not enough to prevent a crash. Practice the following maneuver on a large, unoccupied parking lot or back street: Take a friend and a broomstick or yardstick with you. Have your friend suddenly press the gas pedal with the stick when you aren't expecting it. *Quick,* turn off the key and hit the brakes! Do so several times until you can do it well.

Avoiding UA

You can decrease your car's chances of undergoing unintended accelera-tion by observing the following guidelines:

- ✔ *Do not* drive with the cruise control on unless you're using it.

- ✔ Press the brake hard when moving the gear selector into drive or reverse (in cars with automatic transmissions).

- ✔ *Do not* idle in park for long periods of time. Instead, shut off the engine until you are ready to move; restart the car and then put it in gear.

- ✔ *Do not* drive with two feet, using your left foot for the brake. This can totally confuse the computer.

- ✔ Have a professional install your car phone, sound system, or CB radio. Improperly installed speakers and power wires can affect computer sensors; screws can interrupt chassis wiring; and improperly shielded antennas can irradiate computer circuits and induce resonance, confusing your car's computer.

- ✔ Have high quality, original equipment spark plug wires installed. Make sure that the wires are factory length and are secured in their holders. Spark plug wires lying near a sensor wire can induce current in the sensor wire.

Most vulnerable situations and types of cars

Unintended acceleration is more likely to occur under these circumstances:

- ✔ In cars with automatic transmissions
- ✔ In cars with computer-controlled idle speed

✓ When you engage the transmission immediately after starting the car

✓ When you shift the transmission into drive or reverse

✓ After you idle for long periods in park and then shift into drive

✓ While you're traveling in the speed range of 45 - 55 mph

✓ When you apply the brake and gas pedals simultaneously

What to Do after an Accident

One out of every five people reading this book will have an automobile accident of some consequence in the next 12 months. The question that everyone should be able to answer is: "What do I do after being involved in an accident?" Here's a handy checklist to follow just in case you are involved and need to be reminded about what to do — and what not to do — first:

✓ Activate your four-way flashers.

✓ Calm yourself by taking five to seven deep breaths.

✓ Call an ambulance for the injured; call a fire truck if gas is spilled; and call the police.

✓ *Do not* leave the scene of the accident.

✓ If you're not hurt, get out and start moving around. Doing so helps to clear your head so that you can more rationally appraise the situation. Try not to yawn; it might appear suspicious — like you were driving under the influence or were asleep at the wheel.

✓ If the vehicles are blocking the flow of traffic, quickly mark their locations on the ground and move them out of the roadway.

✓ Get out your safety kit and set up reflectors, flares, or triangles.

Take pictures

After you take these preliminary steps, you should prepare for the next step: dealing with the insurance company. If you have a camera handy, get it out and take pictures of the accident. Tell your story with pictures. Shoot positions of everything before anything is moved. Photograph the following:

✓ Other vehicles as they are going down the road

✓ The other parties, especially if they are moving about in apparently uninjured fashion

✓ Any passengers and their positions in the vehicle(s)

✓ Traffic control devices; skid marks; shiny, wet, or icy pavement; or obstructions

✓ Rusty or dirty damage to the other vehicle from previous accidents. Be shrewd. Does the damage correspond to where your vehicle hit their car? What looks fresh and what doesn't? Look for rust and dirt build-up on old damage. If you don't get this on film now, you may be held responsible for damage that you didn't cause.

Safety kit items

I suggest placing the contents of this kit in a sturdy plastic shoebox, tackle box, or toolbox and keeping the kit in your trunk. You can add your own items as you wish. Also, you may want to combine this kit with the Emergency Roadside Kit described in Chapter 15.

✔ Roadside flares, fuses, a blinking flasher light, or emergency reflector triangles

✔ "Send Help/ Send Police" cardboard sunscreen dash cover

✔ Disposable camera

✔ Notepad

✔ Crayons, colored pens, or markers

✔ First aid kit

✔ Bright orange safety vest

✔ Pancho or lightweight raincoat (a jumbo plastic garbage bag will do)

✔ Nutz & Boltz Personal Reflector (call 800-888-0091 for information)

✔ Fire extinguisher

✔ Flashlight with alkaline batteries (keep the batteries in a separate plastic bag to preserve them)

✔ Small, portable CB radio

Gather information

Next, get this important information about the driver and his or her vehicle:

✔ Name, address, home phone number, and work phone number

✔ Place of employment and name of someone to contact (perhaps a coworker) in case the driver is absent

✔ Insurance company, policy number, and coverage period

✔ Make, model, year of the vehicle, condition, color, and tag number

In addition, get names and phone numbers from witnesses. Make sure that the names are spelled correctly, and double-check all numbers. Ask for names of others who can speak for the witness if he or she is not available.

From the police officer, get this important police information: name, rank, badge number, precinct, phone number, and an address to write to get a copy of the police report. Get the facts regarding all injured parties, including passengers. Take down names, addresses, dates of birth, sex, and the extent of injury.

Look for suspicious signs

If you wind up taking the accident to court, you should be especially alert. A little sleuth now can pay off in big rewards later — in court! Here are some things to watch out for:

✔ Watch for things that the other driver(s) may have tossed away or is busy tucking out of sight. Do you see alcoholic beverages being hidden? Is a marijuana cigarette being tossed out the window?

✔ Do you smell drugs or alcohol?

✔ Do you smell gasoline? Leaking gas may have affected the driver's judgment.

✔ Listen to what the other parties are saying to each other. Are they blaming one another for the accident?

✔ What are the other parties saying to the police? Are they making up a story about how you were at fault?

✔ Is anyone acting in a way that seems strange or out of place?

✔ Is the other driver sleepy? Yawning? Lethargic?

Get out your notebook and write down everything at the scene. Draw a diagram, making sure to note road names, numbers, accesses, mile markers, lanes, and the direction that each vehicle was heading. Try to make your view as wide as you can. Don't trust your memory; your emotions may erase big parts of the scene.

With the colored markers or crayons from your safety kit, color the events with colored pens to identify their relation to each other, which helps fix them sharply in your mind. Consider the following examples:

✔ White cars against snow or sand

✔ Gray day, overcast, fog, rain, sleet, smoke, and so on

✔ Red cars at dawn or dusk

✔ The driver wearing a green parka that could restrict head movement or obstruct vision

✔ Rear of the car full of junk or other objects that prevent proper rear-view vision

✔ Driver wearing sunglasses at night

✔ Car windows covered with sun-blocking tint so dark that you can't see in or out

Keep your cool

Watch your behavior. Don't be arrogant. Here's the ideal attitude:

✔ Remain a little on the positive side of neutral.

✔ Choose your language carefully; use small words and talk politely.

✔ Don't admit fault or distraction.

✔ Avoid further discussion with the other parties. They may be fishing for information to use against you.

✔ Do not volunteer information about the extent of your insurance coverage.

See a doctor

If you are injured, don't try to tough it out. Never admit in conversation or in writing that you have not been injured. You may regret it later. Until you are examined by a medical professional, you really don't know.

 If you have any type of injury, even if the soreness doesn't start to appear until a day or two later, see a doctor. You *must* establish that you were injured by creating a medical history. Even a visit to the emergency room for a once-over examination is important if you expect to seek damages for pain and suffering later on. If you wait to see a doctor, establishing that you were injured by the accident — and not from something else — will be very difficult. Don't tough it out.

Chapter 9

Blowouts and Breakdown Blues

· ·

In This Chapter

▶ Knowing how to react when you have a blowout

▶ Changing a flat tire

▶ Spotting the warning signs of brake failure

▶ Making a panic stop

▶ Understanding how anti-lock brake systems work

▶ Dealing with dash-light warnings

· ·

K nowing the right way to change a tire is critical — a mistake here could cost you your life! How do you know when your brakes are about to fail? If you don't know, you might not be able to stop, which is certainly a life-threatening situation. What to do if you have to make a panic stop? What do you need to know about ABS brakes? What if you have a blowout? What does that angry dash warning light mean? Read on for answers to all these questions and more.

Taming a Blowout

Tires almost always go flat when you're on your way somewhere, especially when you are late. There you are, cruising along, brain occupied with the details of life and — *pow!* A blowout in the front tire.

Let's say your right front tire just went flat. Quick — what do you do?

A.   Slam on the brakes.

B.   Keep pressing the gas pedal.

C.   Steer into the flat.

D.   Steer away from the flat.

E.   All of the above while babbling hysterically.

Your first reaction to a blowout is to hit the brakes. Maybe you think stopping the car will save the tire. It won't. That tire is already destroyed.

Hitting the brakes is the *last* thing you want to do. The vehicle is stabilized by its forward momentum. A collapsed tire doesn't cause serious instability until the vehicle slows below 50 mph. Vibration and noise are worst at between 50 and 40 mph, the range at which some people lose control of their vehicles. As the car slows, the sideways pull of the flattened tire has a greater effect.

Against all instinct, you need to keep your foot on the gas pedal when a blowout occurs. Choice B is the correct answer. The vehicle's forward momentum is your ally because continuous engine power helps you steer the vehicle. Maintain it and steer as you would in a sudden strong crosswind.

Don't let those strange noises generated by the flat tire worry you. Grip the wheel firmly at the 10 – 2 or 9 – 3 o'clock positions, and only make steering corrections as needed — no wild wrenching on the wheel. Begin decelerating gently, all the while looking for a good place to pull off the road. Soon enough, the side with the blowout will begin to drop lower to the road.

Forget the tire and wheel. Avoiding an accident is far more important than some silly pieces of rubber and metal. And besides, stopping in a traffic lane will almost guarantee an accident. Keep going slowly until you find a safe place to get off the road. If you are on a traffic-filled freeway, it may be better to continue to the next exit. A flat is good for up to $1/3$ mile before you are riding only on the rim, and the rim can go for up to two miles before it becomes scrap metal. Remember, your life is more important than the tire.

Flat-Tire Blues

No matter how much you try to avoid it, tires occasionally go flat. Knowing how to deal with it can help you avert a disaster.

First, calm yourself. You can't fix or inflate a tire with steam, so blow off your steam later. Take heart in the fact that practically anyone can change a flat with a few important instructions.

Remember, it's more important to get off the road safely and avoid an accident. If you save the tire but die in the process, no one will be impressed.

 If your flat is on the driver's side and you must stop on the shoulder, park *way* off the road. Changing a driver's side tire close to traffic could get you killed.

Put on the emergency flashers and place flares or reflectors 75 – 100 feet behind your car. Flares and/or roadway reflectors are must-have items for your car safety kit. (See Chapter 15 for a complete list of items to keep in your emergency road kit.)

Changing your flat tire

 Changing a flat tire is a dangerous job. The car could slip off the jack and roll onto you. Always work on a level place. Never lie under the vehicle. Be sure that any passengers are out of and away from the vehicle.

To change the tire, you need the following items:

- ✔ A working jack
- ✔ A lugnut wrench or tire spanner
- ✔ Firm ground below the car to support the jack
- ✔ A spare tire that is inflated and ready to use

Ten tire-changing commandments

I. Immobilize the vehicle. Put the shift lever in Park or leave the manual transmission in first gear (engine off). Set the parking brake. Look around for a rock or other object to chock the wheels.

II. Mount the jack in its place on the body or bumper of the vehicle. Check the owner's manual if you're not sure where you should mount the jack. Ditto for assembly and jack operation. There are many types of jacks and jack mounting points for various makes and models. Don't assume that the car is the same as your last one — read the manual! Operate the jack until the vehicle just begins to raise up and then stop.

III. Remove the wheel cover (hubcap) and set it nearby to hold the lugnuts after you remove them. To remove some wheel covers, you need a special tool. The tool should be in the glove box and looks like a lugnut with the adapter part built right into one end of it. Be careful; wheel covers have sharp edges and can cut you!

IV. Loosen the lugnuts maybe halfway, but don't remove them. Getting them to move may take muscle work. Don't hurt your back! Push with one arm and pull with the other simultaneously. Use your legs to help muscle the lug wrench.

V. Play it safe. Put the spare tire on the ground next to the jack. Slide the spare tire under the vehicle as soon as there is enough clearance so that it will serve as a catch if the vehicle falls from the jack.

VI. Raise the vehicle with the jack until it is high enough that you can put the spare tire on the vehicle.

VII. Install the spare after you remove the lugnuts and place them in the wheel cover. Remove the flat tire and put it under the car for added safety.

VIII. Tighten the lugnuts, but not too tight yet. Make sure that the metal wheel is snug against the hub or brake drum and not cocked at an angle. A cocked wheel can give the false impression of being correctly mounted but later break loose and cause an accident. When you're certain that the wheel is not cocked, tighten the lugnuts snugly with the lug wrench. Tighten them until the wheel begins to move.

IX. Lower the car carefully. Move the old tire out of the way. Now tighten the lugnuts with the wrench some more. Use a star-shaped pattern, skipping over each second nut until all are very tight.

X. Pack up. Put the flat tire and wheel cover in the car. Go to the next service station or garage and have the wheel lugnuts torqued to the correct foot-pound tightness required for the vehicle. Consult your owner's manual for the exact torque value.

Lugnut lessons

Your car's lowly lugnuts are more important than you might think. These simple fasteners can make the difference between a safe car and a death trap; if the lugnuts suddenly fail to hold or come loose, the wheel could come off, resulting in a total loss of control.

The simple act of tightening the lugnuts to the proper torque value has been generally overlooked by mechanics. The importance of this simple task cannot be stressed enough. I heard about one woman who will never walk again because the lugnuts on her wheels were not tightened properly. They came loose; the wheel came off; and the car rolled over. In the accident, she broke her back and instantly became a quadriplegic.

The initial tightening should be done in whatever manner is easiest. Most mechanics prefer to use an air impact wrench for this step. Next, tighten the lugnuts in a star-shaped pattern using a torque wrench to achieve the proper torque.

 Failure to torque the lugnuts properly often results in a dangerous condition. If the lug bolts are torqued too tightly, the brake rotor usually warps, causing brake pedal pulsation and poor braking. If the lugs are not tightened enough, the wheel can come off.

Lugnut tips

If the repair shop has removed your wheels for any reason, check the lugnut torque before driving away. If the lugnuts were improperly torqued (the usual situation), you can prevent the brake rotors from warping by retorquing the lugnuts before the brake rotors become hot.

Use a *beam-type* torque wrench to check the torque on the lugnuts after the wheel is mounted. This tool allows you to determine whether your wheels were torqued properly by the repair shop.

Improper lugnut torque is the most common cause of warped brake rotors. Warped brake rotors cause the brake pedal to pulsate when applying the brakes. A man with an expensive car came to me complaining that his brakes kept on pulsating — no matter what the dealer did. He had returned to the dealer several times and was charged for a brake job and machining of the rotors each time.

I explained that the car's lugnuts were probably installed with an impact-gun rather than a torque wrench, causing the problem. He insisted that the dealer had used a torque wrench because he had asked about it and was told that the lugnuts were properly torqued with a torque wrench. I said, "Let's see," and tried to loosen the lugnuts using a beam-type torque wrench. The lugnut torque ranged from 40 – 150 pounds of torque on the same wheel! The dealer lied to him and was, in fact, the cause of his brake problems. The problem was the same from the beginning — the mechanic was lazy and installed the wheel with an impact gun.

If you are a mechanic and have a hard time remembering to properly torque the wheels when you are finished, lay the torque wrench on the driver's seat. That way, you have to pick up the torque wrench to move the car out of your service bay. This technique will remind you every time.

Application of lithium grease or antiseize compound to the lugnut threads and contact areas helps to maintain proper torque values consistently, especially with aluminum or mag wheels (because lugnuts are always steel). Steel and aluminum create an electrolytic action against one another and become stuck to each other. Every time the wheel is removed, metal is galled from the rim. Over time, the rim is ruined by this process.

Antiseize is preferable to lithium and can be bought from any hardware or parts store. Just wipe some antiseize on the threads and mating surface of the lugnut, wheel stud, and rim mounting hole. While you're at it, put a dab on the mounting/centering hole where the wheel meets up with the hub so that you can get the wheel off the hub more easily next time.

 If a lugnut or bolt is frozen in place and is too difficult to remove, try smacking the head of the bolt with a large hammer. Doing so can free a stuck lug, especially when the rim is aluminum or alloy.

No Brakes!

It's a motorist's worst nightmare. You're zooming along the open road, you step on the brakes, and — nothing. The pedal is mushy and won't slow the car. Or it goes all the way to the floor with no effort. What do you do? Here are some ways that you can slow down in a panic situation:

- **Pump the brake pedal:** Pumping may repressurize a leaking circuit temporarily. After the pedal comes back and gets firm, stop pumping and hold it.

- **Use the parking brake:** They don't call it the emergency brake anymore because it does a poor job of stopping the car. The faster you are going, the longer it will take to slow down.

- **Scrape the rails:** Race car drivers call grazing the nearest guardrail, wall, or curb "scrubbing off speed." Let the friction of car-against-object slow you down. It means body work later, but it's still better than a fatal crash.

- **Don't shut off the motor:** Shutting off the motor won't stop the car. Besides, you need to keep the engine running in order for the power steering to work.

- **Downshift (manual transmission only):** Be careful. Doing this can slow the car dramatically. If you are not traveling in a straight line, downshifting can make the car spin out. You may also damage the transmission. If your car has an automatic transmission, downshifting will probably have no effect.

- **Put the car into reverse:** The only way to stop an automatic-transmission-equipped car by using the transmission is to throw it into reverse, possibly ruining the transmission. Brace for a shock when doing this — the wheels will quickly lock up. As it turns out, this procedure is more complex on some cars and trucks, so here are some extra tips on this emergency maneuver:

  - *Never* put the transmission in reverse while going forward unless absolutely necessary. This is not a trick to play around with. Each time you do it, you risk causing significant damage to the transmission, transaxle, or driveshaft(s).

  - *Always* be concerned about the wheels breaking loose and causing the vehicle to "spin out" or become impossible to steer, especially if one wheel is on a slick surface and the other wheel has more traction. The wheel with the most traction will grab the pavement, sending the vehicle into a spin.

  - The amount of throttle is critical to making this maneuver work. If you take your foot off the gas pedal when you slam it in reverse, the engine will most likely stall, and the transmission will lock up the wheels. To get the transmission to engage in reverse on some vehicles, the engine speed must be raised slightly. This will cause the drivetrain to engage in the opposite direction instead of just freewheeling without any engagement of the wheels.

  - Too much gas, and the wheels will smoke and spin out of control. Too little gas, and the engine will stall. In actual application of this procedure, the throttle pedal becomes a pseudo-braking system, with pedal application directly related to braking action of the wheels.

  - This doesn't work with computer-controlled transmissions, which are found on many cars of the mid-90s. If you don't know whether your car has one, ask your local dealer. In general, a computer-controlled automatic transmission will not let the transmission engage reverse while rolling forward.

Ten Brake Failure Warnings

Have you ever had the brake pedal fall to the floor — a complete loss of brakes? It has to be the worst experience that a driver can have. Your brake warning light is only one indication of impending brake failure. Always be sure to check your vehicle for any of these ten brake failure forewarnings and their possible causes.

Low brake fluid

Random checking of brake fluid levels in cars by the Car Care Council found that one out of three was low on brake fluid. Some cars have warning indicators for low fluid level; some do not. Modern cars have clear brake reservoirs that allow you to see the level without removing the cap. Low fluid means one of two things:

✔ The brake pads are worn thin, making the caliper pistons extend, which causes a drop in the fluid level. This condition is normal and indicates the need for new brake pads.

✔ The car has a leak somewhere in the hydraulic system.

In either case, the brakes need immediate attention. If you don't know how to check your brake fluid level, consult your owner's manual or have a local mechanic show you.

Low brake pedal

The brake pedal goes close to the floor when applied. With the engine on and brake pedal pressed, you should be able to get your foot between the pedal and the floor. A low pedal can mean something as simple as maladjusted brakes. It can also indicate much more serious problems, such as bent/distorted brake shoes, improper shoe/drum fit, or a loose wheel bearing that's causing caliper piston kickback.

Pedal sinks to the floor

In this condition, your vehicle is an accident waiting to happen. Typically, the master cylinder is about to fail or there is a leak in the system. If the fluid level isn't dropping, the master cylinder is at fault.

Hard brake pedal

You have to put strong leg pressure on the brake pedal to stop the car. When power brakes don't have any power, the booster or pump may be malfunctioning. Other causes of a firm pedal include grease-soaked, glazed, or hard brake linings, vacuum supply problems, or frozen wheel cylinders. All of these possible causes are pretty complicated and technical and will necessitate a visit to the shop for further diagnosis if you are not very technically minded and are not inclined to look into it yourself.

Spongy pedal

The brakes apply when you press down, but the pedal is mushy. The usual cause of a soft or spongy pedal is air trapped in the system. Other causes include vapor locking from old brake fluid, brake hose(s) ballooning (and about to burst), warped brake shoes, new shoes or pads that don't fit properly, or brake drums worn too thin, causing _bellmouthing_ of the drums. Bellmouthing is where the brake drums are too thin and expand outward when the brake shoes put pressure on the inside of them — making the drum assume a bell shape.

Sensitive pedal

Your brakes apply almost as soon as you touch the pedal. Brake "grab" can cause loss of directional control, particularly on slick roads. Oil/grease/brake fluid contamination on the friction material is the usual culprit. Other causes include a faulty metering valve, system failure for the rear half of split brake systems, a slipped power booster reaction disc (located between the master cylinder and booster), organic pads installed where asbestos is required, or a loose caliper.

Pedal pulsation

When you apply the brakes, the pedal bounces or pulsates against your foot. A pulsating brake pedal means a rotor or drum is out-of-true. Like a washing machine with all the clothes on one side, it is a likely cause of pedal pulsation when the drum or rotor has more metal on one side than the other. If the wheels have been removed recently, the rotors were probably warped by improper tightening of the wheel lugnuts. Other causes include loose wheel bearings, a bent drive axle, and warped rotors from using metallic pads on rotors designed for organic brake pads. If your brakes were relined recently, the wrong type of brake pad material could have been installed or the wheels could have been put on with an impact gun. The root cause is difficult to discover after the fact. See the section "Slaying Dragon Brakes" in Chapter 2 for more information about brake pad material.

Note: Some ABS-equipped vehicles have a normal pedal vibration when you apply the brakes with force.

Dragging brakes

Dragging brakes are usually accompanied by a loss of fuel mileage and a burning smell from the affected wheel(s). This condition causes brake fade (spongy pedal) and will probably lead to complete brake failure. Typical causes are a restricted flexible brake hose or driving with both feet — resting your left foot on the brake pedal. Other causes include improper brake adjustment, sticking parking brake cable, frozen hydraulic piston(s), brake pedal linkage binding, loose/worn front wheel bearings, weak brake spring(s), overfilling the master cylinder, debris in the master cylinder compensating port, or a defective quick-takeup valve in the master cylinder. See the section "Slaying Dragon Brakes" in Chapter 2 for more information about dealing with this problem.

Brake pull

When you apply the brakes, the car pulls to the left or right. Brake pull can cause you to lose control and have an accident. The brakes always pull toward the side on which the brakes function properly. The most common cause is a restricted brake line or hose. Other causes include contamination of the friction elements; frozen or tight wheel cylinder/caliper pistons; incorrect, unmatched, or unevenly worn linings; non-parallelism or excessive runout of the rotor; a drum that is out of round, threaded, cracked, glazed, bellmouthed, or damaged; brakes out of adjustment; a broken shoe return spring or a grooved backing plate; a faulty combination valve in a cross-type system; and eccentric radius arm bushing worn on one side of the car and new on the other.

Whew! This is a lot of technical stuff to digest and may not mean much to you — all these possible causes are pretty complicated and necessitate a visit to the shop for further diagnosis if you are not very technically minded and are not inclined to look into it yourself. But if you are a do-it-yourselfer and want a list of possible causes, here it is. Also, if your mechanic is stumped and needs suggestions, go armed with this book.

Noise

The brakes make a loud noise when you apply them. Many cars today have built-in brake pad wear detectors that make a high-pitched chirping noise when the brakes just begin to apply. This noise tells you that the brake pads have become thin and need to be replaced. The other most common brake noise is caused by the brake pads vibrating against the rotor. This awful squeal is usually caused by worn or weak anti-rattle clips or springs, glazed pads, or corrosion buildup between pad and caliper.

Another dangerous brake noise is a scraping sound, possibly accompanied by a squeal. This noise can be caused by caliper mounting bolts that are too long, a loose rotor rubbing against a caliper, or brake pads or shoes that are worn down to the metal. A rattle at low speeds on rough roads with the brakes not applied usually means that there is excessive clearance between the pad and caliper, worn, missing, or improperly positioned anti-rattle clips or springs, or that the rotors were turned at too slow a feed speed. A chatter noise accompanied by pulsating pedal during brake application means excessive lateral runout or parallelism of the rotor, a loose wheel bearing, a bent drive axle, or improper lug bolt torque.

Panic Stop!

Do you know what to do and what not to do when making a panic stop? Quick thinking and lightning-fast reactions can eliminate or at least minimize your injuries and losses in a panic situation; it's a good idea to rehearse these items in your mind beforehand so that you are mentally prepared for the day when you have to make a panic stop. Here are some tips:

- ✔ Are you clear to the left or right? If so, a quick turn into an empty traffic lane may allow you to avoid a collision. Truckers make a habit of checking to either side for this very reason.

- ✔ Look in the rearview mirror. Someone may be so close behind you that he or she can't avoid hitting you and causing a rear-end accident. If you have time, pump the brake pedal to catch the attention of the driver who's on your tail. No way to avoid being rear-ended? Then let that driver hit you first and force you into the car in front of you. Otherwise, your car will be against the vehicle in front and the collision will have a more violent hammer-and-anvil effect. Also, for insurance reasons, it's better to be "forced" into the vehicle ahead.

The best defense against panic stop problems is to follow the Coast Guard motto: "*Semper Paratus,*" or "Always Prepared." The time to think of the following items is *before* you have to slam on the brakes:

✓ Seatbelts are a must! Make sure that they are snug against your body. Don't forget that lap belt if your shoulder belt is automatic.

✓ All loose baggage, including packages, groceries, and personal belongings, should be secure inside the car. You can use the seatbelt to secure briefcases and purses as well.

✓ Don't keep items on the rear deck of the car. Even a small item like a library book can cause a nasty blow to your head in a panic stop.

✓ Secure pets with an auto pet harness. Otherwise, a panic stop may throw your pet against the door frame or windshield. Never allow the pet to ride in your lap, or you may crush it against the steering wheel, even in a minor accident.

✓ If you are transporting a load of cargo in the back seat or behind you in a station wagon, make sure that the cargo is secure. If the cargo is high enough to hit you in the back of your head, you are asking for trouble. In a panic stop, the cargo will slide forward and can snap your neck or slam into the back of your seat with tremendous force.

✓ Install the best tires you can afford. Your tires might make the difference between a near-miss and a disaster.

✓ ***Crash avoidance tip:*** If someone suddenly pulls out directly in your path, aim for the rear fender. By the time your vehicle has gotten to that point, hopefully the other vehicle will have already passed and you will miss it.

✓ Make sure that your brakes are working properly. Practice a few panic stops in an empty parking lot or deserted road to check your brake system. If your vehicle pulls to the left or right or stops poorly, get the brakes repaired before they cause you to take someone's life. That life may be a small child darting out from between parked cars . . . or your own!

Anti-Lock Brake Systems Explained

Is ABS best? Since the advent of air bags, many people have become complacent about driving safety. Some think that an air bag is all that is really needed. In reality, air bags deploy in only about one percent of all emergency situations. According to General Manager of Pontiac, John Middlebrook, "The average individual will use an air bag once every 175 years but will use anti-lock brakes in an emergency once a year." Really, it's better to avoid a dangerous situation, and that is where anti-lock brake systems come into the picture.

The advantage of ABS is twofold: In most cases the vehicle can be stopped faster with better directional stability, even under adverse conditions. Think of the last time you slammed on the brakes and skidded. Were you able to steer when your vehicle was skidding? If you tried to turn when the wheels were locked, you found that the vehicle didn't respond. Why? Because the wheels didn't have any traction.

A vehicle with ABS acts differently. The wheels don't skid; instead, they continue to have traction, which allows the driver to steer through a panic stop. The vehicle can still be controlled and, in many cases, steered out of harm's way.

ABS Flaws

ABS isn't always best. Sometimes, ABS can actually work against the driver, so some car-makers offer an ABS OFF switch to allow the driver to turn off the anti-lock function. Consider the following situations:

- ✔ In conditions where the entire road surface is slick, ABS may not function properly and can keep the driver from having full control of the car. Some examples are driving on gravel or dirt roads or driving on sheet ice. In these cases, the anti-lock computer cannot tell what is happening because the computer uses input from each wheel to compare to the other wheels. In this particular type of situation, the computer releases the braking effect on the first wheel that starts to slip, causing the other wheel(s) to lose traction more quickly. After the second wheel loses traction, the computer releases both wheels, which can cause instant directional instability.

- ✔ The driver is not familiar with ABS brake operation and doesn't know not to pump the pedal when making a panic stop.

- ✔ The driver is likely to panic when the ABS system starts to work and makes the brake pedal pulsate. The driver gets frightened by the pulsating brake pedal and releases it.

TIP If you don't use it, you'll lose it! Use your ABS at least once a month or the ABS controller can fail prematurely from lack of use. Find a deserted parking lot and make a full-on panic stop, causing the ABS system to operate. Also, periodically testing the ABS system gives you practice in using ABS, so you will not be inclined to let up on the brake pedal in a panic braking situation when the ABS starts cycling and the pedal vibrates against your foot.

Before blaming the ABS computer for turning on the yellow ABS light, check the basics. Some of these items are easy to fix without the need for a repair manual and high-tech tools.

The heart of the ABS system's logic is the rotational speed of the tires. If one or more tires are worn or are of a slightly different size, the ABS system is affected. The ABS system has built-in look-up tables for the tires and their handling characteristics. Logic for tire height, profile, traction, and slip ratio is part of the ABS computer program. If tires with lower stability are installed, for example, the ABS computer can become confused. The system may still work, but hard braking can cause the car to shimmy and possibly slide sideways. Even a badly underinflated tire can throw the system off and trigger the ABS light.

The wheel sensors cause most of the havoc in ABS because these parts work in a grueling environment. Moisture, salt, dirt, slush, small rocks, and metal particles can cause problems. The sensors usually have a critical gap between the sensor and the tone wheel. If dirt or a small rock gets into the gap and moves the sensor, the ABS light triggers a failure.

Cleaning the engine compartment contaminates the sensors' connectors. When the ABS does its self-test procedure and the sensor doesn't respond as it should, the ABS light is triggered. This condition can be easily cured by cleaning the weatherpack connector. Road salt can do the same thing and can also be cleaned off. Use electric contact or electric motor cleaner to service the connector. Coat the terminals with silicone grease to prevent further problems.

Metal particles are the biggest headache of ABS. The roadside environment is full of iron particles from brake drums. The ABS wheel rotation sensor contains a permanent magnet, and the magnet starts to collect metal filings. Pretty soon it looks like a porcupine with metal particles sticking all over it. The presence of the extra metal eventually prevents the wheel sensor from correctly responding to the tone wheel as it turns, triggering the ABS light. You can easily clean the sensor, curing the problem.

ABS speed sensors installed in the differential housing are also a problem. During the differential break-in period, the ring and pinion gears seat against each other. Small metal particles are worn off these gears and become attached to the ABS sensor magnet. The magnet can be cleaned. Even better, change the gear lube after 5–10,000 miles and eliminate the source of the problem.

The heart of any computer system is the power source. Battery voltage is critical for the proper functioning of the system. ABS requires a constant supply of voltage. If the supply is too high or low, the ABS fails and turns the light on. If the charging system doesn't keep the battery charge up at least 9.5 volts, even for a fraction of a second, the ABS shuts down. If the alternator is producing non-rectified alternating current (AC voltage) levels in excess of a few volts, the ABS computer can be damaged. One of the first things to check when troubleshooting the ABS is the battery voltage, both DC and AC. If there is more than about $^1/_2$ volt AC in the electrical system, the alternator is shot because it has a bad rectifier (diode).

Dash Warning-Light Dilemmas

For the past decade or so, car-makers have been producing dash warning lights in two colors: amber and red. When the amber (or yellow) light is on, a problem exists. When a red light is lit, the problem is much more serious, usually requiring immediate action. One of the more serious things a warning light can indicate is a charging system failure.

What do you do when the alternator or battery symbol comes to life on the dash? Is it necessary to stop immediately, or can you drive until the next opportunity to stop? How long can you go without hurting anything?

The answer really depends on the drive belt configuration of your engine. If your water pump is driven by the same belt as the alternator, stop immediately. Don't turn off the motor until you check whether the belt has broken or is not turning the water pump and alternator. If the belt is still there, the alternator has failed, and you can probably drive for a little while — at least to the repair shop. If you don't know whether the water pump is also driven by the alternator fan belt, ask your mechanic to look and let you know. This is an important fact you should know about your vehicle!

If the alternator belt has broken and the water pump isn't turning, shut the engine off immediately. If you drive any further, you may blow a head gasket and maybe even crack the engine block. If your vehicle has an engine temperature gauge, you can use it to determine whether the problem is the belt. If the engine temperature goes up, you should stop your car immediately!

If you are satisfied that just the alternator is out of service, try to find a place to stop where you won't have to start the car again. After you shut off the engine, it is quite likely that you *will not* be able to start the car again because the battery will be too weak. Look for a garage or service station that might be able to fix the problem, or at least find some place that you can safely leave the vehicle until you can have it fixed.

 Before you just go out and have the alternator replaced, consider having the entire charging system checked. You should have the charging system checked both before and after the alternator replacement. It's a good idea to get a printout showing how much amperage your old alternator was producing and how much the new one is making. Some replacement alternators can be as defective as the one they replaced. Having this test done both before and after gives you some insurance that the new alternator was installed correctly and is putting out a good amount of charging amperage.

If you plan to tough it out and want to drive as far as you can go on battery power, don't use any accessories. Turn off the radio, heater, and air conditioner. Don't use the turn signals and try to stay off the brakes as much as possible. Try to maintain a minimum speed limit of 45 mph, the most efficient speed.

If your vehicle is carbureted and the battery still has a good charge, you may have four to five hours of driving left. Fuel-injected vehicles use much more energy and will only go for about one hour on the battery. Pay attention to the engine. As the battery weakens, the engine will begin to misfire, especially at higher rpms. When that happens, cut your speed. You have only a few minutes of battery life left at this point, so look for a safe place to come to a final stop.

If you are driving at night, the driving time will be cut considerably. Watch for the lights to begin dimming. When they do, start looking for a place to get off the road. This is illegal, but in an emergency, and if another vehicle is going along with you, arrange to have the other vehicle drive in front while you drive with your lights off. Use your emergency flashers and follow directly behind the other vehicle.

I once had my charging system go out while leaving Tallahassee, Florida on my way to Tampa. I had already driven for over an hour and knew that my battery wouldn't make it. It was a Sunday night and everything was closed except for a gas station. I purchased a new battery and was able to complete the trip by using the new battery.

Chapter 10

Stalled Cars and Other Nightmares

In This Chapter

▶ Starting a stalled or unwilling engine

▶ Using hand signals for safety

▶ Knowing what to do if your engine overheats

▶ Making the engine run cooler

▶ Dealing with a car fire

▶ Understanding how to tow and not to tow

*J*ust when you least expect it — the engine won't start. It just cranks and cranks. In this chapter, you'll find out all the mechanics' tricks for starting an unwilling engine. What if it's running hot? How do you deal with an overheated engine in the breakdown lane, and what steps do you take to remedy that hot condition? What if the car catches fire? Here, you'll learn the three things the fire department would like you to do before you leave a burning vehicle.

You may have to give up altogether and have your car towed. In that case, you should know that all tow trucks are not equal — some types can damage your car and should be avoided. Read on for all this information and more.

Starting a Stalled or Unwilling Engine

Have you ever wondered whether you can do anything to get your car to start after it stalls? The engine cranks over but doesn't catch — it cranks and cranks and never fires up. This section gives you some "mechanics' magic" tips for getting it to start. Some of these hints are simple, and some are a bit technical. If you don't understand them, have your mechanic review them with you so that you will be able to carry them out in the event that you are stranded and your car just won't start!

 A no-start condition is when the engine turns (cranks) over but fails to catch. This condition is different from a no-crank condition. If nothing happens when you twist the key — the starter motor doesn't turn the engine at all — go to the flowchart in the Appendix of this book that shows you how to troubleshoot an engine that won't crank.

Also remember that excessive cranking ruins the starter motor. Crank for 30 seconds at the most, followed by a one-minute rest. Doing so lets the starter motor cool down. Be sure to turn the ignition key all the way off between cranking attempts.

 Some of the following procedures can cause a fire if you are not careful. Always have a fire extinguisher handy, wear safety goggles, and dress appropriately (short sleeves, no jewelry, hair tied back). Please be careful!

Here's the procedure for getting that engine to start:

1. **Lift the hood and let the engine cool down.**

   You can overcome heat-induced ignition module problems by letting the module cool down. Ditto for vapor lock problems. You would be surprised at how many unwilling-to-restart engines are happy to cooperate after they cool down. That's why the darn thing starts when the tow-truck driver arrives!

2. **Remove the air filter.**

   If the engine is flooded or the air filter is dirty, removing the air filter helps to clear out the unburned gas. This trick works great if the engine has been cranked and cranked and may be flooded.

3. **Pop the gas cap and let the fuel tank breathe.**

   Sometimes the fuel tank vapor vent valve fails, preventing fuel from being drawn from the tank. This vent valve is located under the car, above the gas tank, and is very difficult to get at. Sometimes, it clogs up and makes the tank build pressure — or, the opposite, the tank won't vent properly and the gas can't come out. You can circumvent this problem simply by removing the gas cap.

Turn the key all the way *off* before you crank the engine so that you reset the computer. After you do so, the engine control computer is able to recognize a failure of some sensor. If turning the key off doesn't help, try disconnecting and reconnecting the battery cable. Make sure that the car and all accessories are turned off before you mess with the battery cable, or you can fry the computer. Disconnecting the battery may cause the engine to idle funny for a short while, and you may lose the memory in your radio. Also, if your radio has a security alarm, this trick may shut it down until someone re-enters the code.

If you own a GM car, take note: You can easily put the engine in limp-home mode by connecting two of the leads in the ALDL connector. If your engine is equipped with a Mass Airflow (MAF) sensor (which is a fairly common component that causes problems), disconnect it when the engine is off, forcing the computer into limp-home mode. Ask your mechanic to show you where the ALDL and MAF connectors are.

Create a spark

If you get no spark at the spark plug or from the coil in an engine *with* a distributor, stress the module. Remove the coil wire from the distributor, holding it one inch from a good ground. As the engine cranks, slowly move the wire closer to the ground until it begins to spark. Repeat this procedure as necessary. After it starts to produce spark, plug it back in the distributor and start the engine.

If you get no spark at the spark plug or from the coil in an engine *without* a distributor, check the connections to the electronic ignition module, the coils, and the crankshaft sensor. Try wiggling them to check for a tight fit and unplug them to look for corrosion and terminal ends that may have backed out of the holder.

Dry wet plug wires

Use any type of lubricating spray or, even better, a silicone spray, to dry off the plug wires and coil wire. If none is available, use a dry rag or towel. Don't forget to remove the distributor cap (if your car is so equipped) and dry it inside. If neither a spray or dry rag or towel is available, just open the hood and let the sunshine and air dry things out. It may take a little longer, but eventually the moisture will evaporate.

Give it a shot of fuel

If your vehicle is carbureted or throttle-body fuel-injected, put a little fuel ($1/2$ shot glass full) in the throttle inlet to get the engine to fire up for a moment. This should cause it to start up and run, at least for a moment. Sometimes the extra rpm surge that occurs when it fires up causes the stuck float, fuel injector, or weak fuel pump to come back to life. After the car has started and is running, you can get it into a shop and have a mechanic fix the problem. If you don't know whether you have a carburetor, throttle body, or what, have your mechanic go over the engine compartment and show you what you have and how it works.

While this procedure is not applicable to multiport fuel injected engines, you can use ether or starting fluid to achieve the same result with a fuel-injected car. Follow the instructions on the can to give it a shot of gas and get it to fire up for a moment with the same results described in the preceding paragraph. Be careful not to use too much or you can cause a fire.

Jump it

What if no fuel is going into the engine, and the engine just starts and dies when you give it a shot of fuel or ether? Listen at the gas filler hole while someone else turns the ignition key. Do you hear the fuel pump run for a few seconds? If not, the electric fuel pump may be the cause of your no-start. Just about every car made since 1980 has an electric fuel pump. When the pump fails to run, you can sometimes coax it to life with a jump start (see the procedure in Chapter 2). After you connect to another vehicle, start the other vehicle and run it for 15 minutes at a fast idle (give it some extra gas to make it idle fast) to put an additional charge on your battery. Leave the jumpers connected and try starting your vehicle. The extra voltage sometimes makes the fuel pump motor come to life.

Thaw it out

Is freezing weather causing your no-start? Is the engine cranking over v-e-r-y s-l-o-w-l-y? If so, try a different battery or a jump-start. If you already did so, the viscosity of the motor oil may be too thick. Try draining the oil and installing 5W-30 oil in the engine. Does the electric fuel pump run? (See the preceding procedure for instructions on checking the fuel pump.) You can revive a frozen fuel pump by using a drop light to heat it and thaw the frozen fuel/water inside it. You can revive frozen crankshaft position sensors the same way. If using a drop light isn't possible, try pushing the vehicle into a heated garage. No, it's not a good idea to build a fire under the car to warm it up. This will do more than warm the car. Be sure to call your insurance company and find out whether you have fire coverage!

Air it out

You suspect that the engine is flooded because you smell gas (I'm talking about the gas smell after several attempts at cranking it). First, make sure that you don't have a gas leak! If you see any visible signs of gas leaks, *stop!* You can start an engine fire. If you smell gas, the engine is probably flooded. Simply remove the air filter and let the engine air out for 15 minutes. Now crank it over. Hold the gas pedal on the floor to clear out the extra gas and let the engine draw in fresh air. If you don't know how to remove the air filter, consult your owner's manual or have your friendly mechanic show you.

Dry the ignition wires

Stalled because of rain or going over a big puddle? The car may have stalled because the ignition wires are wet. It's best to remove the plug wires and dry them out one by one (so you don't get them mixed up, silly). Ditto for the distributor cap. Spray the wires, cap, and rotor with WD-40, 5-56, LPS, or silicone spray. In a pinch, you can displace the moisture by using any spray solvent (such as brake cleaner or carb cleaner).

 Be careful not to start a fire! Let the solvent dry thoroughly before you attempt to start the car. If an appropriate spray isn't available, just open the hood and let the air and warm sun dry out the underhood area. It may take longer — but it works!

Unplug the exhaust system

What if the engine cranks okay and seems like it is trying to start, but it just can't seem to catch? It almost starts but then pops or sputters, and you see no exhaust fumes coming out of the tailpipe. This is a good indication that the exhaust system is plugged. An easy way to get the engine to start is simply to remove one spark plug. More difficult ways are to remove the oxygen sensor or loosen the exhaust pipe somewhere in front of the muffler (or catalytic converter) to let the exhaust leak out. Removing a spark plug lets the car start, but you can't drive it to the shop this way. You should loosen the exhaust flange or remove the oxygen sensor to make the car drivable.

Hand safety signals

Use this familiar peace sign in the event that you want to apologize to another driver.

This time-out sign means that you are in need of assistance (your face should reflect this as well).

This signal, followed by a circular motion of the index finger, lets another driver know that his or her tire pressure is low.

Use this signal to advise oncoming drivers to slow down because danger is ahead.

Overheating? Don't Blow Your Cool!

What do you do if your engine is drastically overheating, steam has started to spurt from the hood area, and the temperature warning light is on? Follow these steps:

1. **Pull over as soon as possible.**

    Another mile or two can turn a minor repair into a blown head gasket or, even worse, a cracked block. In some cases, the cost of repairing the damage can exceed the value of the car.

2. **Turn the heater to its high setting and open the windows.**

     This draws heat away from the engine and helps to cool off the radiator.

3. **Unless the engine is steaming, smoking, or on fire, don't turn off the ignition.**

    If allowed to idle, the engine can throw off more heat because the engine's coolant is circulating. Shutting off an overheated engine can turn the oil to varnish, which can cause engine bearings to seize up, ruining the engine.

4. **If you have access to a hose, spray water into the grille of the car in the area of the radiator.**

    Make sure that you cool down the hood area to avoid getting burned when you lift it. The engine should still be running.

5. **After the water has cooled off the radiator to the point that it is cool to the touch, carefully open the radiator cap and pour water into the radiator until it is full. Then replace the cap tightly.**

    If water isn't available, leave the engine on but use gloves or towels to open the hood.

6. **Remove the oil filler cap carefully — it's hot — and add a quart or two of oil.**

    You should add oil even if the dipstick indicates that the engine is full. For a short period, the engine can handle the excess, and the oil will help cool the internal engine parts.

     Be careful not to spill oil on the hot engine; doing so may cause a fire!

Wait until the engine/radiator is cool — about an hour — before driving again. Just be sure to have the oil drained as soon as possible — which is a good idea anyway if the engine overheated and burned the oil beyond its useful life.

Important: If you do not have water or oil and turning on the heater doesn't help, turn off the engine as a last resort. You should wait until it is cool before trying to start it again an hour or so later.

Beating the Heat

How important is heat reduction in an engine? The cooling system of a diesel engine, running under load, has a great deal of heat to remove. So much, in fact, that if it weren't properly cooled, the heat generated could reduce the engine to a molten blob within an hour. About 9,000 gallons of coolant pump through the cooling system each hour. In one day's operation, that's enough coolant to fill a large swimming pool. Consider this: The cooling system accounts for less than 60 percent of the engine's cooling capability. The rest of the heat is left for the oil to dissipate.

Here's a compilation of tricks and tips for preventing overheating in the first place. Look over the list and pick one or more that will work best for your situation. Some are simple, and some are very technical. If you don't understand a particular suggestion, consult your mechanic.

- ✔ Use a 50 – 50 mix of coolant and water. Too much coolant can cause overheating. People think, "A little is good — more must be better." Then they drain out all the coolant/water mix and refill with straight coolant. Bad idea! Coolant doesn't cool. They should have just called it antifreeze. I told them but no one would listen!

- ✔ Have your thermostat and radiator cap changed every four years or 60,000 miles. The thermostat is the most common cause of cars running hot and/or overheating. Be sure to buy only name-brand parts, such as Stant or Robertshaw. Cheap imitations will fail and cause a major breakdown. Is it worth it to save a few dollars?

- ✔ Use synthetic oil in your engine and drive-train. Synthetic oil can reduce engine oil temperature by 50 degrees and is much better at getting rid of engine heat. It is also much more slippery, which lets the engine run with less internal friction — something that also contributes engine heat.

- ✔ Put the gear selector in neutral if your transmission is an automatic. If you are stuck in a traffic jam and not moving, let the engine and transmission idle freely in neutral. Doing so speeds up circulation through the transmission cooler, which helps to cool both the engine and the transmission.

- ✔ Be sure that the radiator is clean inside and outside. Have the inside checked when the coolant is flushed every two years. With the nozzle on your garden hose or a self-serve car wash spray wand, spray high pressure water from the inside of the engine compartment toward the outside remove bugs, dirt, leaves, and so on.

- ✔ With the engine cool, squeeze the lower radiator hose. You should feel a spring inside. If the spring isn't there or has corroded away, the water pump's suction can cause the hose to collapse. This condition usually indicates that all the hoses are old and need to be replaced. Ditto for the coolant. If it was acidic enough to dissolve that spring, think what it must be doing to the rest of the cooling system!

- ✔ As a general rule of thumb, change the cooling system hoses every 4 – 5 years or 40,000 – 60,000 miles. Doing so helps to prevent a hose from rupturing and leaving you on the side of the road. Pay a little now or a lot later!

- ✔ To help avoid overheating, try using a *heat transfer agent,* a cheap and easy method for reducing cylinder head temperatures. A small amount of the product added to the radiator can decrease cylinder head temperatures by as much as 30° F.

Overheating First Aid

If your car does overheat, *do not under any circumstances open the radiator cap until it's cool.* A safe procedure is to spray water into the grille with the engine running. Direct the water into the radiator and keep spraying until the engine is cool. Turn off the engine and continue to spray the radiator until it's no longer hot to the touch. Now you can safely open the radiator cap.

Causes of overheating

Stubborn, hard-to-find overheating problems are caused by the items listed here. Some causes are simple, and you can easily rectify them yourself. Others are a bit technical and require the assistance of a mechanic or radiator repair specialist. Rest assured that if your car is running hot, the reason is to be found in this section.

Leaks in hoses, water pumps, timing covers, radiators, and heaters/hoses often leave green puddles on the ground under the car (see "Trouble Puddles" in Chapter 11). If the source of the leak is not evident, use a cooling system tester to pressurize the system. Do this on a hot engine using 15 – 20 psi and let it cool down. Repressurize as needed to maintain this amount of pressure. Some components leak only when hot; others leak when cold. If you don't have a pressure tester, stop by a radiator shop and have the shop test your car for you.

 Don't drive your vehicle with a low coolant level and overheat the engine, or you may turn a leak into a blown head gasket! If you do need to drive, loosen the radiator cap and keep adding water (bring along a few jugs full) as needed until you reach your destination.

Both the radiator cap and the cooling system should be able to hold the tester's pressure for at least five minutes. Loss of pressure means that the coolant is able to leak out somewhere. Also, the radiator cap must hold the correct rated pressure printed on the top of the cap.

Do you see coolant being forced out the overflow of the radiator or out the top of the overflow bottle? If so, you may be seeing the effects of a blown head gasket. If your car has a blown head gasket, you are in for a pretty big repair. It's probably not a good idea to drive the vehicle with it acting this way because the leaking head gasket can cause further engine damage. Get it checked out right away!

A low coolant level can cause all kinds of mischief. For one thing, it can cause the coolant temperature sensor to read incorrectly and cause air bubbles to form in the hot parts of the engine. The heater may not work properly, and, most importantly, the engine may overheat.

If the coolant solution is mixed with too little or too much coolant, the system may overheat. Too much coolant causes the engine to run too hot because it cannot transfer heat into the strong mixture of coolant (more than 75 percent coolant). Too much water can cause the system to boil over because coolant is supposed to raise the boiling point 20 degrees above that of water.

If the engine oil level is too high, it causes oil to foam at high speeds. Oil that is foamy doesn't lubricate the inside of the engine, which results in a hotter-running engine. A low oil level causes overheating from friction caused by the poorly lubricated engine parts.

Rear-wheel-drive vehicles only: If the radiator fan clutch fails to keep the fan engaged, the fan clutch is the wrong type or is made to turn in the opposite direction. The engine will overheat only when you drive at slow speeds. On the highway, it will behave okay. With the engine hot and not running, give the radiator fan a good spin. Does the fan spin more than five revolutions? If so, the fan clutch is definitely bad.

Front-wheel-drive and some rear-wheel-drive vehicles with electric cooling fans: If the electric fan does not come on soon enough or does not come on at all, the engine will overheat only when you drive at slow speeds. On the highway, it will behave okay. The fan should operate when the temp sensor is grounded (except for Mazda and some Toyota models).

Radiator blockage causes internal restrictions and reduced flow rate. A quick check for internal radiator blockage is to feel the outside of the radiator (with the engine turned off). The radiator should feel hot at one end and then cooler as you move your hand across it. A blocked radiator will feel cool in the center and hot around the edges. Another test is to remove the radiator cap and look inside the radiator with a penlight. First, open the petcock, drain out some of the coolant, and check whether fluid is left standing in the tubes. Standing coolant indicates that the tubes are blocked. Next, run the engine with the coolant level still low and check for good flow. It should have plenty of circulation, kind of like a waterfall.

New cars have air dams and use airflow channeled through the bottom of the grille opening. This design is called the "bottom feeder" airflow design. If airflow through the radiator is blocked by missing or damaged air dams, or leaves and debris are blocking the air scoop, overheating will occur.

Internal engine cooling system restrictions in the engine water jacket caused by scale or blockage are the hardest types of cooling system problems to find. Usually, you have to remove the engine block core plug (also known as a *freeze plug*) to look inside the engine cooling jacket for blockage. The only way to clean out this type of blockage is to pressure flush and back fluids from the engine block. In extreme cases, the freeze plugs will have to be removed and the junk physically cleaned through the plug openings.

If the hood felt insulation liner falls down in front of the radiator, it will restrict the airflow. This problem is plainly visible. A similar, less visible probem is where the sealing rubber around the radiator and air intake area is damaged, falls off, or is not reinstalled after the car is repaired for some reason. This sealing rubber channels and forces the air to go through the radiator. Without it, the air can simply bypass the radiator and not do its job of cooling.

The cooling system thermostat may be sticking closed, be the wrong type, or be installed upside down. To pinpoint this problem, remove the radiator cap and run the engine at high rpms (2,000 or so) for a few minutes to get it hot. Turn the engine off and let it heat-soak for a minute so that the heat travels throughout the engine and cooling system. This procedure should cause the thermostat to open fully. Next, have someone start and rev the engine while you watch for the fluid level. If the thermostat is working and has opened as it should, the liquid level will drop in the radiator and you will see lots of coolant flow. It will really churn the coolant! Now, continue to idle the engine and as the engine cools down to normal temperature. The coolant flow should slow down, indicating that the thermostat is working properly and has begun to close.

The water pump impeller blades are broken or eroded, or the impeller itself has come loose. If you see a great deal of red rust accumulation inside the cooling system (like the Rio Grande River), this condition may be caused by the engine block or water pump impeller blades rusting. The pump must be removed and examined for further diagnosis of this very tough-to-find problem.

The air conditioning may have been overcharged during a recent A/C service, which can cause the engine to labor and run hot. Does running the A/C make it overheat? Does the engine seem to have much less power (than usual) when the A/C is running? This condition is very easy to correct. Have some of refrigerant removed from the A/C system. Go back to the shop that serviced the A/C and have them check the A/C system pressures to see whether the pressure is too high — an indication of an overcharge.

The brakes may be dragging. If so, the wheels will be hot to the touch and the car will not coast very well when put in neutral. (See "Slaying Dragon Brakes" in Chapter 2.)

The exhaust may be restricted, causing the engine to run hot. This is another difficult one to pinpoint. The best way to find out if there is an exhaust restriction is to have the exhaust system back pressure tested. It should not have more than about 2 pounds of back pressure with the engine running at 2,000 rpms (no load on the engine).

The engine may be getting hot air all the time, meaning that the EFE (Heat riser) is stuck closed or the THERMAC is stuck on hot — depending on the type of vehicle you have. You can easily pinpoint this problem by removing the air filter and filter cover letting cool air into the engine all the time. If this makes the problem go away, the "heated air" system must be checked out by a mechanic.

Timing for the ignition system may be retarded. Many things on many different engines can retard the timing. Finding the cause will require the help of a tune-up or engine drivability specialist.

A worn camshaft causes poor engine efficiency. This condition usually is reflected in a lowered engine vacuum. A simple engine vacuum test should nail this cause down. The vacuum should be 18–21 inches at idle, without any fluctuations. Ditto for a timing belt that has jumped off just one tooth.

The lower radiator hose may be collapsed, restricting coolant flow at highway speeds. A missing spring inside this hose usually causes this problem. Give it a squeeze to feel for the spring.

Air locked in the system may be preventing coolant flow. Anytime the cooling system is opened up for service, there is a possibility of getting air locks in the system. If the air is not removed (burped) from the cooling system, the engine can overheat. In extreme cases, this can damage the head gasket!

Install the thermostat with two aspirins, holding it open to bleed the air out, especially where the thermostat is mounted on the water pump. This simple procedure can prevent air locks and make the cooling system purge itself of bubbles more easily.

Any source of air leaking into the suction side of the water pump (between the pump and the lower radiator hose) will allow air into the cooling system and cause air locks. Loose hose clamps are the usual cause for air sneaking into the system.

If the radiator is too small or the wrong radiator is installed, your engine will never run cool — especially on the highway under heavy loads or when going up hills. Heavy-duty Core radiators are available at your local radiator shop.

The engine belts may be tight, worn, smooth, or frayed or may not fit on the pulley properly. Slipping fan belts can prevent the water pump from turning at the proper speed and coolant from circulating as it should. Also, the fan belt is running the water pump in the wrong direction.

If the pump has a smooth pulley, it is made to rotate counterclockwise. If the pulley has a groove or V, it rotates clockwise or the same direction as the crankshaft.

A lean air-fuel mixture causes combustion temperatures to be too high. Have the exhaust gas analyzed in order to pinpoint excessively lean mixtures. This condition usually is accompanied by the presence of engine ping, knock, or detonation.

Chariots Afire!

You smell smoke. It's coming from under your hood! Your engine is on fire. What do you do?

 If the fire is coming from underneath the car or from the rear, get off the road and a safe distance away from the car as fast as possible because the gas tank may explode. Be sure to turn off the ignition when you stop because this simple act may stop the fire from spreading and help the fire to go out on its own.

If you are squeamish or don't care if the car burns up, just pull over and get at least 100 feet away from the vehicle. If you have time, gather up your personal belongings because you don't want to have to go back after them. If you have children on board, get them out first — as fast as possible!

Stand away from the car. If possible, wave down a passing truck — truckers carry fire extinguishers. (Don't forget to offer to pay for the fire extinguisher afterward.) Another source who can summon more help is someone with a car phone.

If you want to attempt to put out the fire or do some things that may assist the fire department when they arrive, read on. Attempt these procedures only if you have been trained in working with cars, the fire is small, and you are in dire need. Otherwise, leave the job to a professional.

First, try to shut off the ignition *immediately*. Shutting off the ignition shuts off the fuel pump, which stops the flow of fuel.

Important: If your car will let you, don't lock the steering wheel when you turn off the ignition. Also, stopping the engine causes the power brakes and power steering to stop working, so be prepared to really struggle with the steering wheel and push hard on the brakes to stop.

Get to the side of the road as quickly as possible. While you're rolling, air flowing through the grille fans the fire. Make sure that the doors are unlocked because the battery may soon lose electrical power. After you are certain that the doors are unlocked, close the car windows and sunroof, making the inside as airtight as possible.

You may need to turn the ignition back on again for a moment to get the windows to go up. However, the fire department says that doing so before exiting the car is smart because it keeps the fire from spreading into the passenger compartment.

Before you get out of the car, release the hood and gas cover. The fire department will need to get into the engine compartment and will have a harder time if you haven't released the hood latch.

After you are out of the car (if you have time and the fire isn't spreading too fast), loosen the gas cap to prevent fuel tank pressure from forcing more gas into the engine.

If you plan on fighting the fire yourself, open the trunk and get out the trunk mat, blanket, floor mats, or anything else that you can use to smother flames. Take the jack handle or tire iron as well.

 The hood will probably be too hot to touch. If so, use the tire iron to work the safety catch. ***Important:*** Leave this job to firefighters if the heat is too intense.

If you open the hood and are greeted with flames, do not try to smother the fire. Shutting the hood may slow the fire until help comes. Don't close the hood completely; the fire department will need to open it again when they arrive.

If the fire is small, smother it with the trunk mat. You may be able to find sand nearby that you can use to smother the fire. In some cases, you can pop off a hubcap to shovel sand onto the fire.

If the fire is caused by an electrical short and appears to be in the electric wires, try to disconnect the battery. If you can't get at the battery or the clamps are too tight to wrestle free, you may need to cut the battery cable. Always try to disconnect the ground cable because it won't make sparks if you accidentally ground it to the frame. If no tools are handy, you can try using the jack handle and pry or knock the post off the battery to disconnect it. Be careful and forewarned: Sparks can cause the battery to explode!

Note: Electrical fires are not affected by CO_2 fire extinguishers unless you can spray the CO_2 directly onto the short, cooling it down and depriving it of oxygen. In general, electrical fires continue to create heat until the battery is disconnected. Also, if the engine block or wheels are made of magnesium-aluminum alloy and catch fire, they can be extinguished only with a special purple foam (Class D) fire extinguisher.

Fire extinguishers

A fire extinguisher is an invaluable piece of equipment. Purchase one and keep it in your car. Be sure that the fire extinguisher is F.M. or U.L. approved and is specified for class A, B, and C fires. The best ones have gauges that let you know they are still full.

Water-charged

This type of extinguisher is practically useless unless you are trying to put out an upholstery or carpet fire. Water is likely to cause burning gasoline to spatter and spread the fire to other parts of the engine compartment.

CO_2 or Halon

This type of extinguisher is good for all types of fires except electrical and magnesium-alloy metal fires. CO_2 is discharged at a temperature of less than $-210°$ F and is not very effective in open areas where the wind can dissipate the discharge stream. Use CO_2 for fires in confined spaces under the dash and in the engine compartment where wind isn't a factor. CO_2 does not leave a chemical residue behind and will not damage expensive electrical equipment.

Dry chemical

This type of extinguisher is good for most automotive fires with one serious drawback — it leaves a caustic powder behind that is highly corrosive. If used, the chemical must be washed out of the area as soon as possible before it attacks wiring and paint. Also, this type of extinguisher must be recharged once triggered, regardless of how little is used. After the seal is broken, all the propellant leaks out.

Metal-X or Purple "K"

This type of extinguisher uses a potassium-based chemical that stops magnesium fires. Engine blocks, transmission cases, and magnesium wheels can burn, and these fires are impossible to stop without this type of extinguisher.

To Tow or Not to Tow

Your car has a problem, so you call a tow truck. What are the chances that towing your car from your driveway to the garage will do additional damage?

Towing isn't what it used to be. With the advent of computerized transmissions, front-wheel-drive, four-wheel-drive, unibody construction, and plastic air dams or fascias, towing modern cars is a big problem. If the vehicle is towed on its drive wheels, the damage to a transaxle can run as high as $5,000. The following sections describe the three commonly used tow methods and list the pros and cons of each type.

Sling towing

Sling towing is the traditional tow method, and is the one most likely to damage your car. When the sling is attached to the car's front end, it is likely to damage the front bumper. The sling also attaches to the frame under the car and, if the operator is careless when placing the hooks, front end parts of your car can be damaged. A sling should never be used if there is an air dam or if the car has plastic front bumpers. Automatic transmissions in rear-wheel-drive cars will be damaged if the car is towed more than 25 miles.

Wheel-lift towing

Wheel-lift tow rigs are the accepted norm of the towing industry today. They don't require attachment to the undercarriage and don't use the bumper to stop the car like the sling. However, because this type of towing lifts by the front wheels, cars with air dams can still be damaged. The same problems with rear-wheel-drive cars exist: Automatic transmissions in rear-wheel-drive cars will be damaged if the car is towed more than 25 miles.

Flat-bed towing

Flat-bed towing is the most expensive type, but it is also the best. The drawback of flat beds is that they are unwieldy, requiring more room to maneuver into place. Also, the process of loading the car is more time consuming. After the car is on the truck, the car is essentially out of harm's way. If not properly secured, however, the vehicle can still be damaged by the securing hooks or by shifting and hitting the front of the tow truck's headboard.

A good towing operation will have both wheel-lift and flat-bed tow trucks. Although sling-style tow trucks are relics of the past in big cities, rural towing services still use them. If you have a late model car and a sling tow truck shows up to tow you, refuse it! A reputable towing operation will ask you the year, make, and model of your car when you call. You might consider asking the towing service what kind of truck it intends to dispatch.

Part IV
On Your Way to the Shop

SLING-TYPE

In this part...

This part tells you what you should know before you take your car into the repair shop so that you can be an informed consumer.

Chapter 11

Trouble Sounds and Bad Vibes

● ●

In This Chapter

▶ What's that puddle under your car?

▶ Smell something burning or unusual?

▶ Got a new "clunk on bumps" or some other noise?

▶ Talking in mechanics' language to get your car fixed right

▶ Checking for bad alignment problems the quick-and-easy way

● ●

*W*hen it comes to letting you know that it is having a problem or is about to leave you stranded, your car will usually give you tell-tale signs to alert you ahead of time. This chapter shows you how to recognize what your car is trying to tell you so that you won't wind up stranded on the side of the road — or even worse, broken down in the middle of the road. Your car can't talk, but it may still be trying to communicate with you. Here's how to listen!

Recognizing Trouble Puddles

The puddle under your car can mean a lot of trouble if the puddle is not water. You can tell a great deal by checking out the color of the puddle.

If you can't tell whether it is coming from your car, or if you park your car over gravel, cut open a large cardboard box and lay it under the car. Make sure that the cardboard isn't touching any of the hot exhaust parts. Leave the car overnight, and check it the next morning.

Match the color to the problem, making careful note of the puddle's location:

✔ **Green puddles** mean leaking cooling system parts. If the leak is from the front engine area (where the drive belts are), the water pump is suspect. Leaks from the grille area are probably related to the radiator. Leaks from the dashboard area could be from a hose or heater core. Fix the leak before you ruin the engine!

✔ **Red puddles** are made up of automatic transmission fluid if the leak is in the area of the transmission. If the leak is from the radiator area, the cooler hoses from the transmission to the radiator are leaking. Fix the leak before it ruins the transmission.

✔ **Clear or light red puddles** indicate power-steering leaks. This fluid is usually clear in color, although some cars use red automatic transmission fluid in their power-steering units, which may fool you. It is important to pay attention to the exact location of the puddle.

✔ **Dirty, dark, or black puddles** mean that you have motor oil leaks. Keep track of your oil consumption. If the engine is using more than a quart every 800 miles, the engine oil leak can be dangerous. If the oil is leaking on the exhaust system, it can cause a fire! *Tip-off:* Does the engine show signs of smoke after you shut it off?

- **Clear, thick, oily puddles** point to manual transmission or differential leaks. Gear lube has a strong, heavy-machinery smell. Finding the source of the leak will tip you off to what is leaking.

- **Blue puddles** indicate a leaking windshield washer bottle.

Recognizing Trouble Smells

Your nose can be a great diagnostic tool. Take note of when a smell comes from your car. Is it when you start up, after you drive awhile, at night, or when it is raining or damp out?

Match the smell to the problem:

- **Acrid chemical smells** arise after the car is hot and mean that coolant is leaking on hot exhaust parts, causing a strong odor. This smell is similar to the smell of the inside of a new plastic bag — a plastic smell. You may smell it coming out the tailpipe if the coolant is leaking into your combustion chamber. Carefully check the coolant level and watch for a loss.

    Get this checked out right away! This can cause a fire because coolant will catch fire and burn.

- **Chemical smells** inside the car after you've been driving it indicate that coolant is leaking from the heater core inside the car. This is sometimes accompanied by oily film deposits on the inside windows, especially the windshield. Sometimes it smells like an old refrigerator or new Styrofoam.

- **Rotten egg smells** can occur when you first start the car and at other odd times. This is a normal condition of an overly rich fuel mixture. This smell is caused by the catalytic converter being too cold to properly burn off the rich mixture coming out of the engine. If this smell persists, something is causing the engine to run rich all the time.

- **Burned plastic smells** are most commonly caused by overheating wiring. Turn off all electrical accessories to see if the smell goes away. Carefully feel the fuse box to determine whether it is the source of the smell. Unplug the fuses one at a time, feeling each for telltale evidence of the heat problem. Also smell each wheel for dragging brakes (see "Slaying Dragon Brakes" in Chapter 2 for more information about this problem).

- **Burning leaves smells** may arise if you park under a tree. Sometimes leaves get into the heater duct and fall against the blower motor resistor. This resistor gets red-hot and burns any debris lodged against it. Try removing the resistor to determine whether burned leaves are stuck to it.

Recognizing Trouble Sounds

Does your car make a clunk when hitting a bump? Do you hear a squeak throughout the week? Tracking down persistent automobile noises is a real chore, but you can narrow the search by familiarizing yourself with some common causes.

Speed-sensitive noises that change with vehicle speed include the following:

- Brake pad wear indicators rubbing on the rotors make a scraping noise. A stone caught in the rotor housing also makes this sound. Does pressing the brake make the noise go away?

✔ Loose, glazed, or slipping fan belts cause noise such as chirps, squeaks, clicks, and rattles. These noises are more common when you first start the car or when you're using an accessory such as the air conditioner or rear window defroster. Does the noise happen when you're turning the wheel, when the A/C compressor cycles, or when you call the alternator into action by using the accessories?

✔ Clutch chatter or clunking when accelerating or stopping can be caused by a broken engine mount or engine strap. Pinpoint the problem: Does the noise become worse when the engine is in gear and the brake is applied (automatic transmissions) or when the clutch is released with the brake applied (manual transmissions)? Try reverse as well. Also check for driveshaft noises by putting the car on a lift and listening to the driveshaft while someone inside the car shifts between reverse and drive with the brake applied.

✔ Exhaust noises come and go when the engine rocks back and forth. The exhaust doughnut sometimes leaks exhaust gas when the engine flexes the pipe. Do you feel exhaust residue at the pipe junction? Just take your fingers (with the engine cold) and rub the area around the exhaust joint. Do your fingers come up black from the leaking exhaust soot?

✔ U-joints (in rear-wheel-drive vehicles) make a clunk when they are too loose. U-joints can also become tight and cause a hard-to-find vibration at speeds greater than 45 mph. Remove the driveshaft and physically check the U-joints. Are they too loose or do they bind?

✔ CV joints (front-wheel-drive vehicles) may knock, click, or cause steering wheel vibrations. Inner CVs clunk like U-joints when worn and loose. They also cause vibration at speeds over 50 mph.

✔ Wheel bearings make noises similar to U-joints and CV joints but usually occur at lower road speeds, especially on curves and turns.

✔ Driveshaft center bearings (RWD and FWD vehicles) make noises similar to bad wheel bearings but are not affected by turns.

✔ A driveshaft imbalance condition (RWD and FWD vehicles) is apparent at speeds above 45 mph, causing a high-speed vibration.

✔ Radial tire runout (egg-shaped tire) is most noticeable at low speeds.

✔ Lateral tire runout (bent rim) is most noticeable at higher speeds.

✔ Unbalanced tires (weights missing) are noticeable at speeds above 50 mph.

✔ Transmission tailshaft bushing (RWD and FWD vehicles) causes a scraping or squealing noise that is detectable when you're accelerating and decelerating.

Engine-speed-sensitive noises that change with engine speed include the following:

✔ Misaligned pulleys and broken brackets for the alternator, A/C compressor, or power steering pump cause underhood engine noises. Do you see a broken brace?

✔ Timing belts make noise when loose. If the belt strikes the belt housing, it rattles or knocks. Loose timing belts cause backlash snapping inside the distributor (a knock or rattle), similar to a worn distributor bushing. Take a long hose and listen for the source of the sound. Where do you hear it coming from?

✔ Exhaust leaks make noise when cold and are quiet when hot. This is especially common in exhaust manifold leaks. The cast iron manifold "expands" as it gets hot, partially sealing off the leak. Use a long piece of hose, such as a stethoscope, and listen for the source of the noise. You will hear the sound of escaping exhaust gases.

✔ Poorly installed exhaust systems clunk, rattle, buzz, or make droning noises. Sometimes the noises happen when you're accelerating, stopping, going over bumps, or idling.

✔ Air pump silencer mufflers lose the dampening material in the muffler and make noise when the air pump is vented to the outside. This sound is normal.

✔ Air conditioner or power-steering hoses can make a drone or hum. Check for contact areas by looking for shiny rubbing spots where the hoses have been rubbing against something nearby.

Describing Sounds of Trouble

Your car can't talk about its problems. The engine can talk to you only by making noise. When your car starts sending you signals that something is wrong, you should take heed. Table 11-1 lists sounds that you can describe to your mechanic to help him or her diagnose your problem.

Table 11-1   Describing Trouble Sounds to Your Mechanic

Sound	What to Call It
Continuous bass drum roll; distant thunder	Boom
Door buzzer; buzz saw far away	Buzz
Camera shutter; retractable ball-point pen	Click
Heavy door closing	Clunk
Sharpening an ax on a grinder; garbage disposal	Grind
Air escaping from a tire; steam from a radiator	Hiss
Someone knocking on your door	Knock
Marbles rattling inside a can; popcorn popping	Ping
Champagne bottle cork popping	Pop
Baby's rattle; stone bouncing around in a can	Rattle
Lion roaring; waterfall	Roar
Bowling ball rolling down an alley; distant thunder	Rumble
Screaming on an amusement park ride	Screech
Drop of water on a hot skillet	Spit
Branch breaking	Snap
Tennis shoes on a wooden court; door hinge needing oil	Squeak
Silverware being hit together	Tap
Bowling ball being dropped	Thud or thunk
Fan rubbing against its cage	Whir
Electric drill motor; mosquito	Whine

Explaining Car Problems

Often, the description of an automotive problem gets lost in translation. Communication is vital if you want to have the problem corrected the first time. Table 11-2 lists some new vocabulary you can use when describing a problem to your mechanic. Study this list so that you'll be able to speak your mechanic's language.

Table 11-2   Describing Automotive Problems to Your Mechanic

Problem	What to Call It
Pressing the brake pedal produces less and less braking.	Brake fade
The brake pedal moves when you apply the brakes.	Brake pulsation
The suspension runs out of travel and the body hits the rubber stop with a heavy thud.	Bottoming (also called bottoming out). This is like there are no shock absorbers and the chassis is hitting the frame with a thud.
You use the starter to turn the engine a slight amount without actually starting it.	Bumping the engine
The engine is being turned by the starter but is not starting. The engine just turns over; cranks over.	Cranking
Your car experiences a temporary or complete loss of power. The engine quits at sharp intervals. The problem may be intermittent or repetitive, and it may happen during acceleration or deceleration. It's like someone turning off the ignition.	Cuts out
A job done incorrectly has "come back" to be done again. A bad word to a mechanic.	Come back
The engine pings or pre-ignites. This problem can be mild or severe, usually worse during acceleration. The engine makes sharp, metallic knocks that change with the rpms.	Detonation
The engine keeps running after you turn the key off.	Dieseling (named after diesel engines, which don't need ignition power to run)
The brakes apply too much with too little effort; overly sensitive brakes.	Grabby brakes
You get a momentary lack of response as you press the accelerator. This condition occurs at all speeds but is most apparent when first starting. Severe cases can cause the engine to stall.	Hesitate (see also "Sag")
There is unwanted harshness, looseness, or reverse feedback in the steering wheel.	Kick-back
The engine gives a sharp jerk or pulses. This problem is related to engine speed; it is most noticeable at idle or low speed and disappears at higher speeds.	Miss (also known as a *misfire*)
The car steers left or right by itself either while you're driving or when you apply the brakes.	Pull
The engine runs unevenly at idle, sometimes making the car shake.	Rough idle
The vehicle doesn't respond immediately when you press the gas pedal.	Sag

(continued)

Table 11-2	*(continued)*
Problem	**What to Call It**
A mechanic has done an incomplete alignment job without checking or setting two of the other important alignment angles, mainly the camber and caster angles.	Set the toe and let it go
The engine delivers limited power when accelerating, under load, or at high speeds.	Sluggish
Your car gives less than anticipated response. With accelerating, refers to little or no increase in speed when depressing the gas pedal. With braking, refers to a soft or mushy brake pedal when stopping.	Spongy
The steering wheel rapidly moves side to side when you hit a bump or use the brakes. Shakes.	Shimmy
The action of the engine coming to life. Firing up. Igniting.	Starting
The steering wheel is hard to turn first thing in the morning and is okay the rest of the day.	Steering morning sickness
The steering wheel must be turned farther than normal to make the car change direction. Looseness in the steering wheel.	Steering play
The vehicle speeds up and slows down without your moving the gas pedal.	Surge
The steering wheel as well as the car shakes, caused by an out-of-round/balance tire. This happens all the time, regardless of stopping or starting.	Tire tramp
The steering wheel pulls, associated with acceleration or deceleration; this is typical of front-wheel-drive cars.	Torque steer
You feel that you are pulling a trailer behind you. Sudden or sharp onset/release. Bucking.	Trailer hitching
The vehicle is hard to keep on a straight course, requiring frequent steering corrections to maintain direction.	Wander

Dog-Tracking Blues: Rear-Wheel Misalignment Problems

Have you ever noticed the car or truck in front of you "dog-tracking"? That is when the rear tires don't line up with the front ones. The term comes from observing how dogs' rear legs don't track with their front ones when running — they go off to the side. Dog-tracking is symptomatic of a rear-wheel misalignment problem.

If you draw a line between the rear tires and make a perpendicular line forward from the center of that line, it should pass exactly between the center of the front tires. If the rear tires are not pointing exactly to the front, the line will be off center. This is called the *rear thrust line,* and when it isn't exactly in the middle of the front tires, the car dog-tracks down the road. Figure 11-1 shows you an out-of-alignment vehicle and a properly aligned one.

OUT OF ALIGNMENT | **PROPERLY ALIGNED**

Figure 11-1: The vehicle on the left is dog-tracking.

Dog-tracking usually goes unnoticed by the driver of the vehicle because it is impossible for that person to see what the rear wheels are doing. What the driver can notice is the steering wheel not centered or the vehicle pulling to one side. Careful examination of the front and rear tires may reveal uneven wear on one side.

 Bad alignment can shorten the life of a tire by one-third. It also causes a small loss of fuel economy. Of the more than 170 million passenger cars and trucks on the road, some estimates say that 30 million could use a good four-wheel alignment.

Four-wheel alignments can find dog-tracking problems by measuring the thrust line of the rear wheels in comparison to the front wheels. The alignment mechanic can then make adjustments to the rear wheels to solve the dog-tracking problem. When having your car aligned, ask whether the shop offers four-wheel alignment.

 Shops that have four-wheel alignment equipment often don't check the rear wheels for thrust line problems. An estimated 59 percent of wheel alignment jobs done at dealerships are performed only on the front wheels.

 To ensure that you get a real four-wheel alignment, ask the mechanic to print out the specifications for all four wheels before and after the alignment. Ask to have the readings explained in terms of which angles were out of specifications and how the changes were accomplished. Some corrections are adjustable right on the car; some require that special shims or correction kits be installed.

If you suspect that your car has a rear-wheel alignment problem, here are a couple of easy ways to find out:

✔ **Visual test:** Have someone follow your car while you drive down a straight road. That person should look along the outside edges of both left tires, like "sighting down a fence." Does the rear tire line up with the front along the left edges?

✔ **Tracking test:** Find a flat, smooth driveway and hose down a ten-foot patch with water. Drive slowly in a straight line across the wet area. After you cross the wet patch of driveway, the wheels will leave wet tracks on the adjacent dry area. Stop the car and slowly back up for about six feet without moving the steering wheel. Are the rear tire tracks in the same place for both forward and backward? If your car is dog-tracking, the rear tire tracks will not match up when you back over the tracks that your car made while going forward.

Chapter 12
Finding a Good Mechanic

* *

In This Chapter

▶ Knowing whether a shop is a good or bad pick

▶ Finding the shop that is right for you and your car

▶ Understanding how the shop decides what to charge you

▶ Preparing for the questions that the mechanic may ask

* *

Remember *The Andy Griffith Show,* in which everyone lived in the mythical town of Mayberry? Their cars all ran great thanks to Goober, the World's Best Auto Mechanic. Good ol' Goober. He could just pop a car's hood, listen for a moment, and reach an accurate diagnosis without the aid of computer diagnostic machines. Using only a screwdriver, he would then dive under the hood, make a tiny adjustment to the engine, and — poof — the car was fixed!

Does such a person exist in the real world of auto repair? Are there still places where you can count on the best treatment, the lowest prices, and most importantly, honest service? The answer is yes . . . provided that you know where and how to look.

Understand Shop Typology

As any experienced diner knows, you don't order burgers in a Chinese restaurant. The same holds true for repair shops: Going to a discount tire store for tires may be okay, but going there for transmission service may be a bad idea.

There are four basic types or categories of repair shops: dealerships, specialty shops, independent general repair shops, and mass merchandisers. I'll compare them in the following paragraphs.

The *dealership* is where cars are first introduced to the motoring world. Dealerships usually have the best equipment and mechanics available — and sometimes the highest prices. When other mechanics give up on a problem, the car usually ends up at the dealership.

Dealerships are the place of choice for warranty repairs, extended service contracts, and emission repairs. Car owners who insist on factory-trained mechanics and original-equipment parts typically take their vehicles to dealerships.

 A popular misconception is that all repair and service work must be done at the dealership or the vehicle factory warranty is voided. Anyone can do the work provided that he or she performs all the necessary adjustments and services detailed in the owner's manual.

Specialty shops were born when the first factory-trained mechanics left dealerships to work on their own. These shops are generally a good bet, offering service equal to the dealership at a lower cost but usually concentrating on just a few specific makes or models.

Independent general repair shops are as much an American tradition as apple pie. These shops handle all types of services and repairs on a wide variety of vehicles. Often, the owner is on the premises (one sign of a good shop), and the mechanics who work at a given independent shop are usually specialists for one type or make of vehicle. Independent shops tend to specialize in only one or two makes. Good independent shops develop a *following* of satisfied customers and generally provide the best service for the best price.

Mass merchandisers, or chain stores, offer bargains galore. To the unwary, they can also prove to be the most costly repair option because they may have quotas and use high-pressure sales tactics (see Chapter 13, which discusses rip-offs in detail). Also, these places may be staffed by poorly trained, entry-level employees. In some cases, low-quality repairs can cause expensive damage to other parts — unbeknownst to you until you discover it much too late to do anything about it.

Example: David wants his Mercedes battery replaced. The dealer wants almost $200 for a battery, so David decides to have a department (chain) store auto shop install a new battery. While there is no installation charge, almost two hours are needed to complete the job. When David later examines the car after paying the bill, he finds spilled battery acid in the battery tray, a loosely mounted battery, and grease prints on the white fender.

 Shop chain stores for good prices on tires, batteries, and accessories, but don't take your difficult drivability problems to them. If you decide to go to a chain store repair shop, be sure that the repair is done properly and that other items are not damaged in the process. If possible, don't leave until you check what was done.

Stick Around

If a shop isn't any good, it will soon be put out of business either by bad reputation or by the state's attorney general. The bad guys don't stay in one place very long. Typically, after a couple of years in a location, the shop closes and reopens under another name. As soon as word to stay away from the place gets out in the new neighborhood, the shop moves on to yet another location.

 Ask how many years a shop has been in its location. A smart shop advertises the number of years that it's been in its current location. In many of the best independent and specialty shops, the name of the shop reflects the name of the owner or someone in his or her family.

Example: Mr. Ripp U. Off opened a shop on a busy street in town and advertised heavily in the newspaper. His gimmick was a two-year, 24,000-mile warranty on all repairs. Ripp had a big sign painted to hang along the highway proclaiming his marvelous guarantee.

People came from all over to take advantage of Ripp's incredible warranty — incredible because most repairs are warranted only as long as the parts, typically 90 days. Some parts carry a one-year warranty, but labor is extra. In other words, the part is replaced free, but you must pay for the labor to replace it.

How could Ripp make such an offer? Maybe Ripp was counting on people moving too far away to take advantage of the warranty. Or perhaps he hoped that people would lose their receipts or forget that the repair was still covered when it failed again. Could it be that Ripp really believed that his parts and workmanship could actually outlast the warranty? Or did he secretly plan on moving before all those people came back for free replacements?

That's exactly what happened. Complaints started to mount. People were disgusted with Ripp's repair shop. What was formerly a full parking lot became empty. Finally, he closed the doors and moved to another town, presumably to open again under another name.

Look It Over

Give the shop a good once-over. Is it well lit and properly ventilated, or is the air foul, with junk piled to the ceiling? Take a good look at the shop floor. Is it covered with a decade's worth of grease and grime? That muck and mire will eventually wind up inside your car, probably on the carpet!

Conversely, if the shop seems more like an operating room than a garage, look out. The mechanics may not have anything to do but clean floors all day. A busy and efficient shop will be somewhat messy — especially by the end of the day — but not festooned with junk and old, worn-out parts.

Example: I once worked in a shop called Don's Custom Auto Restoration Service. Don was an alcoholic who, at one time, had been a good mechanic. He didn't care about anything but beer and would consume several six-packs a day. The place was a mess. The parking lot was completely full of junked cars left behind because they were not worth fixing.

The lifts were old and rickety. Don never fixed them, and they leaked hydraulic fluids, dropping cars without warning. He used old driveshafts to prop up the lifts so that they wouldn't fall on us when we were working under them. The floors were so covered with filth that it was impossible to tell where the dirt parking lot ended and the shop floor began. If you dropped a small car part on the floor, it was lost forever.

Ask about Membership Affiliations

A good repair shop is involved in its community. Look for signs of involvement, such as photos, plaques, and trophies. Look for membership in groups like Lions Club, Rotary, Better Business Bureau, Little League, Boy Scouts, and so on. A shop owner who cares about the community usually takes extra measures.

Professional and trade organization memberships are also a plus. Look for signs that acknowledge the shop's affiliation with groups such as AAA (American Automobile Association), ASE (National Institute for Automotive Service Excellence), ATRA (Automatic Transmission Rebuilders Association), ASA (Automotive Service Association), and ASC (Automotive Service Council).

Take the Diagnostic Test

Equipment is an important measure of any service facility. Does the shop have modern diagnostic machines? Do the machines appear to be in good working order? Does the equipment look like it is in use, or is it shoved into a corner and out of the way?

Look around the write-up area for the credentials of the mechanic staff. Ideally, you should see certificates that match the name brand of the diagnostic equipment. For example, if the shop has an Allen Smart Engine Analyzer, at least one mechanic should have a training degree from Allen. Also, make sure that the certified mechanic listed on the certificate still works there!

Inspect the Cars in the Lot

One way to tell whether a shop is the right place for your car is to check out the other cars parked in the lot. Are there any cars like yours, or does your car stand out like a horse among donkeys? Is your car the only imported car in a lot full of domestics or vice versa? Is your car the only new one while the rest look ready for the boneyard? Is the lot fairly deserted? What chased all the other customers away? Is the place about to go out of business? These signs are not good!

While you are looking around the lot, check the dust level on the parked cars. Do they look as if they have been there a long time? Does it look like your car might join their ranks of the living dead? Maybe you should escape while you still can.

Size Up the Staff

Check out the staff and get a feel for their attitude. Do they seem helpful? Ask a few simple questions: How much is an oil change? What about a tune-up? How much time does a simple repair take? If the person waiting on you is in a bad mood and barks at you, acts angry, is upset for some reason, or gives you an uneasy feeling, take your business somewhere else. Take heed of the writing on the wall.

Determine Whether the Shop Wants Your Business

Is the shop booked for days or even weeks? Some shops really don't want any more business, so they treat regular customers with respect and treat newcomers so badly that they don't come back. You may be told that your car can't be worked on for an unreasonable period of time, or you may be quoted an unusually high price because the staff is trying to chase you away.

Example: Hojo John's repair shop had been in the same location for many years. Everything about the place was right. The owner was on the premises, the shop had been in the family for two generations, and it was located on a busy highway. The shop was always so loaded with work that it was difficult to find a place to park in the lot.

The shop's reputation in the community was great, but new customers were treated rudely and were often quoted very high prices. One man was told to get rid of his car because it was going to be very hard to fix, even though there was nothing wrong with it in the first place. Another person was told that the catalytic converter was cracked (a very expensive repair) when, in fact, the muffler had cracked open again. The reason? This new customer had recently purchased a muffler with a lifetime warranty from Hojo, who didn't want to replace the muffler and was trying to get rid of him.

 Talking to the customers sitting in the waiting room on a busy Monday morning may be a good idea. Candidly ask how fairly they have been treated. Explain that you are considering the shop for your own car and that you'd like to know what they think about the shop. If everyone jumps up and starts yelling and shaking their fists, you'd better skip this one.

Get to Know Shop Procedures

Before choosing a repair shop, check the length of the guarantee on the parts as well as labor. Some shops give the standard 90-day guarantee. Others offer guarantees for six months or even a year. Be sure to ask, or you may find out that you paid for a "tail light guarantee". This means that the shop guarantees the job for only as long as they can see your tail lights. As soon as you leave the repair shop lot and your tail lights are out of view, there is no guarantee.

Ask about the parts that the shop intends to use. Does it use original equipment parts, rebuilt or remanufactured parts, or name brands? What brands does it install? If you aren't sure about the quality of the brand, check with several parts stores and ask how good that particular brand is.

How Do You Figure?

In these days of making the dollar stretch, many people are looking around for a less expensive or more reliable repair shop. Hard economic times are also forcing people to wait until it is absolutely necessary before repairing their vehicles. Repair shops are noticing that customers are bringing their vehicles in with huge lists of work to be done all at once or waiting until the vehicle won't run at all before fixing it. In fact, more vehicles are being towed in than ever before.

When shopping around for a repair shop, you need to know some important things about how repair shops operate. If you understand the advantages and disadvantages of the different types of pricing systems, you are probably in a better position to pick and choose which type of shop will best meet your needs for a particular type of repair. Here are the relative advantages or disadvantages of each type of pricing.

Hourly clock rate

In this system, you pay the posted garage labor rate per hour multiplied by the clock time necessary to complete the job.

Advantages

- It's easy to understand how the cost of each job is calculated.
- Implementing the cost of each repair is simple.
- It promotes quality work because the mechanic is paid to be on the job, not to hurry and finish it as fast as possible.

Disadvantages

- Poor (slow) work habits can be passed on to you by adding to labor time.
- Technical problems encountered during the job increase the hourly time needed to complete the job and end up costing you more than preset prices.
- Accurate estimates are impossible because the shop has no way of knowing how long a particular mechanic will take to complete the job.

Menu of prices

Some shops have a pre-established price list for all jobs that they perform. These prices are usually set to compete with other shops in the area. Repair jobs are sometimes lumped together into a package (such as shocks, struts, tire rotation, and alignment).

Advantages

- ✔ It's easy to understand costs up front, before the job is started.

- ✔ The system is simple to implement, involving no variation from customer to customer.

- ✔ The customer is not penalized for poor (slow) work habits of the mechanic.

- ✔ The system is good for selling the total preventative maintenance job.

Disadvantages

- ✔ This system is not as profitable for the shop — an incentive to oversell.

- ✔ The shop must continually survey the local marketplace for competitive pricing.

- ✔ Package pricing can irritate customers who want only one particular job and not the whole package of items that the shop wants to sell.

Flat-rate or commissions

The job cost is based on a published, flat-rate manual, which lists the time it is expected to complete every type of repair possible on every make, model, and year of vehicle.

Advantages

- ✔ Job profits can be controlled by adjusting labor rates.

- ✔ Cost estimating is simple.

- ✔ The customer is not penalized by poor (slow) work habits of the mechanic.

- ✔ The system encourages high mechanic productivity.

Disadvantages

- ✔ Problems with the job (frozen or rusted bolts; parts that don't fit right or are defective) can cause headaches for the mechanic, who is not paid for them. He or she then tries to make up time and winds up cutting corners on the rest of the repair.

- ✔ Flat-rate manuals can be inaccurate, either undercharging or overcharging. Some flat-rate manuals published in the aftermarket give the mechanic the most time for the job. The manuals published by the car-makers list the least amount of time for a given job. This standard encourages mechanics to try and get back at management and beat the system. The result is shoddy repairs.

- ✔ Mechanics may skimp and cut corners to beat the flat rate, not carrying out all the job functions called for in the job description. You wind up with an improper, incomplete, or shoddy repair.

Variable flat-rate

The job is priced not only by the flat-rate manual but also by the skill level necessary to carry out the job. A tire balance or oil change is a low skill level job and is priced much less per hour than repairing a fuel-injection problem.

Advantages

- Mechanics will look for more problems and try to sell more work so that the shop can make more money. So the mechanic will take the time to go over your car and tell you about the things you need.

- The labor talent is maximized, so the mechanics with more skill receive more compensation than mechanics with less skill. This arrangement makes for a happier work environment and better job performance.

- The system encourages high productivity by creating a productive environment and happy workers.

- Customers don't pay high labor rates for unskilled work such as changing tires and mufflers.

- Job profits can be controlled by adjusting labor rates.

- Cost estimating is simple; the shop can offer competitive pricing.

- The customer is not penalized by poor (slow) work habits of the mechanic.

- Customers can still question the skill levels required to carry out a particular task.

Disadvantages

- Problems with the job (bolts are frozen or rusted; parts that don't fit right or are defective) can cause headaches for the mechanic, who is not paid for them. Job price estimating becomes more difficult. Also, flat-rate manuals can be inaccurate, either undercharging or over-charging. Mechanics may skimp and cut corners to beat the flat rate, not carrying out all the job functions called for in the job description.

- Mechanics resent being paid at lower pay scales when called to do repair jobs below their functional level.

Flat-rate and parts commissions

In this system, the mechanic shares in the profits of parts sales as well as labor. The more parts sold, the more the mechanic makes on the job.

Advantage

- Mechanics will look for more problems to sell more work so that the shop can make more money. This pricing structure means your car will be carefully looked over and any impending problems will be brought to your attention.

Disadvantages

- Mechanics will have less of a tendency to fix a problem part and will call for a replacement instead, making the shop more money.

- The customer may be sold parts not needed or will be sold new parts when the old ones can be easily repaired.

The following table tells where you are most likely to encounter which type of repair billing system.

Table 14-1   Where You'll Find the Different Types of Billing

Billing Type	Where You'll Find It
Hourly clock rate	Specialists, dealerships, and family-run independent repair shops; example: automotive electrical repairs
Menu of prices	Specialty shops like brake, muffler, and transmission repair shops
Flat-rate or commissions	The most common method used today by all types of shops
Variable flat-rate	Dealerships
Flat-rate and parts commissions	Chain stores and mass outlets; example: tire and department stores

Fixing It "Write" the First Time

When you take your car to a repair shop, you have less than a 50-50 chance of getting the problem fixed the first time. Communication is a major problem. You ask for one thing to be looked at or repaired and wind up having something different done, maybe something you didn't even know was necessary.

The best way to go to a repair shop is equipped with a complete, written description of the problem, typed neatly if possible. Here are some questions that the mechanic may ask when doing the vehicle pre-write-up:

✔ When does the problem occur: hot, cold, or while warming?

✔ Does it happen when you first start the car or after you have been driving? How far do you have to drive before it happens?

✔ Is the problem intermittent? Can it be duplicated so that the mechanic can witness it?

✔ What is the engine speed when the problem occurs? Does it happen at road speed? At idle?

✔ Does it occur on the highway?

✔ Does it happen during acceleration, deceleration, at steady speeds, or during braking?

✔ Does the grade of the road have anything to do with it?

✔ Does turning the car cause the problem to happen or stop?

✔ When did it first start happening? Did it begin after the car had been worked on?

✔ Does running the defroster, air conditioner, or other accessories have anything to do with the problem?

✔ If your car has power steering, does turning the wheel change anything?

✔ Does hot, cold, rainy, snowy, or damp weather have any bearing on the problem?

Also be prepared to provide the following:

✔ The car's basic statistics: Is it automatic? Does it have power steering or A/C?

✔ The size of the engine

✔ A history of the problem: when it began and what has been done to fix it

If you are not sure what has been done, bring copies of repair orders to help determine the repairs previously done.

Part V
Automotive Self-Defense

In this part...

*T*his part tells you how to spot the bad guys and what to do if you get caught in their traps.

Chapter 13

Meeting Mr. Ripp U. Off: Mechanics and Other Rip-Off Artists

. . . .

In This Chapter

▶ Mr. Ripp U. Off: What he looks like and how to spot him at work

▶ Coming to your own defense to prevent being ripped off

▶ Preparing a complaint letter if you have problems with a repair

▶ Avoiding insurance fraud

▶ Discouraging rental car rip-offs when you're traveling

▶ Protecting yourself from foreign shortchangers

. . . .

Automobile service and repair can be big cash-makers for rip-off artists. Anyone can rent a garage, don some overalls, put out a sign that says "Mechanic on duty," and start fixing cars. In most states, licensing of mechanics is not a requirement and probably never will be one. Meanwhile, scams and flimflams abound.

Recognizing Mr. Ripp U. Off's Trademarks

When visiting a repair shop for the first time, look for Mr. Ripp U. Off's signposts. You can spot his trademarks by looking for one or more of the following indicators:

✔ The shop does a diagnostic on your car and charges you for the work even though you didn't request it. When you ask why a diagnostic was ordered, Ripp tells you something like, "We have to do this to establish a baseline for your car," or, "We do this to all first-time customers."

✔ Ripp doesn't offer a written diagnosis of the problem. You are told only *what* your car needs. He never bothers to tell you *why* your car needs it.

✔ Ripp tells you that it is impossible to give you a written estimate before starting to work on your car. He says, "I have no way of knowing how much your transmission problem is going to cost until I remove it and take it apart." By then, it's too late to leave.

✔ You don't see any mechanics' credentials posted (Ripp doesn't have any).

✔ The atmosphere makes you uneasy, and your intuition tells you to stay away. Maybe it's the 13 junked cars out back.

✔ Ripp always tries to scare you with statements like, "I wouldn't trust my family in that car anywhere. You could be stranded at any time."

✔ You see Ripp's favorite signs posted: Cash Only. No Checks. No Credit Cards.

Protecting Yourself

Here are some general tips for protecting yourself from being ripped off:

Communication is the key to getting a successful repair. Find a shop where you can talk with the mechanic directly. If you can't, prepare a neatly printed or typed page describing *exactly* what is wrong with and/or what you want done to the car. Attach the note to the dash.

Ask for an estimate written on shop stationery or a work order. Scribbled numbers on a note pad are useless in court. Many states require a written estimate, but *you must ask for it.*

Shop around for the best hourly rates and job costs. Hourly rates vary, as do parts markups. Ask how much the *total* job will cost — including incidentals like solvents, shop rags, environmental fees, and surcharges.

Ask how long the work is guaranteed and how long the parts are warrantied. Ask who pays for the labor if the part fails. Get a written guarantee.

Write on the repair order near the bottom, "No other work is authorized without owner's consent." Point this statement out to the service advisor.

If the job involves interior work, paint, body work, and frame work, ask whether the shop plans to subcontract the work. Go to the shop and talk with the subcontractor. Tell him or her that you will not settle for anything less than top quality work.

If the shop tells you that providing a realistic estimate for the entire job is impossible, get costs for teardown and reassembly alone. Doing so provides you with a ballpark estimate *and* a built-in escape hatch if you want to bail out on the repair and decide that you don't want to go through with it.

Example: Billy had 140,000 miles on his car when he started to hear a knocking from his engine. The shop diagnosed the sound as a rod bearing but said that it couldn't give him an estimate until a mechanic tore down the engine and looked inside. He asked for a tear-down estimate. The shop estimated $485 to remove the engine, open it up, and determine the cause of the knock. Additional costs would crop up, depending on the actual problem and the cost of reassembly. Instead, Billy decided to have a used engine with low mileage installed for $800. By knowing the cost of the tear-down before he told the shop to do it, he was able to avoid spending money on an engine too old to be easily repaired. He saved over $300!

When signing the repair order, write neatly across the bottom, "Save replaced pans for customer inspection." The mechanic doesn't know whether you are from the Consumer Protection Division of the State Attorney's office, the Better Business Bureau, or what. This statement alerts the mechanic that he or she had better be careful.

Women: Take a man along when you go in for the write-up. Find a male friend who looks like "Mr. Clean" to go along and watch. He doesn't have to say a thing, just observe the process. If he says something, he may tip off the mechanic as to his lack of knowledge. If your friend remains silent, however, the mechanic has no way of knowing what Mr. Clean knows. Unscrupulous service people still see women as an easy mark. Having a silent observer can make a big difference in how you may be treated.

Place several quarters in plain sight on the dash, console, or floor. If any are missing when you pick up the car, look out! You are in the clutches of Ripp! Anyone who will steal change will also cheat you on repairs.

Understanding the Rip-Off Doctrine

Sometimes it would be good to have a lawyer in your back pocket, especially when it comes to dealing with unscrupulous repair establishments. Lawyers can see the earmarks of a swindle in process and can carefully take the right legal steps to prepare for the possibility of future litigation. Wouldn't it be great to be able to spot the makings of a rip-off beforehand?

If you know the signs of a scam in the making, you may be able to avoid the situation in the first place or at least engage in *damage control* to minimize your losses. If you suspect that something is amiss after work has begun, it is vital to carefully document the exact process. Do so by making notes as you go along. Write down the names, dates, and people you deal with. Then you can prevail in litigation should it become a necessity.

The following sections give you a short field guide to the different types of rip-offs that you might encounter.

Parts? What parts?

You ask for the return of replaced parts — a law in most states — but the repair shop fails to return them or returns only some of the items. When pressed about where the remaining parts are, the shop representative or service advisor is unable to offer an adequate explanation.

Example: When asking for the return of his parts, a customer noticed that there were only six items returned when the bill listed eight. When asked why there was a difference, the shop could not offer any reason for the discrepancy.

 Write — in bold capital letters — on the repair order: "Keep replaced parts for customer's inspection."

Value added

When you ask for a certain type of repair to the vehicle, the representative or service advisor automatically adds another type of service or labor operation. Or after the customer leaves, additional repairs are added to the work order.

Example: When you ask for a tune-up, the shop charges an additional $75 for a diagnostic analysis that you "have to have."

 Authorize only those repairs necessary to cure the problem. Ask, "Is this repair going to cure the problem?"

Example: You bring the vehicle to the shop for a brake special. You sign the repair order and leave, thinking the brake pads will be replaced for $39.95. When you return the bill is almost $600. In addition to the brake special, the repair order lists new calipers, rotors, wheel cylinders, and shoes.

 Always ask for a copy of the repair order after you sign it. Sometimes a shop will get in a hurry and forget to get your signature. Remember, the document is not legal until you sign it!

The shop is doing routine scheduled maintenance and calls with terrible news about the vehicle. It was in perfect condition but suddenly needs a high-dollar item. It's entirely possible that a mechanic made a mistake and destroyed the part, creating the problem. The vehicle owner is told that the problem "definitely" existed before the vehicle arrived at the shop for the routine service.

Example: A vehicle is undergoing routine maintenance. The owner receives a call from the mechanic, who tells him that the engine is in terrible shape and will not last much longer. The shop pressures the customer to have another engine installed immediately. The *real* story is that the mechanic changing the oil didn't tighten the oil filter when he originally installed it during routine maintenance, and all the oil leaked out. Now the engine has a bad rod knock.

 Have the vehicle inspected by a different shop before authorizing anything further.

Invoice shock

A relatively minor electrical repair is being performed and suddenly the shop calls saying that the car has *major* electrical problems. The shop tries to scare the vehicle owner into having several items replaced because the charging system is "too weak to keep the new battery charged." The vehicle didn't exhibit these problems when it was brought into the shop, but now it is *discovered* that several expensive items need to be installed.

Example: The owner is having his battery replaced because it is nearing the end of its five-year warranty, and he doesn't want to be stranded. The service advisor calls him to the counter and informs him that the alternator and voltage regulator are faulty and need to be replaced as well. Those items were functioning when the vehicle was brought into the shop. In reality, no one ever opened the hood or performed any diagnostics on the vehicle. The shop is just trying to sell additional parts and labor without ever properly checking the system.

 Only authorize replacement of the item that you agreed on and ask for proof that the other electrical items are faulty. If necessary, get a second opinion.

Milking the cow

A vehicle won't start and is towed to a garage for starter problems. The garage lists several items in addition to the starter that need to be repaired. In reality, only one item involved in the starting system is needed to repair the vehicle, but the shop wants to replace other items because it says they are also defective.

Example: The vehicle fails to turn over one very cold morning. The vehicle is towed to a garage, and the owner is told the car needs a starter, alternator, and battery. In reality, the starter and alternator are perfectly good; only the battery needs replacing.

 Have the vehicle inspected by a different shop. Make this a rule for any repair costing more than $100.

The big con

Replacing a clutch or transmission is often used as an opportunity to sell a new engine, even though the current engine is in perfect working order.

Example: The clutch is being replaced because it is slipping. The shop calls the owner and says that the engine will need replacement in the very near future. The shop encourages the owner to replace the engine now since the vehicle is already apart.

 Authorize only those repairs necessary to cure the problem. Be on the alert for "snowballing" repairs. Get a second opinion.

Warranty wringer

A repair is covered under warranty; therefore, the owner doesn't expect any cost. But warranty repairs are sometimes viewed as an opportunity to gouge the owner for other non-warranty items. The shop insists that the other repairs are necessary to carry out the warranty work.

Example: A vehicle is towed to the dealer because it won't start. The owner is told that the computer was bad and is covered under warranty. When he picks up the vehicle he is presented with a bill for a major tune-up including a new distributor and ignition coil. He is told that the other work was necessary because those things caused the computer to go bad.

When warranty repairs are made, write on the bottom line of the repair order, "Only warranty repairs are authorized."

Line up the loot

Alignments are one of the biggest scams. The vehicle owner may be told that an alignment was performed, but the steering still pulls or the tires wear out quickly. In reality, no standard exists for what items are to be adjusted or corrected in an alignment.

Example: You are buying a new set of tires because the original ones wore out quickly. You purchase an expensive set of tires and the vehicle is aligned. The new tires wear out prematurely. The shop blames it on the owner, claiming that he must have hit a pothole or curb. In reality, a proper alignment was never done on the front end of the vehicle. (The factory alignment may have been thrown off when the car was unloaded from the truck.)

Ask for a printout of the vehicle's alignment specifications before and after the alignment is performed. The printout will show the normal readings along with the current readings. If something is still wrong with the alignment, you have printed evidence of it, especially if the alignment wasn't carried out properly and some alignment angle wasn't adjusted. Also, you now have a document showing the alignment angles were correct when the car was given back to you.

Missing pieces

The vehicle is dropped off without any body damage or missing parts. When you pick it up, there is a missing hubcap or a new dent in the door. The shop claims that the problem was there before you left the vehicle.

Example: A vehicle is dropped off before the shop opens using the early bird key drop. When the owner picks up the car, the expensive wire wheel covers are missing. The shop claims that the covers were never there.

Bring the vehicle in during working hours. In the presence of the service advisor, walk around the vehicle and point out to the service advisor that there are no physical problems (scratches, dents, and so on) and that all the wheel covers are present. For example, say, "Look, there are no missing hubcaps. My car has no dents in the doors and there are no grease prints on the fenders. I would like it returned that way!"

Automatic dollars

Be careful when getting your automatic transmission serviced. This service can be used as a big scam. The shop often scares the owner by showing the drain pan, claiming that the material in the pan is reason to rebuild the transmission. Remember that it is normal to find solid material (clutch pieces and metal shavings) in the drain pan.

Example: The vehicle is taken to a transmission repair chain for a $19.95 service special. The owner is told that the transmission is in horrible shape and is about to fail. The drain pan is offered as testimony of the problem. The pieces of material in the pan are said to be evidence of impending doom.

 Tell the repair shop that you are going to have the transmission inspected by a different shop.

Chain store shuffle

Chain stores often use alignments to produce additional revenues. Customer are told that additional items are required or the alignment cannot be done.

Example: You bring the vehicle to an auto repair chain for an alignment special. You are told that the vehicle's springs are sagging and that the shop will need to install spring inserts between the coil springs to correct the sag so it can perform the alignment. The inserts are sold for $10 to $20 when, in reality, spring inserts cost less than a dollar and are not needed in the first place.

 If it sounds fishy, get a second opinion. *Never* let anyone install spring inserts; they are a rip-off!

Dumb or rip-off?

Some situations aren't really an intentional rip-off but rather the product of employee stupidity. Nevertheless, you're the victim, so watch out. Dealing with fly-by-night operations or places known to employ many novices, such as discount department store chains, chain auto stores, or parts stores with repair facilities, is just asking for trouble. Here are two examples:

1) Routine service is performed, and not long afterwards a major electrical fault occurs. The repair shop denies any responsibility. In reality, its carelessness inadvertently caused an expensive high-tech solid-state item to fail, even though the failure didn't occur immediately.

    Example: The vehicle is tuned up, battery cables are cleaned, and the oil is changed. A few days later, the digital dashboard or the on-board computer fails. A novice mechanic left the ignition key in the on position when the battery cables were disconnected to be cleaned. This action weakened the transistors, which failed within a few days.

2) The vehicle is having its cooling system worked on. Afterward, the engine overheats and is damaged. The shop is sympathetic, but the repairs will be very expensive.

    Example: The vehicle owner takes the vehicle in to have the coolant flushed and replaced. A routine maintenance to the cooling system is carried out. Suddenly, the mechanic discovers major problems with the cooling system: The head gasket is leaking, and the vehicle will over-heat unless repaired immediately. There was no coolant loss before the vehicle was brought in for the routine maintenance.

    As the vehicle owner drives away, the engine overheats almost immediately. The owner returns to the shop and is told that additional items, including a new head gasket, are needed to repair the problem. The vehicle wasn't overheating initially and now needs a major repair. When the mechanic drained and refilled the radiator, air bubbles were trapped inside the engine and the mechanic didn't properly purge the air. The engine overheated and blew the head gasket.

Have the vehicle serviced only by a trained, veteran mechanic. Ask how long the mechanic assigned to your job has been working as a mechanic. Ask to see credentials, certificates, and any other thing that makes him or her qualified.

Defending Yourself

Time for some automotive self-defense training. The following tips could save you hundreds of dollars in the long run.

Avoid disreputable shops

If you don't take your car to Mr. Ripp U. Off's shop, the chances of his chiseling you are zero. Do a little homework. Never mind the Yellow Pages ads. Whom do your friends and coworkers recommend? Whom do they say to avoid? You may not escape Ripp altogether this way, but you'll narrow your exposure considerably.

Use plastic

Whenever possible, pay with a credit card or gas company charge card. Your credit card is the best defense if a dispute arises because federal law allows you to refuse to pay the charge. Phone calls are a waste of time. Write a letter stating why you are unhappy with the work for which you were charged. Send a copy to the charge company and the shop. The charge card company charges the bill back to the shop forcing them to sue. Courtrooms give Ripp headaches because all the dirty facts of his bad job will come out.

 That's why Ripp posts a sign saying: No credit cards, no checks. Cash only. If you see this sign, leave!

Complaining Effectively

What do you do if you get the car back and it's not fixed? Or they broke something else? Or you're not satisfied for some other reason?

Your first response may be to run right down there and throttle somebody. Okay, not really throttle but . . . holler a little. The trouble is that service managers and shop owners get this treatment all the time. Most have developed a callous on the conflict resolution area of their brains. They may even see your ranting and raving as justification for ripping you off, so save your shouting for the ball park. If you want satisfaction, you need to use calculated diplomacy.

Call first

Alert the shop of your return. Just showing up with the problem will generate animosity. Worse yet, the shop may be so busy that they either can't get to your problem immediately, or they do a quick fix with no lasting results. A phone call paves the way.

Be calm

Determine in advance to be calm. After all, you may be mistaken. Even if you're right, the best way to get your car fixed is to deal person-to-person in a rational manner. Statements like "I'll sue you for every penny you've got" are much more effective on second or subsequent visits. Keep in mind that you may have to stage a blowup at some later point; it will mean more if you've previously been calm and cool.

State the problem

Do not attempt to diagnose what has gone wrong. The problem may or may not be related to the repairs. Don't blame the shop until it is apparent that the shop caused the problem. If the problem persists from a previous visit, make it very clear that you want your money back or the problem fixed.

Get a second opinion

You may want to have a different shop look at the car before you return it to the first shop. Have them examine the suspect repairs and generate a work order spelling out what was done wrong.

Example: You have a clutch installed. Now your car lacks power. You have a second shop look over the work done by the first shop. The second shop finds loose vacuum hoses, missing bolts, and so on. If you had returned to the first shop, it would have covered up the sloppy work and you would never have known.

Tell the boss

Always let someone in upper management, preferably the owner of the business, know about the shoddy work. His or her employees aren't going to tell that they messed up. If you don't write, the owner will assume that everything is fine. Give him or her a chance to be involved and make it right.

Document everything

Always plan ahead for your day in court. Without a written record, it's your word against theirs. Not only do well documented facts further your case, but producing them says you mean business and are determined to prevail. Keep all old repair orders.

Take notes on all telephone conversations and keep records of each visit. Write down the names of everyone you talked to, his or her position, what was said, and the date and time of the conversation. Put your complaint in a letter after the problem begins to document the event, and send a follow up letter after each visit. Describe what transpired and what, if anything, has been done to rectify the problem.

Suggest a solution

How can the shop satisfy you? Suggest a way for the shop to make good, a solution that lets it off the hook. Be realistic about the remedy. If you don't know a good solution, have someone from another shop give you suggestions.

Go to the top

Don't waste your time arguing with someone who likes to argue with customers. Ask to speak to someone in the next management level. Be prepared to go all the way to the top of the organization, if necessary. Be sure to document every person's name, the date, and time of the conversation.

It may take some time before you reach someone who actually cares if you are satisfied. Persist. Don't waste your time with people who have neither the power nor the authority to help you.

Get help

If you can't seem to get the problem resolved at the shop, try bringing in the big guns — not literal weapons, but the following powerful allies available in your own community:

- ✔ **Attorney General:** Routing complaints through this office is typically a slow process but sometimes effective. At the very least, your complaint against that business will be registered and kept on record. If the shop receives enough complaints, its business practices may be investigated.

- ✔ **Autocap:** This arbitration board deals with problems with certain brands of new cars (Alpha Romeo, BMW, Honda, Isuzu, Jaguar, Mazda, Mitsubishi, Nissan, Rolls-Royce, Subaru, Toyota, and Volvo).

- ✔ **Better Business Bureau:** This agency deals with new car arbitration for certain brands only (Audi, GM, Honda, Nissan, Peugeot, Porsche, Saab, and Volkswagen).

- ✔ **Department of Motor Vehicles:** This agency can revoke the operational license of a car dealer — now there's power! The DMV deals with problems in warranty coverage and abatement.

- ✔ **Media:** Your local TV stations, radio stations, and newspapers may have consumer action services that could be of some help in resolving the problem.

If you are complaining to more than one community resource, it's better not to mention the others that you've contacted. Each agency has its own system of operation. Some can take months to respond to your complaint, and if it appears that other agencies are involved, some will drop your case in deference to the others.

Example: If the local TV station's Call for Action line sees that you're taking your problem to the Attorney General, your case may be ignored.

The best way to circumvent a problem with the repair shop is to have a good working relationship in the first place. Get to know your mechanic and stay with that person. Let him (or her) know how happy you are about his work, and don't forget him on the holidays. Also, send a thank you note (and maybe doughnuts or cookies) after your car has been fixed.

Writing a Complaint Letter

Communication is crucial for having a satisfactory repair experience with a shop. First, communicate the exact state of the car. Second, communicate exactly the repairs you expect to receive or the result you want. And finally, communicate exactly why you are satisfied or dissatisfied with the results.

When the repair doesn't fix the problem, people often immediately assume that the shop is at fault. In some cases, the problem was never properly communicated in the first place. Then the shop is never informed that it did something wrong. Over 90 percent of the customers who stop doing business with a repair shop make no effort to tell the shop about their dissatisfaction. They simply don't go back.

About 70 percent of unhappy customers will not complain to the shop because they feel it's not worth their time and the shop probably won't be interested in what they have to say anyway. On average, an unhappy customer tells nine or ten others, but a happy one tells only five. Nearly 95 percent of unhappy customers would come back again if the shop solved their problem quickly and satisfactorily.

Following is a list of tips and techniques for writing an effective complaint letter. This list is for both shop owners and the motoring public and is written to help improve people's satisfaction with the repair process. You can apply these letter-writing guidelines to any type of problem or service.

Document, document, document

Start by taking notes at the very first hint of a problem. Be sure to get the whole name of those with whom you deal. Never trust your memory. Your emotions may cause you to jumble things together; complete events may be forgotten and others may be colored by your frustration. Write down everything that comes to mind. Also, get the date, time, place, rank of management, and anything else that might prove valuable in writing an effective complaint letter. Months later you might be asking yourself, "Who was the gruff guy who was rude to me on the phone?"

If your car has been back more than once, or if other repair shops have attempted the same repair, include copies of the documents associated with those attempts. Never send the originals. Make sure that the copies are dark and legible. If you haven't already done so, be sure to keep the original copies of every receipt — even if you are satisfied with the repair.

State the problem clearly

Don't beat around the bush. State your problem with the shop as clearly and succinctly as possible. If your car still clunks on bumps, keep your discussion to that topic. Many people state the entire repair history of the vehicle before getting to the point and relating the current problem. Don't volunteer all the details of the car since you purchased it. Save it. If the need arises for a detailed chronological history of the vehicle, you will be asked. Don't waste time telling how your neighbor had a car with the same problem, and he had the widget sensor replaced and. . . .

Get a second opinion

Have a family member, coworker, or business associate read your letter before mailing it. You may not have stated something clearly. Sometimes a neutral third party will see other aspects of the problem that you haven't. If you have a difficult time composing the letter, spend the money to have an attorney do it on his or her letterhead. That action always gets immediate attention.

Paint the outcome

A letter that doesn't steer the shop in the direction of resolution isn't likely to produce the result you intend. If you come right out and state your desire for an amenable solution, you give the shop something to work toward. Tell it what you want it to do. At the same time, don't make unreasonable requests.

Share responsibility

Sometimes both you and the shop share responsibility for the problem. If this is true, say so in your letter. Offer to help with the resolution. This gesture will make you appear as less of an enemy to the shop and will more likely resolve the problem.

Set a deadline

Your letter should have a timetable. Make it clear that there is a time limit for resolution, or you will go to more drastic measures. Typically you should give them ten working days to smooth out the problem before you, "Seek resolution with the courts."

Watch that attitude

Keep the tone slightly on the positive side of neutral. Name calling and threatening will only serve to further alienate the shop. Remember the saying, "Honey attracts more flies than vinegar." Your letter is not a place to vent your frustration, especially if you really want to motivate the shop to fix your problem. Remember — your letter may be the first time management becomes aware of your plight with their staff. They may be very grateful that you took the time to share your problem with them. Most people just leave and never come back again.

Document pain and suffering

Keep careful records of all out-of-pocket expenses involved in your attempts to resolve the matter. Record the time you spend on the phone, trips back and forth, and time you spend talking with others as part of the resolution process. Did you lose time at work? Did the improper repair jeopardize your safety? Did you make any long-distance calls? Did you have to borrow or rent a car?

State the case

Tell the shop up front exactly what you plan to do if it fails to take care of the situation. Give the name of your attorney and your intention to litigate if the shop doesn't take care of you. Keep the tone of the letter as neutral as possible. Just let the shop know you mean business.

Photocopy it

Be sure to list several other consumer agencies (either inside or outside the company) to whom you are sending copies of the letter. When the shop sees the list of agencies receiving a copy, it will be motivated to solve the problem as quickly as possible. No one wants the Better Business Bureau or the Consumer Protection Agency breathing down his or her neck.

Write neatly

Don't send a handwritten letter. If necessary, pay someone to type it for you. The more professional the letter looks, the more impact it will have. Be sure to keep a copy for your own records.

Use good grammar and make the letter simple, plain, and easy to read. Don't belabor the point. Don't repeat yourself. Provide a summary of the letter in the opening paragraph, and reread it to make sure it is sensible and easy to understand. Ask a friend or coworker to read it to see if it is easily understood.

Be available

Be sure that the shop can easily contact you to resolve the problem. Give both work and home phone numbers or the phone number of someone with whom they can leave word. Forcing the shop to resort to answering your letter with another letter can really frustrate them and drag things out. If you are afraid to deal with them by phone, seek the help of a friend or family member.

 If the matter involves a large amount of damages, you may be well-advised to seek the cooperation of an attorney to help in the negotiation. If so, let the attorney handle the letters and follow-up phone calls with the shop. When an attorney is involved, the shop very likely will resolve the problem quickly.

Targeting Insurance Fraud

Ripp is the modern equivalent of a carpetbagger. He and his cronies have bogus birth certificates and driver's licenses under fake names. They rent a cheap apartment and have a phone installed. They connect an answering machine to the phone jack, leaving the rest of the apartment vacant.

As Ripp and his cohorts set the stage for their scam, they buy cheap, older vehicles and insure them with the minimum required liability insurance. Next, they purchase a wrecked car from another state — a car that was totaled but is still drivable — making it almost impossible to track insurance records and vehicle ID numbers.

Now the final step: a staged accident between the older car and the out-of-state totaled (yet drivable) car. The accident scene is set in a parking lot or some other location, always on private property so that the police do not have to be involved. The older car is smashed badly enough to be totaled and the drivable total is totaled again. Then the insurance companies pay for it twice!

Insurance scams like this one are operating in all of America's major metropolitan areas and could well be responsible for the escalation of insurance rates. These scams involve no personal injury, and because damages are purposely kept below $5,000, they easily escape notice. Insurance adjusters are quick to reimburse small claims of a few thousand dollars and don't play hard ball when it comes to settling. They just want to move the claim through the system quickly and get on to more serious accidents.

When Tijani Momoh, a Nigerian émigré, was caught, he had at least 15 aliases, 4 social security numbers, and 9 different driver's licenses and is believed to have fleeced insurance companies for more than $1 million in the past few years. Another fraud ring was caught after filing 11 different claims worth more than $45,000 while using the same car, a totaled BMW that was still drivable.

You can help fight the rising costs of car insurance. Fraud is a major component in insurance price escalation, and only consumers can really fight the battle. One of the most significant ways to fight insurance fraud is to avoid insurance scams. Some of the more common types of fraud are staged auto accidents, arson-for-profit, exaggerated injury claims, and phony or inflated theft claims. Here are some tips from the AAA to help fight this problem:

- Always have the police respond to the scene of an accident when there are any injuries. Be sure the police officer makes a complete list of the passengers in the other vehicle on the accident report and that he crosses out the spaces for additional names. Make a list of all passengers in the other vehicle, noting their physical descriptions, names, and addresses. Be sure to get license and registration numbers. If possible, take pictures of the accident scene, including the injured victims.

- If you're injured, verify that the bills submitted by your doctor to your insurance company list only services that were actually performed. Never sign a blank medical form!

- If you suspect insurance fraud, check it out. Get involved. The end result will be lower premiums for you and everyone else. Call the insurance fraud hot line for confidential help or to report suspicious activities at 800-327-3202. Or call the National Insurance Crime Bureau.

Avoiding Rental Car Rip-Offs

When renting a car, pay attention as the final bill is being totaled. If you are entitled to a discount on the rental costs, be sure that the discount is applied toward your final bill. Rental agents have been known to "forget" discounts. Once you sign the charge slip and leave the rental agency, you may have a difficult time recovering the discount due.

Whether on the phone or at the rental counter, get the name of the person assisting you. This information becomes especially important when questions arise about who quoted you a special price, authorized an upgrade, or gave you a discount.

Be sure to have your confirmation number handy, as this may be the only thing you have to prove the rate you were quoted, especially when a discrepancy arises.

Dealing with rental car gas policies

Be aware of the gas policy when renting. Some rental companies require that the car be returned with the same amount of fuel it had when you picked it up. If you return the car and the rental company has to fill the tank, odds are you will pay much more than the current market rate for the gas. Rental agents don't have the time to fuel the car on the spot, so they rely on a chart which calculates mileage, approximate miles per gallon, and other factors — phases of the moon, perhaps? — to arrive at a dollar figure that no one in his or her right mind would pay.

You say you've fueled the car to the original level but the rental agency claims that you haven't? The problem is that gas gauges can take several minutes to reach the actual fuel level of the tank. When you first receive the car, take a moment to check the fuel level. Doing so will require turning the ignition on for a few moments. Complete this step before loading your luggage to give the fuel gauge a chance to reach the correct reading. If this reading doesn't match the amount of fuel shown on the rental agreement, go back inside and request that the agreement be modified to reflect the real fuel level.

When filling the tank to a certain point, do not overfill. Fuel gauges respond slowly to change, making it easy to overshoot the mark. For example, if you need to return the car with three-fourths of a tank of fuel, leave the key turned on (engine off) when pumping. Set the filler nozzle latch on the slow-fill position and watch the fuel gauge as it goes up. For example, when the needle shows half full, stop pumping. Usually the needle will continue to climb to the three-fourths mark.

If you have to return the car with a full tank, put the pump nozzle into the filler neck as far as possible. Pump fuel into the tank as fast as the equipment allows. When the pump nozzle clicks off, stop the process. This way, the gas gauge will read full, though you will save as much as two to three gallons of fuel.

Never buy the gas offered by the rental company, even if they say they are selling it to you for less than the going rate. This claim is almost never true. The going rate will usually be at least ten cents per gallon cheaper. Also, the rental company will assume that you will use the whole tank, which is almost never true.

Always decline the rental company's gas offer and fuel up the car yourself.

Sedating rental car rip-off headaches

Check the car for any dents, scratches, missing hubcaps, or other damage and compare it to the damage report on the rental agreement before driving off the rental lot. Be sure that you are not held financially responsible for any damage done to the car before you rented it.

If you find a scratch, dent, or any damage on the rental car, make sure you have a person representing the rental company sign a waiver absolving you from the damage — before you leave the rental lot.

If you are renting at night or the rental garage has poor lighting, drive the car over to a well-lit area of the rental lot and examine the car in the light so you can see hidden damage that might not show up in the dim lights.

Check the car before leaving the parking lot. Make sure the tires are filled and have fairly new tire treads. They are your best protection against losing control and having an accident on slippery or wet roads. If the tires are low, or in marginal condition, refuse the car and ask for another. Turn on the lights and make sure that all the bulbs work.

While the vehicle is warming up (winter) or the A/C is cooling it down (summer), try every control in the cockpit. Take time to become familiar with the location of all the controls and to determine if they operate correctly. Pay attention to the important controls and immediately check their operation. Be sure to locate and check the operation of the horn, turn signals, wipers, locks, trunk release, and fuel door/gas cap. Adjust the seat to suit your driving comfort and adjust the rearview mirrors.

With the key on, engine off, check out the various dash warning lights. If you don't know what they mean, ask the attendant.

If the car doesn't work properly when you're driving away, go back. If a problem exists, you're better off to turn around while you are still close than to have to return after you have driven miles away. Also, remember to check the operation of the heating and air conditioning systems. A car with a broken heater, defroster, or air conditioner can be really uncomfortable and in some cases, even dangerous.

As soon as you have the opportunity, take the vehicle up to the speed you intend to drive. Does the steering shake? Does it seem like a tire is out of balance? Does it seem to have square tires? Don't be afraid to go back and ask for another car.

Try several stops from highway speeds. Do the brakes work properly? Does the car pull one way or another? Does the steering wheel or brake pedal shake or vibrate when you forcefully apply the brake pedal to make quick stops? Wheel pull or pedal/steering wheel shake can mean the car needs brake service. If the brakes don't stop you in a panic situation and you have an accident, you will still be held responsible for the accident. Proving brake problems after the fact can be difficult, if not impossible.

Make sure that you know whether the car is equipped with traction control and/or antilock brakes (ABS). How to tell? Turn on the ignition and look for the amber ABS warning light. All ABS systems illuminate this light as a bulb-check for the system. If the vehicle has traction control, there may be no way to know it. However, some vehicles have a traction control disable button. If you have any questions, ask the attendant before you leave the lot.

If the vehicle has a problem and you are some distance from the rental company, ask that a replacement vehicle be delivered to you. Most rental companies will deliver a replacement and take the defective one.

And when you turn in the rental car, make sure the attendant goes over the car while you are there and signs off that there is no damage on it. Otherwise, you can be charged for damage you were not aware of — that may have been already there or that occurred while the rental car was being serviced — and you are charged for it. Many rental car companies will do a final audit of the car's condition long after you are gone. By then, it is too late to disagree with their findings.

If you travel often, here are some rip-off prevention tips:

- Check ahead of time to find out whether your own car insurance will cover rental cars, too. If not, you may want to pay a few dollars more and have your own policy amended.

- The medical insurance offered by the rental agency for coverage may not be valid if you are found guilty of DWI (driving while intoxicated). The fine print may also reveal that the coverage is only for that which your own medical and life insurance doesn't cover.

- The special insurance that covers the contents of the car is duplicate coverage, too. Your homeowner's or renter's insurance probably already covers your personal property while you travel.

- Some policies contain clauses denying coverage if the car was broken into.

- Many companies tack on a mandatory fuel charge, even though the gas tank is half empty. This practice means that you are charged a set amount for fuel, whether you like it or not. Be sure to ask, "How much fuel is there supposed to be in the car for this charge?" Be sure to check the rental car for the proper allotment of gas. If you are supposed to get a full tank, make sure that you do.

- If you are told to take a cab to a hotel to pick up the car, find out who is paying the cab fare, who pays the tip, and who will get you back to the airport when you return the car. Many expenses may be hidden here.

✔ Find out whether there are any discounts and if they apply only on weekend or weekly rentals. The fine print may have many exclusion clauses. You might be surprised to find out that an insurance policy pays off only if you die standing up in the car on the last Monday of the spring equinox.

And what if your rental car is stolen? You could become really stranded without a rental car and without the means to rent another. Theft is a growing problem because car thieves know that rental cars are easy pickings that often have valuable luggage in the trunk. Plus, rental cars are never equipped with car alarms or antitheft devices. They're easy to spot, too. Rentals may have special license plates, decals, and bumper stickers.

Depending on the rental car company and the terms of the agreement, you may be held responsible for the entire cost of the rental car! Since most rental cars are sedans with low mileage, you may be responsible for a $12,000 to $20,000 car. To add insult to injury, the rental company may refuse to rent another car to you until they complete their investigation. They may also tie up all the credit available on your credit card, making it impossible for you to rent a car from anyone else.

Use a separate credit card for renting a car to prevent your credit from being tied up.

Check your driving record before renting. If you have three or more traffic violations in the past five years, even parking violations, you may be denied a rental car when you show up to pick it up. Many of the bigger rental companies have gained access to driving records and are denying rental cars to drivers who have bad driving records or have outstanding parking tickets.

The Foreign Shortchange

If you haven't been out of the US and are planning a trip, you might need a primer on dealing with foreign gas station attendants. Even if you aren't going north or south of the border, some of these tips are useful in avoiding rip-offs everywhere.

One complaint of many RV visitors to other countries is having to deal with service station attendants. It seems that many of them attempt to shortchange tourists, one way or another.

Before your first refueling experience, ascertain the price per liter of the type of fuel you intend to purchase. It is usually listed on the pump. If you cannot find it, ask someone. Further, have a calculator in your possession in case you need it.

Here is a list of guidelines:

✔ Always get out of your vehicle and monitor the entire fueling procedure. Never just sit in your rig and trust that everything will be done for you.

✔ Always check that both the "cost of fuel" and "liters" meters on the pump read zero before the attendant begins to pump.

✔ When the attendant finishes pumping your fuel, immediately write down the cost of fuel and number of liters shown on the pump's meter. Occasionally, you will find a pump that has an inoperable "cost of fuel" meter. In these cases, you will need your calculator to multiply the number of liters pumped times the price per liter. The attendant may have a calculator, too, but don't take his or her word for it.

✔ Ask the attendant for a receipt. When you get the receipt, check to see whether the numbers agree with those on the pump. If they do not agree, do not allow the attendant to ring off the figures on the pump (for the next customer) until you have shown the difference to the attendant and settled the matter. If the figures do agree, pay the amount shown on the pump.

✔ Before you receive your change, figure (on paper if necessary) how much change you are supposed to receive. This way, when you are given your change, you will know exactly how much you should receive. When you are given your change, you should count it in front of the attendant. Do not walk away or turn away from the attendant, and do not allow him or her to walk away from you until you have counted your change and are satisfied that you have received correct change.

✔ Last, check your fuel gauge to make sure that you really did receive the fuel you paid for. If you follow these guidelines, you should not have problems with attendants at gas stations as an RVer. And if the attendant does try to make a few dollars at your expense, he or she will have a little more respect for your savvy.

✔ Never take a rental car across the border without permission from the rental car company. You could wind up in big trouble if you do!

Mexican driving tips

With the signing of NAFTA and all the new free trade that is going on between the US and Mexico, many people head down south to check out our new trading partner. However, you need to know some things about driving etiquette when taking to the roads in Mexico. First, make sure that your insurance will cover your travel. Check with your agent because you may have to purchase special insurance when you get there. Also, be prepared for road conditions much worse than you ever encountered when driving here, despite the fact that Mexico has spent billions fixing up the highways. As for etiquette, here are some tips:

✔ In Mexico, a stop sign is treated just like a yield sign is treated here. If you come to a complete stop at a Mexican stop sign and no one is coming, the car behind you will either run into you or the driver will beep the horn in anger because you stopped for no reason.

✔ Right on red is against the law unless a sign is placed at the intersection.

✔ You use left turn signals to let the driver behind you know that it is okay to pass you, not to signal a left turn. You can cause a big problem if you signal a left, because the driver starts to pass you and then you turn left into the car! If you need to make a left turn, pull over to the right-hand lane or shoulder, wait for the road to clear, and then turn left.

✔ Car horns are used for anything, including expressing joy, showing that you have the right-of-way, saying hello, and venting anger at the crazy drivers around you.

✔ Avoid bus rides unless you want a real thrill. Bus drivers are among the most reckless drivers of all. If you see a bus coming, watch out. The drivers always go too fast and take chances that you would never consider.

✔ Green Angels are the Mexican equivalent of our motorist clubs' roadside assistance programs. More than a thousand Green Angels are employed by the Mexican government and drive around in green trucks to help stranded motorists. If you break down, have someone call the Green Angels for help. Labor is free, but you have to pay for parts.

Chapter 14

Avoiding Car Theft and Other Disasters

In This Chapter

▶ Parking safely

▶ Using security devices

▶ Avoiding carjacking

▶ Carrying a weapon

▶ Breaking into your own car

▶ Outsmarting Mr. Ripp U. Off on the road

C ar thieves, like home burglars, generally have an easy time. Their thievery, unfortunately, is made simple by car owners who obligingly leave doors unlocked (four out of five cases) or leave keys in the ignition (one out of five cases).

Professional car thieves are entering the field in increasing numbers, yet most cars are stolen by amateurs who can be stopped fairly easily. You need all the self-defense you can get to fight both the amateurs and professional thieves who are out to get your car! This chapter outlines some ways to reduce your chances of becoming a victim.

Reducing the Risk

First and foremost, never leave your keys in an unattended car. It is a strong invitation for an amateur thief to take a joyride.

Clever thieves take note of the keyed-lock numbers printed on ignition keys and can obtain duplicates by calling a car dealer with the number while posing as the car's owner. Parking lot attendants, hotel valets, and quick oil-change attendants, who have easy access to these numbers, sometimes double as car thieves.

Have the dealer or locksmith remove the numbers to eliminate this problem. However, you should record these numbers in a safe place if you ever need them to obtain a duplicate.

Leaving your name, address, and phone number on a keytag is inviting trouble. If your keys are lost or stolen, the tag will lead the thief directly to your car — and your home. Never leave more than the ignition key with parking lot attendants, as they can have your keys duplicated while you are away.

Install personalized license plates. Thieves don't want to be identified and will avoid your car.

If your car has a "halo light ring" that lights up the hole for your ignition key, look out. Thieves can easily jimmy the lock, so your car has a higher risk of being stolen. You should invest in a car alarm.

Park carefully

Where you park and how you leave your car can have a direct impact on whether or not your car is a thief's target. Keep these tips in mind when you're parking your car to reduce your chances:

✔ Avoid leaving your car in an unattended parking lot for an extended period of time. Statistics show that a car is five times as likely to be stolen from an unattended lot than from the street or from an attended lot.

✔ Park under a streetlight and/or near a busy entrance. It may be necessary to park further from your destination to obtain a well-lit parking spot, but the extra bit of walking is worth it.

✔ When staying in a hotel, ask the desk clerk for the safest place to park the car.

✔ Driver's or passenger's side vent windows and windows that are not rolled all the way to the top are a favorite means of entry for thieves. Always lock all doors, the rear hatch, and the vent windows and tightly close all windows when leaving the car unattended.

✔ Don't advertise. Before leaving the car, remove valuables from view. Remove car phones, CB radios, tape decks, tapes, CDs, packages, and purses and lock them in the trunk. A desperate thief will find the temptation irresistible. If possible, remove the car phone or CB antenna and stow it in the trunk.

You may think that there is nothing in the car to steal and neglect to lock the car. What about your car? Note that thieves also steal older cars to use in drug trafficking.

✔ Always remember to replace the cigarette lighter — a missing lighter may tip off a thief that you have a valuable car phone or radar detector.

✔ Replace your car stereo with a removable one. These units can easily be pulled out and stored safely out of sight in the trunk. Even better are the types with removable faceplates. You can also use a dummy cover to place over your stereo, making it appear cheap and undesirable.

✔ Park with your front wheels turned sharply right or left to make the car difficult to tow away.

See the section "Staying Safe in Mall Parking Lots" later in this chapter for further information about parking smart.

Operation Identification

For about $10, you can purchase an electric engraver and etch your vehicle operator license number on the car phone, CB, tape deck, or CD player. Engrave the car's Vehicle Identification Number (VIN) on the car in several places: on the underside of the hood, inside the trunk lid, and inside the door edges. Doing so makes it easy to identify your car if it is recovered in a "chop-shop" or if someone alters the VIN tag. Engraving the VIN someplace on the car may also deter the chop-shop from stripping the vehicle.

These types of systems are simple, effective, and usually inexpensive. Some types of VIN applications can be done in the aftermarket or by the vehicle owner. Car dealers offer glass etching kits that can engrave these numbers in all the glass windows on the car.

Note that these devices do not deter the thief. In general, a thief is not on the lookout for vehicles marked with the VIN and will steal the vehicle anyway. Also, auto manufacturers have been reluctant to mark parts with the VIN because of the costs involved. Presently, manufacturers are marking only the most likely theft targets, and the marking is in the form of peel-off labels.

Always carry a copy of your VIN, your license tag number, and a complete vehicle description in your wallet or purse. If your car is stolen, you will be able to quickly give the police the information that they need to apprehend the thief.

 Never leave your driver's license, registration, or any other form of ID in your car. If the thief is stopped by police, he or she can fool the officer by offering it as ID.

Use antitheft devices

You may want to consider purchasing a security device to reduce the risk of someone stealing your car. The investment will be a wise one, especially if your car is at high risk of theft or you live and work in a high-risk area. Read on for details about the different types of security devices and their advantages and disadvantages.

Alarms

Function: Upon entry, alarms trigger a siren, horn, blinking lights, cellular phone, kill switch, or some other device. The alarm can also be triggered by an interior motion detector or similar device. Some release tear gas, smoke, or a nonlethal electrical shock.

Cost: Moderate

Advantages: Designed to deter the theft of the vehicle and can also deter theft of items inside the vehicle. Signs are typically posted on the vehicle indicating that an alarm is present. These systems are usually passive and can offer insurance discounts.

Disadvantages: False alarms are a nuisance and can create resentment from neighbors. False alarms can also negate the effectiveness of the alarm when a thief is actually breaking into the vehicle. For this reason, bystanders may not react when the alarm is sounded. Fines are becoming prevalent for frequent false alarm offenders.

 Auto alarm systems can tell a thief what type of alarm you have. You may not want a thief to know this information. Use a generic sticker instead.

Locking devices

Several types of locking devices are on the market today and can be purchased at auto parts stores.

Manual steering wheel locking devices

Function: Lock the steering wheel or the brake pedal, making it impossible to drive the vehicle.

Cost: Low

Advantages: These devices are inexpensive, requiring no special installation. The high visibility of such devices may encourage a would-be thief to look for another, easier target. The device can be removed and installed on the vehicle as needed and moved to your next vehicle when selling.

Disadvantages: Experience has shown that these devices can be removed in about 20 seconds by sawing the steering wheel. In some vehicles, the thief can simply bend open the steering wheel and remove the device. Because these devices require some effort to install, they are not always installed when the vehicle is unoccupied — especially when the vehicle is left momentarily. Failure to remove the device can lead to a crash. Sometimes, the presence of such a highly visible device is a signal to the thief that this car is worth stealing.

Ignition and steering column locking devices

Function: Encapsulate the steering column, thereby preventing access to the ignition lock and switch mechanism. These devices are intended for use only on vehicles with the Saginaw steering column, which is very easy to force.

Cost: Low

Advantages: The high visibility of such devices may encourage a would-be thief to look for another easier target. These devices prevent thieves from breaking the lower outer steering column covering and working the lock.

Disadvantages: Permanently installed versions are unsightly and crude looking. These make it difficult for a mechanic to service the steering column. Such devices can be removed in a few minutes using a hack-saw. The versions that must be attached before leaving the vehicle require some effort to install, so they are not always installed when the vehicle is unoccupied — especially when the vehicle is left momentarily.

Electronic pass-key systems

Functions: Called *resistant key systems* or *smart-keys*. There are two general classes of electronic pass-key systems:

- Pass-key or embedded coded key, which requires a special key to be recognized by the car's computer before the engine will start

- Electronic lock or keyless device, in which a code is entered by a door-mounted keyboard, key switch, remote control, or similar device

Cost: Moderate to high. In some cases, very high and must be installed at the factory.

Advantages: This passive device is the easiest of all antitheft devices to use. It is also the most effective in preventing theft.

Disadvantages: Failure of the device can render the car inoperative. Usually, these devices must be ordered with the car and are not installed in the aftermarket. The door-mounted keyboard can be pried with a screwdriver. Then an experienced thief can short it out and open the door.

Tracking

Function: When activated via radio-frequency link or via satellite tracking system, these systems notify the police that the vehicle has been stolen and give the car's current location. There are three types in use today.

Triangulation

Function: Requires the police department to be fitted with special direction finders to track down the radio signals from the stolen vehicle. At least two police units are required. Currently, LoJack markets this system.

Cost: High

Advantages: A very high number of vehicles are recovered when fitted with this system. Thieves will shun the vehicle if they know that it has such a system on board because they know that the police are going to track them down. Can also aid in recovery of hijacked vehicles.

Disadvantages: Available only in limited areas (currently). The signal can be blocked by parking garages, tunnels, mountains, and buildings (canyon effect).

Also, this system works only within the city and not out of town. The owner must notify the police before the vehicle is driven out of town or it can't be tracked. It is also costly, and difficulty in installation prohibits universal use.

Global positioning systems (GPS)

Function: The vehicle is fitted with a very small satellite transmitter that continually sends a microwave signal up to several satellite receivers in stationary orbit. The monitoring station can pinpoint the exact location of the vehicle at any time by satellite navigation triangulation.

Cost: High

Advantages: A very high number of vehicles are recovered when fitted with this system. Thieves will shun the vehicle if they know that it has such a system on board because they know that the police are going to track them down. Can also aid in recovery of hijacked vehicles. In addition, these systems can be used to track the whereabouts of the vehicle at all times — trucking companies use them for this purpose.

Disadvantages: The signal can be blocked by parking garages, tunnels, and mountains and buildings. The owner must notify the police immediately after the car has been stolen. If the thief disables the device before the police are notified, the system can be defeated. High cost and difficulty of installation prohibit universal use.

Cellular car phone alarm systems

Function: The car is fitted with a combination car phone and alarm system that triggers the car phone when the car is broken into. The car phone can be set up to automatically dial the local police, informing the dispatcher that the car is being broken into and giving a complete description of the car. The car phone can also be programmed to call the owner or any other number desired. In some systems, the phone can be programmed to send the thief a message, scaring him off.

Cost: Moderate to high

Advantages: The unit is self-activating and does not require the owner to discover that the car is being robbed. It requires no satellite or triangulation, using already existing cellular technology.

Disadvantages: The unit depends upon the existence of a cell-site to connect the call, as well as available lines during peak usage periods. The signal can be blocked by parking garages, tunnels, mountains, and buildings.

Kill switches and starter interrupt

Function: Immobilizes the vehicle unless the driver takes some specific action. These devices can be either passive or active and are most effective when used in conjunction with another antitheft device.

Cost: Low

Advantages: Cheap and easy to purchase in the aftermarket or can be readily installed by the car dealer or car stereo shop. They are easy to install, simple to operate, and take precious time for the thief to locate and circumvent.

Disadvantages: They are not always active when the vehicle is unoccupied — especially when the vehicle is left momentarily. A short or malfunction of the device can prevent the vehicle from starting or can cause the vehicle to suddenly quit running.

Phonies

Function: Fool would-be thieves into believing that there is an on-board alarm system, when in reality the sign is the only antitheft device. Phonies come in the form of window stickers, blinking dash-mounted alarm lights, and alarm boxes.

Cost: Very low

Advantages: Easy to install and very cheap. If nothing else, installing one of these stickers on the window or adding the blinking box to the dash or console is a good idea.

Disadvantages: Professional thieves can readily distinguish the phony from the real thing and will ignore the phony deterrent.

Conventional

Function: Factory-supplied theft deterrent devices offer some protection right from the factory. These devices include tapered or hard-to-jimmy door locks, trunk locks, and hood locks.

Advantages: Already installed in the vehicle. These factory devices can have a dramatic effect on reducing the number of vehicle thefts by non-professional thieves.

Disadvantages: Drivers become careless and do not use the locks or remove their keys every time they leave the vehicle.

Other devices

Bet you didn't know that there were so many antitheft devices out there! Hang on — two more are worth mentioning.

Automatic license plate reader

Function: Installed by police at strategic locations (such as the entrance of a tunnel or at the beginning of a large bridge crossing), these automatically read the license plates of vehicles and check a computer file for stolen vehicles.

Cost: Extremely high

Advantages: The vehicle owner has to install nothing. Can be used to apprehend vehicles stolen for use in other criminal activities. The criminal can be easily trapped once the car has been identified by setting up a road block at the opposite end of the bridge or tunnel. Can also be used to arrest scofflaw drivers who are delinquent with paying parking fines.

Disadvantages: The system is extremely expensive and is only in the experimental stages of development. The stolen car must be reported in a timely manner and entered into the database fast enough for the license plate reader to acknowledge the stolen vehicle.

VIN tracking

Function: Apprehends vehicles stolen from other states by identifying the hidden VIN on the vehicle. Every vehicle has a hidden VIN that cannot be easily changed. When a valuable vehicle is bought or sold, the new owner checks for the hidden VIN to determine whether it matches with the registered VIN.

Cost: None

Advantages: It is extremely difficult to modify the hidden VIN because it is stamped right into the frame. Attempts to modify or grind away the numbers are futile, as they can always be found by using chemical metallurgy.

Disadvantages: The location of hidden numbers is not generally known, making this type of inspection difficult.

Avoiding Carjacking

Carjacking, or stealing cars by force, is the most hideous crime to hit the nation in recent years. It is the modern equivalent of piracy. Expensive and exotic cars are the favorite targets of carjackers, and it's understandable.

Today's cars are much harder to steal — unless you have the keys. It's much simpler to stick a gun in someone's face and demand the keys than to disarm car alarms and ignition interlocks.

Unfortunately, most local and state criminal codes don't define carjacking. It is usually reported as auto theft or armed robbery, so there are no solid statistics to indicate times, places, or victims of this type of crime.

Background news

While it is unlikely that you will fall prey to this kind of crime, preventative actions on your part can reduce the risk. Start by being aware of some common themes among carjackings:

- ✔ Carjacking isn't a problem just in large cities — it happens in suburbs, small towns, and rural areas as well. For some young people, carjacking may be a rite of passage, a way to achieve status, or just a thrill. Teens (and adults) are committing more crimes of violence than ever before.

- ✔ Carjacking is a crime of opportunity — a thief searching for the most vulnerable prey without regard to sex, race, or age.

- ✔ Cars, especially luxury ones, provide quick cash for drug users and other criminals.

- ✔ Sophisticated alarms and improved locking devices make it harder for thieves to steal unoccupied cars.

Presenting an opportunity for the carjacker

Carjackers look for windows of opportunity . . . like you stopped at an intersection with your windows rolled down or your door obviously unlocked. Other such places of opportunity include the following:

- ✔ Parking garages and mass-transit lots
- ✔ Shopping malls and grocery stores
- ✔ Self-service places like gas stations
- ✔ Car washes and automated teller machines
- ✔ Residential driveways and streets where you get into or out of your car
- ✔ Anyplace that drivers slow down or stop

Taking the appropriate precautions

Since an informed public is a good step toward thwarting criminals, here is some information to help you avoid a carjacking:

- ✔ Don't pick up hitchhikers (and don't hitchhike yourself).

- ✔ Park near walkways and sidewalks. Avoid parking near dumpsters, woods, large vans or trucks, or anything else that limits your visibility. Avoid parking where there is little foot or auto traffic.

- ✔ Avoid parking in secluded, poorly lit areas — especially late at night. Most carjackings occur between the hours of 9 p.m. and 3 a.m. The later in the day it is, the more likely you are to be carjacked.

   CAUTION   Be especially alert in unstaffed lots and enclosed parking garages.

- ✔ Keep doors locked and windows up while driving and especially when stopped in traffic. If someone approaches your car, don't open your window for any reason. Remember, you are not safe if you are not moving.

✓ Walk with purpose and stay alert. Don't walk to your car alone at night. Have someone accompany you. If you spot someone loitering nearby, don't go to your car. Turn around and go the other way. Call the police if the stranger lingers.

✓ Approach your car with your key in hand. You don't want to be fumbling around for keys while standing next to your car — a perfect time to get mugged! Also, be sure to look around and inside the vehicle before getting in.

✓ When you're in your vehicle, your horn can serve as a good deterrent. If someone suspicious approaches your car, use your horn and don't get out. Criminals don't like attention.

✓ Plan your trips carefully, especially in unknown areas. Don't get lost. If you do get lost, don't ask for directions from anyone standing around the street. Go to a gas station or other well-lit area and ask for help. Also, be wary of anyone asking for directions or handing out fliers.

✓ Trust your instincts — if something makes you feel uneasy, get into the car quickly, lock the doors, and drive away.

A man was driving in an unfamiliar area of a major city when he decided to ask for directions. When he stopped to ask for help, he was robbed. The man was an easy mark since he appeared to be lost.

✓ Keep your doors locked and windows rolled up (at least part-way if it's hot and you don't have air conditioning), no matter how short the distance or how "safe" the neighborhood.

✓ Drive in the center lane to make it harder for would-be carjackers to approach the car.

✓ When you're coming to a stop, leave enough room to maneuver around other cars, especially if you sense trouble and need to get away. Remember, you're not safe if you are not moving. When approaching a red light, leave space between your vehicle and the one in front of you. If someone approaches in a threatening manner, pull away. If someone tries to stop your car by blocking you, especially if there is a gun, get out of there fast!

✓ Avoid driving alone. Go with someone whenever possible, especially at night.

✓ Don't stop to assist a stranger whose car is broken down. Help instead by driving to the nearest phone and calling police to help.

✓ If you often drive at night or alone, consider a CB radio or cellular phone to make it easier to summon help in an emergency — especially if you have to travel in dangerous areas of town. Even a fake mobile phone will do. If you think that you are in danger, pick up the phone and call for help. A would-be carjacker will shy away from someone who is in the process of reporting the crime that he or she is about to commit!

Preventing future problems

Never combine your car keys and house keys, and never attach a label with your home address to your keys.

Never leave your vehicle registration, insurance card, or driver's license in your car. If you do, the thief will know where you live and may rob your home. Remove any papers that have your home address on them. Put a copy of the registration and your business card under the back seat. If your car is found, this will be one of the first places the police will look for identification. Also, drop business cards down inside the doors.

Take your garage door opener with you when you leave your car. If your car is stolen with the opener left inside it, the thief may try to get into your house.

Reacting in a threatening situation

If someone suspicious runs into you, don't get out of your car. Roll up the windows, lock the doors, and motion for him or her to follow you. Drive to the nearest police or fire station. If none is available, drive to a fast-food restaurant drive-up window and summon help. Another option is to go to a well-lit place where there are plenty of people, such as a convenience store.

If you are threatened by an attacker wielding a club, pipe, or knife and your doors are locked and windows are closed, remember that it will take time to break the glass and get inside. You have time to drive away. Don't panic, but get out of there fast!

 A teenager kept her wits about her when a gang of men approached her car, blocked it, and demanded that she get out. Avoiding untold harm, she stepped on the gas and sped away, almost running them over. She might not be alive to tell her story if she had complied with their demands.

If a gunman demands your keys, turn them over. Resisting can lead to a horrible death. Remain calm. Try not to scream or look nervous. Do whatever you are told. Be polite and tell the carjacker that you will obey all requests. If other people are in your car, instruct the passengers to slowly get out when you do. Keep your hands high and visible. You *never* want to go for a drive with a carjacker, and neither do your passengers.

Identifying the carjacker

Try to get a description of the attacker. Note as many details as possible, such as tattoos, scars, or anything else that might be unusual.

 Wait until the attacker is out of sight before you go for help. Then call the police and give them a description of your car and tag number. Remember, the carjacker might come back to kill you if he thinks that you will identify him later.

Carjackers are often drug-crazed maniacs and act unusual. Look for overanimated behavior or other signs of intoxication. Also, pay attention to clothing. Look for gold jewelry or clothing that seems out of place. Also, beware of anyone whose face is partially covered with a hood.

If you are alert, you can spot a potential attacker before he spots you. If you see that you are about to become a target, take immediate evasive action before the attacker can get close. Awareness is your best defense. Keep a sharp eye. Look out!

Staying Safe in Mall Parking Lots

Modern shopping malls can be the hunting grounds for thieves. Malls project the feeling of security when often just the opposite can be true. Even when the mall has security police and cameras, it is not as safe as you might think. The following sections provide some tips for problem-free shopping experiences.

Parking your car

Park under or near a light if there is any chance that you will return after dark.

Park in the major aisle areas in plain view of the mall entrance. You may walk a little farther, but it's worth the peace of mind.

Carjacking data

Most cars are recovered within a few weeks from the time they are stolen.

While a holdup can be a misdemeanor, carjacking is a federal crime. So is kidnapping.

Stolen cars equipped with homing or tracking devices can be recovered very quickly, sometimes within minutes. If you live in a large city, consider purchasing a tracing device such as LoJack.

Most exotic cars are stolen for parts and go to chop-shops where they are dismantled, while others are shipped to other countries. The chance of recovery in these cases is usually slim.

Cars of lesser value are often stolen for use as getaway cars in other crimes. These cars are usually recovered but are typically trashed inside.

Vehicles that are *most* likely to be stolen for parts are BMW, Mercedes-Benz, Lexus, Cadillac (full-size), Jeep Cherokee, and Corvette.

The *least* likely vehicle to be stolen is a pickup truck equipped with gun-racks and NRA decals on the bumpers (ha ha).

 Don't park next to vans, the vehicle of choice for kidnappers and other criminals.

If you see someone watching you from another vehicle as you pull up, park somewhere else. If you're particularly suspicious of the person, report him or her to mall security.

Jot down your parking location as you leave your car. Include which mall entrance or store is nearest. This may save you a lot of time wandering around when you return hours later, arms loaded.

If you keep valuables in your vehicle, stow them in the trunk before you get to the mall. Doing so at the mall tells a watching thief, "Forget the door locks; the good stuff is in the trunk."

Returning to your car

Just dropping off packages so you can shop some more? Move your car to another part of the lot. It's worth losing your space. Someone may be watching.

 As you come within sight of your car, glance beneath it as well as adjacent vehicles. Muggers have been known to hide under or between parked cars and grab victims by the ankles. This is especially true for vans or trucks, which usually have more clearance under them.

Have your key in your hand and ready to insert in the door lock. Fumbling for your keys is an invitation to be mugged.

 Car keys can serve as weapons. Clench the key in your fist, with the biggest key sticking out — protruding between your index and middle fingers. Use it in a swiping motion across the attacker's face, aiming for the eyes. You can also use the key to punch at the bony parts of the attacker's face.

Take a moment to glance into the back seat of your car or rear area of your van as you're getting into your vehicle.

If you are seriously concerned about reaching your vehicle safely, ask a security officer to walk with you. They're there to make sure that you stay safe!

General parking precautions

If your car won't start when you turn the key and someone walks up offering help, refuse. This may be the very person who disabled your car. Lock yourself in the car and ask the person to call the police or mall security.

Shop with others rather than alone. Be sure to leave word at home as to where you're going and when you expect to return. Running late? Call home.

 The safest time to shop is early in the day, when the mall opens. Criminals prefer working under cover of darkness. Crowds are lighter, too.

Crime-Stoppers: Using a Weapon

It's important to wake up and realize that violent crime can happen to you. These days, it can happen anywhere — no neighborhood is safe. Don't make yourself an easy target. You have to look tough and have confidence that you can protect yourself.

One way to engender confidence is to carry a personal self-defense weapon with you — even in your car. One of the most effective and highly recommended weapons is pepper spray. Unlike tear gas, it contains a spray that is 1,000 times more powerful than Tabasco sauce and will even deter a crack-cocaine-crazed drug user.

Carrying a weapon of deadly force can be risky, however, because your attacker can turn a gun or knife against you. Your choice whether or not to use a weapon depends on your personal convictions about killing or maiming an attacker. Carrying a striking weapon might be a better choice if you have any doubt about your ability to use deadly force.

The final choice of weapon is yours. I recommend that you carry some type of weapon in your car, especially when traveling in strange places and when visiting malls and shopping centers. The following sections give you details about some of the more popular self-defense weapons that are available today.

Offensive striking weapons

The **whippet** comes from World War II and was used by the OSS, the predecessor to the CIA. The second and third part of it are made from heavy spring material that collapses into the handle (see Figure 14-1).

Figure 14-1: The whippet. (Photos by Bonnie Ruddie)

The **asp** is an advanced model of the whippet used by the Secret Service. It is designed for use in close quarters. The Coast Guard uses these weapons when boarding boats because a firearm can set off an explosion (see Figure 14-2).

Figure 14-2: The asp.

The **ninja stick** is a telescoping rod that has three very hard striking balls fastened to it and a chain that allows it to be swung in a circular motion. It collapses to $^1/_2$ its total length, about eight inches long (see Figure 14-3).

Figure 14-3: The ninja stick.

The **slap jack** is a flexible leather strap that contains a lead weight on the striking end. The leather strap prevents it from easily being grabbed from your hand by an attacker. Three sizes are shown in Figure 14-4.

Figure 14-4: Three sizes of slap jack.

The **black jack** has a flexible leather handle with a stiff spring inside. The club end is leather filled with lead. The leather strap prevents it from easily being grabbed from your hand by an attacker. (See Figure 14-5.)

Figure 14-5: The black jack.

The **billy club**, or **nightstick**, is a smaller version of a baseball bat. The tether prevents it from being grabbed from your hand by an attacker. Of the two sizes available, the smaller is shown in Figure 14-6.

Figure 14-6: The billy club, or nightstick.

 The **Electronic Nightstick** is a combination steering wheel lock, flashlight, noise-activated car alarm, and billy club. This weapon is very effective and versatile.

Deadly force weapons

The **knife-pen** looks and works like a ball-point pen but reveals a very sharp knife when you pull it apart (see Figure 14-7).

Figure 14-7: The knife-pen.

The **zip gun** looks like a fat fountain pen but fires one .25 caliber shot. This weapon is illegal in some states (see Figure 14-8).

Figure 14-8: The zip gun.

The **Belt Buckle Derringer** is a five-shot revolver that can be mounted on a special belt buckle, wallet, or pocket pager. It holds .22 caliber long rifle or magnum and is illegal in some states.

Defensive weapons

The **kubaton** is easy to carry in a purse and is intended to be a key chain. The pointed end is for jabbing at an attacker. The circular rings on the rod make it easy to grasp, as shown in Figure 14-9.

Figure 14-9: The kubaton.

The **Key** is similar to the kubaton, but its key shape gives it a sense of humor. You can use it to attack the bony parts of the hands or face.

Slash-guard gloves are made from leather lined with Kevlar. These gloves protect against knives, sharp objects, and abrasive surfaces (see Figure 14-10).

Figure 14-10: Slash-guard gloves.

The **shriek-alarm** (also called a *screecher*) is an air-operated device. It does not immobilize an attacker; it merely makes noise to deter an attacker from approaching you.

 Just like stepping on the attacker's foot, using this device may only infuriate the attacker. In one case, an attacker was so angered by a screecher that he broke the victim's jaw after grabbing her purse.

Personal alarms (also called *squealers*) generate a loud, high-pitched screech when you pull a pin. Just like car alarms, most people ignore them. This device may only serve to infuriate an attacker.

Pepper spray and Mace

Typical spray Mace contains only 5 percent Mace and no pepper spray. Some brands of chemical spray, which are also used by police departments, contain both pepper spray and 10 percent Mace. This combination is especially nasty.

Some brands squirt a stream or foam, while others make a fog. The fog is considered more effective because it can go behind glasses (sunglasses, for example). A stream, on the other hand, bounces off glasses.

These chemicals cause instantaneous blindness and respiratory shutdown. Your assailant can neither see nor breathe. One Baltimore police officer said, "Pepper spray Mace is the best thing we've got."

Dispensing types

Spray Mace and pepper spray have a seven- to nine-year shelf-life and the containers are refillable. Both are available in the following dispensing types:

- ✔ **Key chain:** This type, shown in Figure 14-11, is the most handy and versatile. It easily fits in a purse or pocket and is fitted with a key ring. It also has a safety latch to prevent accidental engagement.

- ✔ **Small can:** Used by police and security guards, this size fits in a belt holster.

Figure 14-11: Spray Mace in key chain form.

- ✔ **Pencil:** This size easily fits in a shirt or coat pocket and is the easiest size to conceal.

- ✔ **Grenade:** Large spray can acts like a grenade: Once the trigger is released, it continues spraying until the can is empty. Can be used against carjackers. Just trigger the can and leave the car.

Using pepper spray and Mace

Always try to spray downwind so that the spray doesn't come back into your face. Turn immediately and run.

Spray in an up-and-down motion from the top of the attacker's head downward. This makes the spray go onto the attacker's hair and head. When he tries to clean it off, he will reactivate it, wiping more of the spray from his forehead onto his face.

 Don't display it; just use it when you need to. If you show it, you will activate an attacker's defenses and the attacker may shoot you or take evasive measures to disarm you. Maintain eye contact with your attacker while you unlock the safety level so that he doesn't see you getting ready to spray it.

 When driving, keep the spray next to you on the seat or between your legs. Have the safety already removed. If someone approaches your car at a traffic light, have the spray in your right hand. If the person wants to talk to you and you roll down the window, the spray will be in your hand and ready to use. If an attacker tries to pull you out of the car, just reach across, spray, and drive off.

Breaking into Your Own Car

Have you ever locked yourself out of your car and desperately needed to get inside? Maybe you are in a very dangerous part of town and must get inside your car quickly for safety. Maybe your child is locked inside. Before you pick up a rock and smash the window, here is a primer on how to jimmy your own lock.

I have included this text not as an inspiration to would-be thieves but as a how-to emergency primer. Thieves already know the procedures listed here and won't be helped. Remember: If all else fails, call a locksmith.

Have an extra key made

First, find out whether it is possible to get another key made. Some dealers keep records of the key codes, and you can call up and have another key made.

If you left a key at home, consider taking a cab home and retrieving the other key. Doing so may be cheaper than having the window that you broke to get in repaired!

Buy a slimjim

 Go to an auto parts store and buy a slimjim. Usually, you will have to bend the slimjim to accommodate the curvature of the door.

Some slimjims come in sets made for more advanced door lock designs. These can cost much more than simple slimjims, but they may be necessary in order to deal with your modern door lock design.

Check with the local police. Some carry slimjims around with them in their cars. Also check with parking lot attendants and nearby garages and gas stations.

Using a slimjim or coat hanger

If a slimjim is not available, use a coat hanger. Try to find one that is made from thick wire, the thicker the better. Bend it straight and put a slight "J" hook on one end. Be careful not to damage the car's rubber weather stripping or paint. Move slowly — if necessary, use saliva to help lubricate the coat hanger.

Always work on the passenger side door, as this lock is usually easier to access. The driver's door may have additional electronic locking and window control units that make it harder to gain access to the lock mechanism.

When working on the lock, put your face against the window and watch the door lock button or lever. When you are right on the lock mechanism, the button/latch should wiggle. If necessary, have an assistant watch the latch and report to you when you are making the latching mechanism wiggle. Now work the slimjim or coat hanger up and down as well as sideways until it opens.

After you successfully make contact with the latch mechanism, it helps to gently bang on the door with your fist or knee while jimmying the lock. Doing so helps the latch slip into the unlocked position in much the same manner that banging on the side of a pinball machine helps the ball go in the hole.

Sometimes the lock will open when you pull up on the latch, sometimes when you press down, and sometimes when you move it to the side. Experiment with different ways. Watch the latch to see which way makes it move a little and continue until it unlocks.

If possible, gain access to where the rubber molding surrounds the window — especially where it seals the rearmost edge of the passenger door window. This is always true in convertibles. Try entering with the coat hanger and snaring the door latch.

Use a strong, stiff wire and press the unlock button. This is the easiest and fastest trick for unlocking cars equipped with electric locking buttons.

Attach together two coat hangers to reach across the vehicle to the other side; this way, you can snare the door handle.

Use a wooden wedge to pry a space between the window and the door so that you can see the lock mechanism. Also use a flashlight to see where you're going with the coat hanger or slimjim.

Getting into an Asian import

On some Asian import models, you can simply bend the top of the door frame away from the body, making access to the latch easy. Bending back the frame when you're done is easy.

Last-resort techniques

If you must break a window, pick the vent window or a small side rear window. These are the cheapest to replace.

Sometimes breaking a window is not an option. As a last resort, destroy the lock mechanism. If the door has the lock separate from the latch assembly (especially in Asian imports), use a big screwdriver to turn the whole lock, tumbler and all. Insert the screwdriver just like a key and force the whole mechanism to turn. You can repair the hole in the door later by using epoxy.

Spotting a Stolen Car

Every year, millions of cars are stolen and resold to unwary buyers who get burned when the stolen car is discovered and confiscated. Some $20 billion worth of insurance money annually goes toward paying fraudulent insurance claims. Some people even arrange to have their own cars stolen! It is estimated that 15 percent of all insurance claims are for fraudulently stolen cars. In major cities like New York, Miami, and Philadelphia, about one in five police reports for stolen cars is falsified. The theft is actually arranged and the stolen car goes to a chop-shop where it is stripped for valuable parts or fitted with phony Vehicle Identification Numbers (VIN) to be resold to an unsuspecting sucker.

I have compiled a checklist of some of the items that you might come across in a stolen vehicle. Take this list with you when checking out a used car — it may save you a great deal of trouble and loss of money by helping you avoid buying a stolen vehicle.

- Is the VIN plate loose or showing any signs of tampering? Are the rivets loose?
- Are the rivets holding the VIN plate original? All VIN plates since 1970 have rosette-style stainless-steel rivets with six "petals" and a hole in the middle.
- Has the VIN plate been repainted?
- Are the VIN plate numbers stamped as the original factory numbers? Do the numbers show any signs of tampering?
- Is the dashboard or instrument cluster loose or mispositioned?
- Are the keys originals or duplicates? If duplicates, where are the originals?
- Do both door locks and trunk lock work with the same key? In cars where the door key should fit the ignition, are the keys the same?
- Is the ignition switch loose? Does it show any signs of tampering or chisel marks?
- Is the steering column original, or does it look like it was recently replaced?
- Does the driver's side door jamb still have the DOT sticker on it? Is it firmly attached, or does it appear to have been tampered with?
- Does the VIN on the door jamb sticker match the VIN on the title and VIN plate?
- Does the engine have its ID numbers, or have they been removed?
- Does the license plate look brand new? Does it have new mounting bolts? Does it match the registration?
- Is the car from out of state? Was the registration recently issued in your state? Is the previous owner unknown?

How to spot a laundered car

When considering the purchase of a used car, you should be aware that thieves often "launder" stolen cars or cars that have been "totaled" by insurance companies. If you wind up buying one, you will get ripped off in a big way. The car will continually have expensive problems and, if stolen, will be recovered by the police — and you will lose your investment!

✔ There is a discrepancy between the VIN (Vehicle Identification Number) on the title and the body, door, or other body part.

✔ The title is made out to a dealer and is in the dealer's name. This ploy is often used to alter a vehicle's identification.

✔ The vehicle is old but has low mileage. Note: Also suspect odometer tampering.

✔ The vehicle is from the East Coast and is being sold on the West Coast. Also suspicious are Canadian vehicles brought here.

✔ The deal is too good to be true.

If you have any doubts, contact your local police agency and have the secretly located VIN checked by the authorities. If you suspect that the vehicle you have inspected is a stolen vehicle, call the National Insurance Crime Bureau at 1-800-TEL-NICB. NICB offers rewards of up to $1,000 for information leading to the arrest and/or conviction of those involved in auto fraud.

Road Unworthy Rip-Offs

Travelers are so busy attending to where they are going that they are perfect targets for Mr. Ripp U. Off. He lurks at rest stops, gas stations, service plazas, and roadside stands, waiting for the unwary, weary wayfarer to happen by. Long-distance driving can create a feeling not unlike jet lag; confusion, dizziness, and lack of mental awareness can set in. When you stop and get out of the car, you may not be paying attention because you're easily distracted by the unfamiliar surroundings.

This is the perfect setup for Ripp to get you. He knows that you're in a dazed and careless condition from all those road miles. He is watching. You forget to lock the rear hatch, vent window, or even the door. As soon as you turn the corner, pounce! You become another victim of travel crime. Here are some tips for beating Ripp on the road:

✔ Always empty the car when staying in a hotel. An innocent suitcase may entice Ripp to break your car window. Your belongings are safer with you in your room than in the trunk.

✔ When parking downtown, pay the extra money and park in an attended parking garage. Choose one that allows the attendant to see all the parked cars on the lot.

✔ When stopping for food, park the car where you can see it while you eat.

✔ Never leave the car unattended while buying gas. The perfect time for Ripp to steal your car is when you go to pay for the gas. Keys in the ignition, full tank of gas . . . what more could he want?

✔ Don't keep important papers all in one place. Make copies of registration documents, insurance data, charge card numbers, and travelers' check ID numbers. Keep them in several safe places; you'll need those numbers if you get in trouble. They won't do any good if they are in your car and the car is stolen.

✔ Use travelers' checks and charge cards. Don't leave home without them, especially if you are going to be carrying large sums.

✔ If you are confused or lost, try not to show it. A lost traveler is a prime target for Ripp.

✔ Take along an inflatable dummy or "Mr. Safe-T-Man" to look like a male passenger.

Outsmarting Roadside Rogues

When you're traveling, waiting all along the way are would-be Mr. Ripp U. Offs. The world is full of new victims for Ripp, and travelers are some of his favorites. Why? Because they are often confused and tired and aren't on the lookout. Business people and vacationers alike are a criminal's bread and butter. Listen and learn as Ripp spills the beans.

The loud-mouthed clerk

"I hang around the front desk, usually pretending to read a newspaper. I wait for someone to check in. When the clerk hands you the key, I listen for the room number and size you up to see if you have anything worth stealing. Now I have a juicy target to rob!"

Don't accept that room key. Demand another in a whisper-quiet voice. Bring all valuables into the room with you and be sure the door is locked with the dead bolt.

The door lock scam

"I check into a room at a motel and immediately make a copy of the key. Then I either complain and switch my room or check out altogether. Now I have a key to your room!

"Or I pretend to be checking in and ask to see a room first. I take the key and go up and down the halls trying each lock. I know that the key will work in several locks. If the key fits, I enter your room and rob you."

Frequent hotels with those coded electronic card keys.

The door connection

"I check into a room with interconnecting doors. These doors have the easiest locks to pick! While you are gone, I'll clean you out and be hundreds of miles down the road before you discover what I've done."

Ask for a room without a connecting door.

The delivery scam

"I call you pretending to be the front desk. I tell you that I have a telegram, pizza, or some other made-up item that you are to come pick up. You step out, and I step in."

Always call back to the front desk for verification. If it sounds suspicious, don't leave your room. Have the delivery sent to you so that you can inspect it with the door chain attached to the door.

The unsafe safe

"You shouldn't leave your valuables in the hotel safe because it isn't safe! My buddy works at the front desk, and when someone leaves a real juicy valuable, he tips me off. I come in, fake a holdup, and rob the safe. Surprise! The hotel is liable only for the first $50."

 If you are staying in town for a while, rent a safe deposit box from a nearby bank. If not, keep your valuables with you at all times.

The credit slip scam

"I work as the janitor and one of my jobs is to empty the trash. I spend a great deal of time going through the garbage from the front desk and restaurant. Why? Because I find the carbon strip from your credit card transactions. I save them until I have enough. Then I quit my job and go on a spending spree using your charge card numbers!"

 Ask for the carbon to be returned to you and tear it up into tiny pieces.

The photo scam

"I offer to take your picture and keep your camera."

 Don't let strangers use your camera.

The accident scam

"I jump in front of your car and pretend that you hit me. When you stop, get out, and help me to my feet, I jump into your car and steal it."

 Lock the car whenever you leave it, even if only for a moment.

The locked-out scam

"I pretend to be locked out of my room and ask the maid to let me in. She happily complies, giving me access to your goodies."

 Always take all your valuables with you. Never leave anything behind that you don't want to see stolen. When leaving, turn the TV on loud enough to be heard outside the room and hang the Do Not Disturb card on the door.

The bump and rob scam

"I drive a real junker. If I need quick cash, I drive around dark neighborhoods until I spot a likely victim. I follow until the time is just right and then I run into the back of your car. You get out to take a look at the damage, and I hold you up. Then I slash your tire so that you can't follow me. Better yet, I steal your car."

 Never get out of your car in a bad part of town. If the surroundings look scary, drive to the nearest public place, convenience store, fire department, or police station. Try to stop where there are people around.

The spill scam

"While at a bar, I 'accidentally' spill my beer or soda on you. The idea here is to lavish you with apologies while I pick your pocket. I use other variations to distract you and steal your briefcase or luggage."

Always keep your wallet in a front pocket. Never let your luggage get out of sight. Even better, keep your luggage close to you or between your legs.

The nothing missing scam

The car has obviously been broken into, yet nothing appears to be missing. The ignition lock shows no signs of tampering, and the police are puzzled. You think that maybe the thief was frightened away while trying to steal the car. You thank your lucky stars and maybe even have a car alarm installed. Months go by and the event is completely forgotten.

When it comes time for your car insurance renewal, you are flabbergasted by the huge increase in the premium. "This can't be!" you exclaim and reach for the phone to call and complain to your agent. You are told the increase is the result of an accident you had a few months back. "What accident?" you ask. After much consternation and further checking, you realize that your insurance card was stolen and someone used it to dupe the insurance company.

Here's how the scam works:

Thieves look for cars parked in places that signify that the owner is probably away from home and in a different city. Convention centers, hotels, and cars with out-of-state tags are targeted.

Once the thief has stolen your insurance card, he calls your insurance company, pretending to be you — the owner of the vehicle.

The thief explains to the insurance company agent that he (posing as you) was involved in an accident in which he was at fault. The "accident" takes place in the city where the car has been broken into.

A fictional name is given of the supposed victim of the crash. For example, the agent is told that "John Doe's" car was hit by your car.

The thief, still posing as you, tells the insurance agent that "you" are out of town and won't be able to settle the claim in person. In fact, you can't be reached by phone for several days either. The agent is asked to settle the claim directly for the repairs of the car belonging to "John Doe."

Later that same day, the thief calls the agent and identifies himself as "John Doe." He wants your insurance company to make immediate arrangements to have his damaged car fixed. Your agent instructs him to take the car to the local claims office so that your insurance company can get an adjuster to examine the damage and settle the claim.

The thief shows up at the local insurance adjuster's claims office in the city you were visiting. He brings a stolen car with some believable damage done to it. The nature of the damage prevents the adjuster from determining how fresh it is. Also, the claim is small enough that any additional investigation by the insurance company is not required.

A check for the repair is issued by the claims adjuster to the thief, who is now posing as "John Doe." The thief uses a fake ID to cash the check and cannot be traced.

The thief repeats the process over and over again, moving from city to city — pocketing huge amounts of cash for his efforts.

 This particular scam is so widespread that it has become a major concern for insurance companies. Don't leave your insurance card in your glove box. Instead, take it along with you in your wallet.

Part VI
The Part of Tens

In this part...

This part gives you lists of tens — ten things to do if your car breaks down, ten things to keep in your emergency road kit, and more.

Chapter 15
Ten Breakdown Commandments

● ●

*W*hat do you do if your car has a problem on the freeway and you need to pull over? Sometimes car problems turn into casualties because drivers don't know what to do when their cars break down. If you don't take the proper precautions, your car may wind up in the junkyard, and you may find yourself in the hospital.

Here are my Ten Breakdown Commandments:

I. Be calm

Clear thinking is very important. If you get excited, you lose your ability to think clearly and react effectively. Stay calm. Stay alert.

II. Move over

Exit the road immediately. As soon as you discover that your car has a problem, you should begin moving to the right-hand lane. Use your vehicle's momentum to get off the road. It is better to tough it out trying to cross traffic to the shoulder while you are moving than to break down in the middle of the road. Hesitation here may be deadly.

III. Flash on

As you're pulling over, put on your right-hand turn signal, not your emergency flashers. If you put on your emergency flashers, traffic behind you won't know which way you are going. After you're off the road, turn on your (four-way) emergency flashers.

IV. Go right

The right-hand shoulder of the road is the best place to stop. Truckers call this the "breakdown lane." Pull as far off the road as possible, within reason. If the road has a hard shoulder and soft dirt beyond the shoulder, stay off the dirt. You don't want to be broken down and stuck, too.

V. Avoid curves

Get as far away from curves in the road as you can. Your car will be very hard to see on a curve. Keep going until you are a safe distance from the curve.

VI. Exit right

If you want to exit your car, slide over to the passenger side and exit from that door. Watch for oncoming cars before you exit.

VII. Seek safety

If possible, climb up an embankment safely away from the car. If you can't get a safe distance from your broken-down car, it is better to stay inside your car with your seat belt on. The passenger seat is the safest place — away from the steering wheel. If there is only a guard rail and no room to get a safe distance from the car, don't leave your car.

Drunk drivers home in on flashing lights like a magnet, which is a good reason to get away from the car.

VIII. Stand alone

Never stand in front of or behind your car or between two vehicles, such as the tow truck and your car. Stand near the front, as far away from the road as possible.

IX. Make yourself become more visible

Open the hood, even if you have only a flat tire. An open hood is the universal signal of a vehicle in distress. Light flares (if you have them) and put them 25 to 50 feet behind your car. Even a lantern or flashlight is helpful in making your car more visible at night. Put the "Send Help" sign in the rear window. Tie a light-colored cloth to the antenna.

X. Beware of strangers when you call for help

 If a stranger stops and offers you a ride, watch out! Don't accept it. Better to ask the stranger to help you by contacting the police than to get in his or her car.

It's best to give the person a quarter and ask him or her to call for some help. If you do leave your vehicle behind, leave a note with your name, the date and time you left, the direction you're going, what you are wearing, a description and license number of any vehicle you get in, and the name of the driver.

Chapter 16

Ten (or So) Things to Keep in Your Emergency Road Kit

● ●

Something as simple as a can of gas might make the difference between an inconvenience and a real emergency. I have compiled a list of things that you should pack "just in case" anytime you travel in your car. Any one of these items could make a life-saving difference if you were to get stuck.

Jumper cables

Don't go cheap! Get cables with copper wire, not aluminum. Heavier is better. Many late-model GM cars are equipped with side battery terminals, so look for a set of cables with built-in side adapters or purchase a pair of these adapters separately. You never know when you'll need a jump from the General!

Flares

Sometimes called *fusees,* emergency flares can keep fast-moving traffic from running into your disabled car. Reflective triangles work okay, but they are not as visible. Keep at least six flares in the trunk, packed in a waterproof plastic bag.

Flashlight

Because of the high humidity found in vehicles, a plastic flashlight is recommended — the larger, the better. Keep the batteries in a separate plastic bag so that they stay fresh. The warning flashers that come mounted on larger flashlights are generally too dim for use with traffic. ***Best:*** A portable floodlight that has its own stand so you can set it up and aim it. *Do not* depend on a light that plugs into the cigarette lighter; your battery may be dead!

Spares

Tires aren't the only spares to consider. Carry an assortment of fuses, light bulbs, accessory drive belts, a spark plug, and windshield wiper blades for your car. Spare liquids to have on hand include water, coolant, washer fluid, motor oil, and gas in a safe, approved gas can.

Fix-its

Useful stopgap materials include radiator leak sealants, duct tape to seal up air leaks or patch radiator hoses, and a tarp to work under in a heavy rain or lie on top of when working in mud or snow. Two kinds of electrical tape are available; get the heavy-duty rubber-impregnated cloth variety. A can of silicone spray will dry wet wires and distributor caps and thaw frozen locks.

Clean-up

Pack a tube of waterless hand cleaner, several rags, a can of carburetor cleaner spray solvent (to remove big grease spots), and a roll of paper towels. You may also want to pack a stain-removal stick for your clothing.

Tool kit

Even the best mechanic is helpless without tools. Pack a good Swiss Army knife with scissors. **Best:** Knives that have blade safety locks. Also pack two pairs of vice grips: one 8" standard pair (with built-in wire cutters) and one needle-nose pair, and a 12-volt test light or small multimeter. A standard socket set works both standard (US) and metric sizes, but add 10mm and 12mm sockets to make it complete. A multipurpose screwdriver with different blades stored in the handle is great. An adjustable wrench works for just about anything else.

Fire extinguisher

Shop around for a fire extinguisher that you find to be the appropriate size for your car's storage space. Too big, and it won't fit and will be in the way. Too small, and it won't be of much help when you need it. The best types are good for Class A-B-C fires. You may want to put the fire extinguisher in a protective pouch or plastic bag for safe storage.

Miscellaneous

A good road atlas is handy when you're lost; so is a compass and a pad of paper and pencil. Seal up a stash of chocolate, pudding, or granola bars for instant energy food in case you are stranded for some time. Five dollars in "mad money" and a CB radio or cellular phone would be useful, too. Take one that has its own battery; again, your battery may be the very reason that you're stuck.

A warm sleeping bag is great if you are stranded in the cold, and don't forget a raincoat. Also, a combination sun visor and "Send Help!" sign is useful. Finally, pack a good book to read while you wait. I recommend *The Grapes of Wrath* because no matter how bad your situation is, reading that book will make you realize that your situation could be a whole lot worse!

Chapter 17

Ten Smog Tricks

• •

*O*ver the years, people have found various methods for getting around the smog check. In some states, anytime a car is sold it must pass an emission test. If you buy a used car that already passed the emission test with flying colors, beware of the tricks listed in this chapter. Otherwise, when the time comes for you to sell or get the periodic emission test, your car will fail and you won't understand why. What was done to get it by, and how can you tell?

I do not advocate that you engage in these tricks of the trade. They are listed so that you won't fall prey to one of these methods. If you suspect that tampering has occurred, you may want to get the car checked a second time just to be sure that it can pass on its own.

Tune it up

A new set of spark plugs, an injector cleaning cap, a rotor, plug wires, and a carb adjustment (if applicable) may be all that are needed to pass the emission test.

Get it hot

Make sure that your engine oil is hot before entering the test lane. The car will have to be operating for at least 30 minutes before the test. Do not let the engine idle for more than a few minutes. If the line to get checked is long, shut off your motor and wait before starting it. Just before your turn, rev the engine at 2,000 rpms for at least two minutes to precondition it for the test.

The hotter an engine runs, the cleaner. In many cases, the engine cools down while you're sitting in line waiting for your turn to be tested. This is typically caused by a defective radiator thermostat, allowing the coolant to circulate even when the engine is not at operating temperature. A simple way to cheat is to put a piece of cardboard in front of the radiator, which causes the engine to run hot. This makes the engine run leaner, thus reducing tailpipe emissions.

Go to the test station during the warmest part of the day. If possible, go on a warm day. Cold weather makes emission systems work less effectively.

Raise idle speed

Engines are less efficient when running at idle. Any problems with low compression, vacuum leaks, leaking injectors, or dirty carburetor jets show up at idle. By raising the idle speed to around 1,200 rpms, you may be able to make these problems disappear.

Add alcohol

The air-fuel mixture has a great deal to do with tailpipe emissions. Alcohol burns much cleaner than gasoline. If the fuel level gets to empty and alcohol is added to the gas tank, the emission levels drop. Typically, an overdose of Drygas or similar fuel additive is used for this trick. Adding three or four bottles just before getting into the inspection line yields passing results.

Remove the air filter

The more air the engine gets, the cleaner it burns. In some cases, removing the air filter cover prevents the crankcase fumes from being burned, reducing emission levels even further. Did your car come with a missing air filter?

Change the oil

Have the oil changed just before you go for the test. Old oil causes crankcase emissions to contribute to the air-fuel mixture. Just changing the oil can reduce emissions enough to make the car pass. Using synthetic oil does a better job of reducing emissions because synthetics burn cleaner. Ditto for thicker oil, like 20 W-50.

Install hotter spark plugs

In some cases, the air-fuel mixture is not burned completely. Installing spark plugs one heat range hotter can further reduce emissions. (Note that hotter spark plugs cause the engine to ping. They should not be left in your car if you find this trick on your car.)

Make the exhaust leak

Small exhaust leaks allow exhaust to escape and oxygen to be drawn in. Every puff of exhaust leaking out is followed by a vacuum pulse, which draws in outside air. The introduction of air into the exhaust system helps to complete burning of the unburned fuel and drastically reduces tailpipe emissions.

Note: This trick will not help the vehicle pass the more stringent IM240 emissions tests. In this case, you may need to repair any exhaust leaks.

Advance the timing

You can overcome problems with the vacuum/centrifugal/mechanical timing advance mechanism by resetting the timing to a higher number. Doing so also speeds up the idle.

Note: This trick will not help the vehicle pass the more stringent IM240 emissions tests.

Maintain your engine

Have the engine tuned up and keep it running in the best shape. Over the life of the vehicle, do not abuse it. Hard and abusive use shortens the life of the oxygen sensor and catalyst. Use the best quality gasoline with the most detergents you can find. But do not use high-octane fuel if your engine requires regular unleaded and vice versa. If you own an older, multiport fuel-injected vehicle, consider having the injectors cleaned before taking your car in for the test.

Keep the fuel tank full

A full tank passes the evaporative emission portion of the test more easily. Also, be sure to inspect your gas cap seal. If it is torn or damaged in any way, your car will fail the test. Better to buy another cap in advance before taking the test.

Appendix
Flowcharts

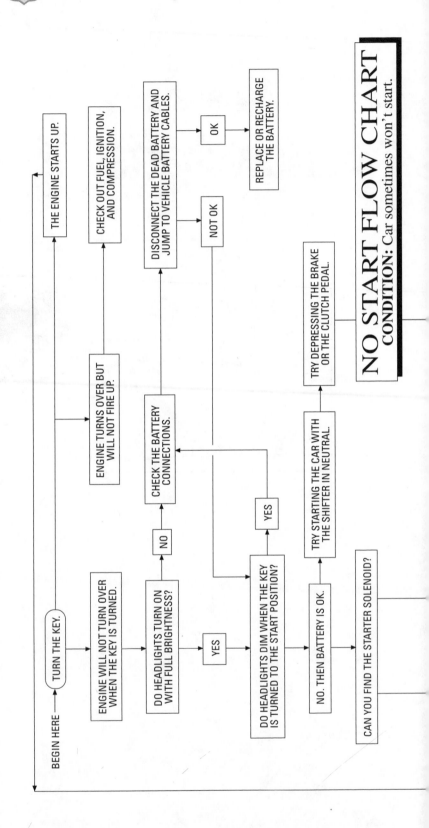

NO START FLOW CHART
CONDITION: Car sometimes won't start.

VEHICLE PULL FLOW-CHART

THE OVERHEATING FLOW-CHART

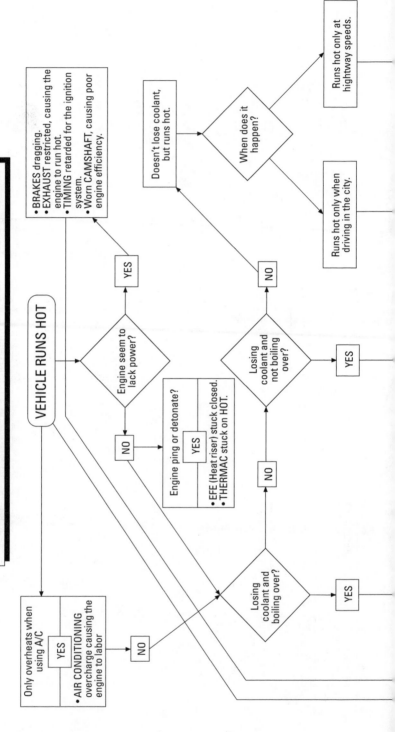

VEHICLE RUNS HOT

Only overheats when using A/C

YES

• AIR CONDITIONING overcharge causing the engine to labor

NO

Engine seem to lack power?

NO

YES

• BRAKES dragging.
• EXHAUST restricted, causing the engine to run hot.
• TIMING retarded for the ignition system.
• Worn CAMSHAFT, causing poor engine efficiency.

Engine ping or detonate?

YES

• EFE (Heat riser) stuck closed.
• THERMAC stuck on HOT.

Losing coolant and boiling over?

YES

NO

Losing coolant and not boiling over?

YES

NO

Doesn't lose coolant, but runs hot.

When does it happen?

Runs hot only when driving in the city.

Runs hot only at highway speeds.

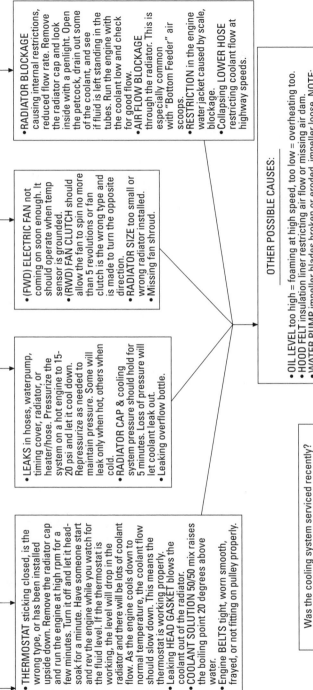

- RADIATOR BLOCKAGE causing internal restrictions, reduced flow rate. Remove the radiator cap and look inside with a penlight. Open the petcock, drain out some of the coolant, and see if fluid is left standing in the tubes. Run the engine with the coolant low and check for good flow.
- AIR FLOW BLOCKAGE through the radiator. This is especially common with "Bottom Feeder" air scoops.
- RESTRICTION in the engine water jacket caused by scale, blockage.
- Collapsing LOWER HOSE restricting coolant flow at highway speeds.

- (FWD) ELECTRIC FAN not coming on soon enough. It should operate when temp sensor is grounded.
- (RWD) FAN CLUTCH should allow the fan to spin no more than 5 revolutions or fan clutch is the wrong type and is made to turn the opposite direction.
- RADIATOR SIZE too small or wrong radiator installed.
- Missing fan shroud.

OTHER POSSIBLE CAUSES:

- OIL LEVEL too high = foaming at high speed, too low = overheating too.
- HOOD FELT insulation liner restricting air flow or missing air dam.
- WATER PUMP impeller blades broken or eroded, impeller loose. NOTE: Heavy red rust accumulation is caused by the impeller blades rusting away. Belt running the water pump in the WRONG DIRECTION. If the pump has a smooth pulley, it should rotate counterclockwise. If the pulley has a groove or "V," it rotates clockwise or in the same direction as the crankshaft.

- LEAKS in hoses, waterpump, timing cover, radiator, or heater/hose. Pressurize the system on a hot engine to 15-20 psi and let it cool down. Repressurize as needed to maintain pressure. Some will leak only when hot, others when cold.
- RADIATOR CAP & cooling system pressure should hold for 5 minutes. Loss of pressure will let coolant leak out.
- Leaking overflow bottle.

- THERMOSTAT sticking closed, is the wrong type, or has been installed upside down. Remove the radiator cap and run the engine at high rpm for a few minutes. Turn it off and let it head-soak for a minute. Have someone start and rev the engine while you watch for the fluid level. If the thermostat is working, the level will drop in the radiator and there will be lots of coolant flow. As the engine cools down to normal temperature, the coolant flow should slow down. This means the thermostat is working properly.
- Leaking HEAD GASKET blows the coolant out of the radiator.
- COOLANT SOLUTION 50/50 mix raises the boiling point 20 degrees above water.
- Engine BELTS tight, worn smooth, frayed, or not fitting on pulley properly.

Was the cooling system serviced recently?

YES

- AIR LOCKED in system preventing coolant flow. Bleed out the air.
- LOW COOLANT level can set a shorted sensor (CTS) code.

Index

• S •

skidding, 101–102
Slap Jack, 184
slash-guard gloves, 186
sleepiness. *See* driver fatigue
slimjim, 188
sling towing, 132–133
slip-stick effect, 40
slipstream, 77
sludge, 16
smart-keys, 176
snake drivers, 74
snow driving
  braking and steering, 90
  getting unstuck, 90–95
  tire ruts, 89–90
soft drink stain removal, 58
sound, trouble. *See* trouble sounds
spare parts, 199
spare tire, 111
spark plug wires, 39
spark plugs, 38–40
specialty shops and finding good
    mechanics, 145
spinning brushes, 59
spotting stolen cars, 189
squeaks
  ashtray cover springs or hinges,
      40–41
  body parts, 42
  dashboard, 40–42
  drylubes, 41
  front-end body bra, 43
  hood-mounted wind deflector, 43
  lithium grease, 41
  lithium, Teflon, or moly com-
      pound sprays, 41
  locating, 40
  noisy sway bar bushings, 41
  powdered graphite, 41
  roof-mounted rack, 42
  silicone spray, 40
  slip-stick effect, 40
  talcum, 41
  tightening mounting bolts, 42
  windshield trim, 42
  windshield wipers, 43–44
squealers, 186
stains, 55–58
stalled cars, starting, 121–124
starter interrupt, 177
starter motor, 121
starting stalled cars, 121–124
static electricity and filling gas
    tank, 8
steering, 142
steering column locking devices,
    175–176

steering wheel
  kick-back, 141
  manual locking devices, 175
  shimmy, 142
  steering morning sickness, 142
  steering play, 142
  torque steer, 142
stick shift cars, getting unstuck, 95
stolen cars, spotting, 189
stopping while unable to use
    brakes, 113
struts, 51
sulphated batteries, 23–25
sulphation, 23–25
sunglasses, 64–66
Sunglasses Association of
    America, 66
suspension
  loose components, 30
  road trips, 63
sway bars, 41
synthetic oil, 16, 55, 126
synthetic transmission fluid, 55

• T •

T-bone side crashes, 102–103
talcum, 41
tapered spark plugs, 39
temperature and tires, 37
temperature
  interior and road trips, 65
  warning light on, 125
ten brake failure warnings, 114–116
ten breakdown commandments,
    197–198
ten emission test tricks, 201–202
ten things for emergency road kit,
    199–200
ten tire-changing commandments,
    110–111
terms, explaining car problems,
    140–142
testing fuel filter, 10–11
Thermac (EFE), 46, 129
thermal air door, 46
thermostat, 128
  bad, 46
  changing, 126
  installing, 129
  never closing, 18
threatening situations and reacting,
    180–181
three-line fuel filter, 47
three-line fuel pump, 47
timing belt
  loose, 139

Title	Author	ISBN	Price
DESKTOP PUBLISHING / ILLUSTRATION / GRAPHICS			
CorelDRAW! 5 For Dummies™	by Deke McClelland	1-56884-157-4	$19.95 USA/$26.95 Canada
CorelDRAW! For Dummies™	by Deke McClelland	1-56884-042-X	$19.95 USA/$26.95 Canada
Harvard Graphics 2 For Windows For Dummies™	by Roger C. Parker	1-56884-092-6	$19.95 USA/$26.95 Canada
PageMaker 5 For Macs For Dummies™	by Galen Gruman	1-56884-178-7	$19.95 USA/$26.95 Canada
PageMaker 5 For Windows For Dummies™	by Deke McClelland & Galen Gruman	1-56884-160-4	$19.95 USA/$26.95 Canada
QuarkXPress 3.3 For Dummies™	by Galen Gruman & Barbara Assadi	1-56884-217-1	$19.99 USA/$26.99 Canada
FINANCE / PERSONAL FINANCE / TEST TAKING REFERENCE			
The GMAT For Dummies™	by Suzee Vlk	1-56884-376-3	$14.99 USA/$20.99 Canada
The GRE For Dummies™	by Suzee Vlk	1-56884-375-5	$14.99 USA/$20.99 Canada
Mutual Funds For Dummies™	by Eric Tyson	1-56884-226-0	$16.99 USA/$22.99 Canada
Personal Finance For Dummies™ For Canadians	by Eric Tyson & Tony Martin	1-56884-378-X	$18.99 USA/$24.99 Canada
Quicken 5 For Macs For Dummies™	by Stephen L. Nelson	1-56884-211-2	$19.95 USA/$26.95 Canada
Quicken 4 For Windows For Dummies™, 2nd Edition	by Stephen L. Nelson	1-56884-209-0	$19.95 USA/$26.95 Canada
The SAT I For Dummies™	by Suzee Vlk	1-56884-213-9	$14.95 USA/$20.99 Canada
GROUPWARE / INTEGRATED			
Lotus Notes 3/3.1 For Dummies™	by Paul Freeland & Stephen Londergan	1-56884-212-0	$19.95 USA/$26.95 Canada
Microsoft Office 4 For Windows For Dummies™	by Roger C. Parker	1-56884-183-3	$19.95 USA/$26.95 Canada
Microsoft Works 3 For Windows For Dummies™	by David C. Kay	1-56884-214-7	$19.99 USA/$26.99 Canada
INTERNET / COMMUNICATIONS / NETWORKING			
CompuServe Starter Kits For Dummies™	by Wallace Wang	1-56884-181-7	$19.95 USA/$26.95 Canada
Modems For Dummies™, 2nd Edition	by Tina Rathbone	1-56884-223-6	$19.99 USA/$26.99 Canada
Modems For Dummies™	by Tina Rathbone	1-56884-001-2	$19.95 USA/$26.95 Canada
MORE Internet For Dummies™	by John R. Levine & Margaret L.Young	1-56884-164-7	$19.95 USA/$26.95 Canada
NetWare For Dummies™	by Ed Tittel & Deni Connor	1-56884-003-9	$19.95 USA/$26.95 Canada
Networking For Dummies™	by Doug Lowe	1-56884-079-9	$19.95 USA/$26.95 Canada
ProComm Plus 2	by Wallace Wang	1-56884-219-8	$19.99 USA/$26.99 Canada
The Internet For Dummies™, 2nd Edition	by John R. Levine & Carol Baroudi	1-56884-222-8	$19.99 USA/$26.99 Canada
The Internet For Macs For Dummies™	by Charles Seiter	1-56884-184-1	$19.95 USA/$26.95 Canada
MACINTOSH			
Macs For Dummies®, 2nd Edition	by David Pogue	1-56884-173-6	$19.95 USA/$26.95 Canada
Macs Programming For Dummies™	by Dan Parks Sydow	1-56884-173-6	$19.95 USA/$26.95 Canada
Macintosh System 7.5 For Dummies™	by Bob LeVitus	1-56884-197-3	$19.95 USA/$26.95 Canada
MORE Macs For Dummies®	by David Pogue	1-56884-087-X	$19.95 USA/$26.95 Canada
PageMaker 5 For Macs For Dummies™	by Galen Gruman	1-56884-178-7	$19.95 USA/$26.95 Canada
QuarkXPress 3.3 For Dummies™	by Galen Gruman & Barbara Assadi	1-56884-217-1	$19.99 USA/$26.99 Canada
Upgrading and Fixing Macs For Dummies™	by Kearney Rietmann & Frank Higgins	1-56884-189-2	$19.95 USA/$26.95 Canada
MULTIMEDIA			
Multimedia & CD-ROMs For Dummies™ Interactive Multimedia Value Pack	by Andy Rathbone	1-56884-225-2	$29.95 USA/$39.95 Canada

4/25/95

OPERATING SYSTEMS / DOS

MORE DOS For Dummies®	by Dan Gookin	1-56884-046-2	$19.95 USA/$26.95 Canada
S.O.S. For DOS™	by Katherine Murray	1-56884-043-8	$12.95 USA/$16.95 Canada
OS/2 For Dummies™	by Andy Rathbone	1-878058-76-2	$19.95 USA/$26.95 Canada

UNIX

UNIX For Dummies™	by John R. Levine & Margaret Levine Young	1-878058-58-4	$19.95 USA/$26.95 Canada

WINDOWS

S.O.S. For Windows™	by Katherine Murray	1-56884-045-4	$12.95 USA/$16.95 Canada
Windows 95 For Dummies™	by Andy Rathbone	1-56884-240-6	$19.99 USA/$26.99 Canada

PCs / HARDWARE

Illustrated Computer Dictionary For Dummies™	by Dan Gookin, Wally Wang, & Chris Van Buren	1-56884-004-7	$12.95 USA/$16.95 Canada
Upgrading and Fixing PCs For Dummies™	by Andy Rathbone	1-56884-002-0	$19.95 USA/$26.95 Canada

PRESENTATION / AUTOCAD / PROGRAMMING

AutoCAD For Dummies™	by Bud Smith	1-56884-191-4	$19.95 USA/$26.95 Canada
PowerPoint 4 For Windows	by Doug Lowe	1-56884-161-2	$16.95 USA/$22.95 Canada
Borland C++ For Dummies™	by Michael Hyman	1-56884-162-0	$19.95 USA/$26.95 Canada
Delphi Programming For Dummies™	by Neil Rubenking	1-56884-200-7	$19.95 USA/$26.95 Canada
C++ For Dummies™	by Stephen R. Davis	1-56884-163-9	$19.95 USA/$26.95 Canada
Mac Programming For Dummies™	by Dan Parks Sydow	1-56884-173-6	$19.95 USA/$26.95 Canada
QBasic Programming For Dummies™	by Douglas Hergert	1-56884-093-4	$19.95 USA/$26.95 Canada
Visual Basic "X" For Dummies™, 2nd Edition	by Wallace Wang	1-56884-230-9	$19.99 USA/$26.99 Canada
Visual Basic 3 For Dummies™	by Wallace Wang	1-56884-076-4	$19.95 USA/$26.95 Canada

SPREADSHEET

1-2-3 For Dummies™	by Greg Harvey	1-878058-60-6	$16.95 USA/$21.95 Canada
1-2-3 For Windows 5 For Dummies™, 2nd Edition	by John Walkenbach	1-56884-216-3	$16.95 USA/$21.95 Canada
Excel 5 For Macs For Dummies™	by Greg Harvey	1-56884-186-8	$19.95 USA/$26.95 Canada
Excel For Dummies™, 2nd Edition	by Greg Harvey	1-56884-050-0	$16.95 USA/$21.95 Canada
MORE Excel 5 For Windows For Dummies™	by Greg Harvey	1-56884-207-4	$19.95 USA/$26.95 Canada
Quattro Pro 6 For Windows For Dummies™	by John Walkenbach	1-56884-174-4	$19.95 USA/$26.95 Canada
Quattro Pro For DOS For Dummies™	by John Walkenbach	1-56884-023-3	$16.95 USA/$21.95 Canada

UTILITIES

Norton Utilities 8 For Dummies™	by Beth Slick	1-56884-166-3	$19.95 USA/$26.95 Canada

VCRs / CAMCORDERS

VCRs & Camcorders For Dummies™	by Andy Rathbone	1-56884-229-5	$14.99 USA/$20.99 Canada

WORD PROCESSING

Ami Pro For Dummies™	by Jim Meade	1-56884-049-7	$19.95 USA/$26.95 Canada
MORE Word For Windows 6 For Dummies™	by Doug Lowe	1-56884-165-5	$19.95 USA/$26.95 Canada
MORE WordPerfect 6 For Windows For Dummies™	by Margaret Levine Young & David C. Kay	1-56884-206-6	$19.95 USA/$26.95 Canada
MORE WordPerfect 6 For DOS For Dummies™	by Wallace Wang, edited by Dan Gookin	1-56884-047-0	$19.95 USA/$26.95 Canada
S.O.S. For WordPerfect™	by Katherine Murray	1-56884-053-5	$12.95 USA/$16.95 Canada
Word 6 For Macs For Dummies™	by Dan Gookin	1-56884-190-6	$19.95 USA/$26.95 Canada
Word For Windows 6 For Dummies™	by Dan Gookin	1-56884-075-6	$16.95 USA/$21.95 Canada
Word For Windows by For Dummies™	Dan Gookin	1-878058-86-X	$16.95 USA/$21.95 Canada
WordPerfect 6 For Dummies™	by Dan Gookin	1-878058-77-0	$16.95 USA/$21.95 Canada
WordPerfect For Dummies™	by Dan Gookin	1-878058-52-5	$16.95 USA/$21.95 Canada
WordPerfect For Windows For Dummies™	by Margaret Levine Young & David C. Kay	1-56884-032-2	$16.95 USA/$21.95 Canada

4/25/95

Fun, Fast, & Cheap!

CorelDRAW! 5 For Dummies™ Quick Reference
by Raymond E. Werner

ISBN: 1-56884-952-4
$9.99 USA/$12.99 Canada

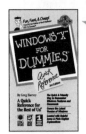

Windows 95 For Dummies™ Quick Reference,
by Greg Harvey

ISBN: 1-56884-964-8
$9.99 USA/$12.99 Canada

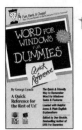

Word For Windows 6 For Dummies™ Quick Reference
by George Lynch

ISBN: 1-56884-095-0
$8.95 USA/$12.95 Canada

Title	Author	ISBN	Price
DATABASE			
Access 2 For Dummies™ Quick Reference	by Stuart J. Stuple	1-56884-167-1	$8.95 USA/$11.95 Canada
dBASE 5 For DOS For Dummies™ Quick Reference	by Barry Sosinsky	1-56884-954-0	$9.99 USA/$12.99 Canada
dBASE 5 For Windows For Dummies™ For Dummies™ Quick Reference	by Stuart J. Stuple	1-56884-954-0	$9.99 USA/$12.99 Canada
Paradox 5 For Windows For Dummies™ Quick Reference	by Scott Palmer	1-56884-960-5	$9.99 USA/$12.99 Canada
DESKTOP PUBLISHING / ILLUSTRATION/GRAPHICS			
Harvard Graphics 3 For Windows For Dummies™ Quick Reference	by Raymond E. Werner	1-56884-962-1	$9.99 USA/$12.99 Canada
FINANCE / PERSONAL FINANCE			
Quicken 4 For Windows For Dummies™ Quick Reference	by Stephen L. Nelson	1-56884-950-8	$9.95 USA/$12.95 Canada
GROUPWARE / INTEGRATED			
Microsoft Office 4 For Windows For Dummies™ Quick Reference	by Doug Lowe	1-56884-958-3	$9.99 USA/$12.99 Canada
Microsoft Works For Windows 3 For Dummies™ Quick Reference	by Michael Partington	1-56884-959-1	$9.99 USA/$12.99 Canada
INTERNET / COMMUNICATIONS / NETWORKING			
The Internet For Dummies™ Quick Reference	by John R. Levine	1-56884-168-X	$8.95 USA/$11.95 Canada
MACINTOSH			
Macintosh System 7.5 For Dummies™ Quick Reference	by Stuart J. Stuple	1-56884-956-7	$9.99 USA/$12.99 Canada
OPERATING SYSTEMS / DOS			
DOS For Dummies® Quick Reference	by Greg Harvey	1-56884-007-1	$8.95 USA/$11.95 Canada
UNIX			
UNIX For Dummies™ Quick Reference	by Margaret Levine Young & John R. Levine	1-56884-094-2	$8.95 USA/$11.95 Canada
WINDOWS			
Windows 3.1 For Dummies™ Quick Reference, 2nd Edition	by Greg Harvey	1-56884-951-6	$8.95 USA/$11.95 Canada
PRESENTATION / AUTOCAD			
AutoCAD For Dummies™ Quick Reference	by Ellen Finkelstein	1-56884-198-1	$9.95 USA/$12.95 Canada
SPREADSHEET			
1-2-3 For Dummies™ Quick Reference	by John Walkenbach	1-56884-027-6	$8.95 USA/$11.95 Canada
1-2-3 For Windows 5 For Dummies™ Quick Reference	by John Walkenbach	1-56884-957-5	$9.95 USA/$12.95 Canada
Excel For Windows For Dummies™ Quick Reference, 2nd Edition	by John Walkenbach	1-56884-096-9	$8.95 USA/$11.95 Canada
Quattro Pro 6 For Windows For Dummies™ Quick Reference	by Stuart A. Stuple	1-56884-172-8	$9.95 USA/$12.95 Canada
WORD PROCESSING			
Word For Windows 6 For Dummies™ Quick Reference	by George Lynch	1-56884-095-0	$8.95 USA/$11.95 Canada
WordPerfect For Windows For Dummies™ Quick Reference	by Greg Harvey	1-56884-039-X	$8.95 USA/$11.95 Canada

4/25/95

*For large quantities call for shipping & handling charges. **Prices are subject to change without notice.

Qty	ISBN	Title	Price	Total

Shipping & Handling Charges

	Description	First book	Each additional book	Total	
Domestic	Normal	$4.50	$1.50	$	
	Two Day Air	$8.50	$2.50	$	
	Overnight	$18.00	$3.00	$	
International	Surface	$8.00	$8.00	$	
	Airmail	$16.00	$16.00	$	
	DHL Air	$17.00	$17.00	$	

IDG BOOKS

Please send this
order form to:
IDG Books Worldwide
7260 Shadeland Station
Suite 100
Indianapolis, IN 46256

Allow up to 3 weeks for
delivery. Thank you!

Ship to:

Name _____

Company _____

Address _____

City/State/Zip _____

Daytime Phone_____

Payment:

☐ Check to IDG Books Worldwide
   (US Funds Only)

☐ VISA

☐ MasterCard

☐ American Express

Card #_____

Exp. _____

Sign. _____

Subtotal _____

CA residents add
applicable sales tax_____

IN, MA, and MD residents
add 5% sales tax_____

IL residents add
6.25% sales tax_____

RI residents add
7% sales tax_____

TX residents add
8.25% sales tax_____

Shipping_____

Total_____

4/25/95